Introduction

In this, the first book of a new series, you will find a wide selection of recipes for soups, hors d'oeuvre, snacks, party savouries and supper dishes for every occasion.

Although we have so many excellent ready prepared soups on the market, there are many occasions when it is well worth while making soup. Perhaps you have boiled a piece of bacon or ham — there is a perfect stock to make a lentil, pea or other soup without spending much time or money. The modern bouillon cubes take the place of stock very adequately, and with either you have the basis of a great variety of soups. In cold weather a really filling vegetable, meat or fish soup is a meal in itself — warming, delicious and satisfying.

I think it a pity we haven't yet adopted the idea of cold soups for summer. On a really hot day nothing is more refreshing than a chilled tomato or cucumber soup. You will find a great variety of familiar and new soups — hot and cold — in the Soup section of this book, as well as hints on garnishing and serving them.

While most of the recipes in the Soup section are for practical and economical soups to make yourself, there are also ideas for adding an individual touch to the ready prepared soups you can buy.

The kind of foods we serve as hors d'oeuvre vary a great deal — you can have trays of a delicious assortment of fish, salads etc.; on the other hand you may be searching for a new hot or cold dish to start a special meal. I think you will find all of these in the hors d'oeuvre section. If your main course is a rather light one then a fairly substantial hors d'oeuvre will turn it into a satisfying meal.

Once upon a time a savoury was just a small dish to serve at the end of a meal — today when so many housewives have their mid-day meal by themselves while the children are at school and their husbands away, a variety of quick and savoury dishes are most useful, for they provide a well balanced and nourishing meal with the minimum of fuss and bother. Television suppers have also made families very willing to have an interesting savoury, rather than a more elaborate dish. All recipes for main dishes will serve four persons, unless otherwise stated.

Modern parties demand a wide selection of tiny, interesting and original savoury dishes — easy to make, easy to eat and attractive to look at. You will find all these types of dishes, as well as the classic 'after dinner' savouries in these sections. They have been divided for quick and easy reference, but it is worth reading through all the sections, and the recipes, as you will often find that a cocktail savoury made in a rather more substantial size will make an excellent family snack — and vice versa. I feel confident you will find this book a great help in planning interesting and practical dishes for your family and friends.

In this, as in other books in this series, I have been wonderfully helped by the team of experts who have provided the pictures and recipes that accompany them.

Marguerite Patten.

Weights and Measures

English weights and measures have been used throughout this book. In case it is wished to translate these into their American counterparts the following tables give a comparison:

Liquid Measure

ONE PINT of liquid may be regarded as equal to TWO American measuring cups for all practical purposes. (American cups are standard '½-pint' measuring cups, but the American pint is slightly smaller than the British and American ½-pint cups are actually equivalent to two-fifths of a British pint.)

3 teaspoonfuls equal 1 tablespoonful.

The average English teacup is ¼ pint or 1 gill.

The average English breakfast cup is ½ pint or 2 gills.

When cups are mentioned in the recipes in this book they refer to a B.S.I. measuring cup which does hold ½ pint.

Solid Measure

English		American
1 pound	Butter or other fat	2 cups
1 pound	Flour	4 cups
1 pound	Granulated or Castor Sugar	2 cups
1 pound	Icing or Confectioners' Sugar	3 cups
1 pound	Brown (Moist) Sugar	2⅔ cups
1 pound	Golden Syrup or Treacle	1 cup
1 pound	Rice	2 cups
1 pound	Dried Fruit	2 cups
1 pound	Chopped Meat (finely packed)	2 cups
1 pound	Lentils or Split Peas	2 cups
1 pound	Coffee (unground)	2⅓ cups
1 pound	Soft breadcrumbs	4 cups
½ ounce	Flour	1 level tablespoon*
1 ounce	Flour	1 heaped tablespoon
1 ounce	Sugar	1 level tablespoon
½ ounce	Butter	1 tablespoon smoothed off
1 ounce	Golden Syrup or Treacle	1 level tablespoon
1 ounce	Jam or Jelly	1 level tablespoon

must be proper measuring tablespoon

French Weights and Measures

It is difficult to convert to French measures with absolute accuracy, but 1 oz. is equal to approximately 30 grammes, 2 lb. 3 oz. to 1 kilogramme. For liquid measure, approximately 1¾ English pints may be regarded as equal to 1 litre; 1 demilitre is half a litre, and 1 décilitre is one-tenth of a litre.

Oven Temperatures

In most recipes in this book reference has been given to the oven temperature or the gas setting. This is an approximate guide only. Different makes of cookers vary and it is a fact that even the same make of cooker can give slightly different individual results at the same temperature or setting.

If in doubt as to whether the temperature given is EXACTLY right for your particular cooker, then do at all times refer to your own manufacturer's temperature chart. It is impossible in a general book to be exact for every cooker, but you will find that the following are a good average in every case.

	Electricity °F	Gas regulo	°C
COOL oven	225 to 250	0 to ½	107—121
VERY SLOW oven	250 to 275	½ to 1	121—135
SLOW oven	275 to 300	1 to 2	135—149
VERY MODERATE oven	300 to 350	2 to 3	149—177
MODERATE oven	375	4	190
MODERATELY HOT oven	400	5	204
HOT oven	425 to 450	6 to 7	218—233
VERY HOT oven	475 to 500	8 to 9	246—260

Basic Methods of Cooking

Baking — Cooking in dry heat in the oven.

Boiling — Cooking by immersing the food in a pan of liquid, which must be kept boiling gently — all the time.

Braising — Almost a combination of stewing and roasting. Meat is placed on a bed of vegetables with a little liquid surrounding, in a covered vessel, and cooked slowly in the oven.

Casserole — Cooking slowly in the oven in a covered casserole dish — usually meat, rabbit, etc.

Frying — Cooking in a little hot fat in an open pan. Deep frying is cooking by immersion in a deep pan of smoking hot fat.

Grilling — Cooking quickly under a red-hot grill: used for small tender pieces of meat, fish, etc.

Poaching — Cooking gently in water which is just below boiling point: usually eggs or fish.

Pressure Cooking — Cooking at higher temperatures than usual, so that food is cooked much more quickly.

Roasting — Cooking with a little fat in a hot oven. Fat is poured from the baking tin over the meat or poultry from time to time, using a long-handled spoon: this is known as basting.

Simmering — The rate of cooking used for stews — just below boiling point, so that the liquid bubbles gently at the side of the pan.

Steaming — Cooking either in a steamer over a pan of boiling water, or in a basin standing in (but not covered by) boiling water.

Stewing — Cooking slowly until the food is tender. It is done in just enough liquid to cover the food, as the liquid is served with it and should be rich. Stews may be cooked in covered saucepans or casseroles, either on a hotplate or in the oven — but always at a low temperature.

Spices and Herbs
for your soups and savoury dishes

Bouquet Garni means a mixture of herbs. When using fresh herbs the sprigs should be tied together or put into a muslin bag, so easily removed. Select parsley, thyme, bay leaf, tarragon or celery leaves.

If using dried herbs instead, remember they have a very strong flavour and use a little only.

Basil has a slight flavour of cloves — a little is good in potato dishes.

Bay leaves are excellent in all types of savoury dishes. Use 1 or 2 only and remove before serving.

Balm gives a slight lemon flavour — good for most savoury dishes.

Borage gives a faint taste of cucumber — excellent when cucumber is out of season.

Capers give flavour to salads and stuffings.

Caraway seeds can be added to some vegetable soups — use sparingly.

Chervil tastes a little like parsley and can be used instead.

Chives taste like a mild onion — an excellent garnish and flavouring.

Cloves are not used a great deal in savoury dishes; use 1 or 2 in soups occasionally, remove before serving.

Curry powder should be used sparingly unless you are certain everyone likes strong curry flavour. Remember to balance this with sweet ingredients too — chutney, dried fruit, sugar.

Dill gives a delicious flavour to soups and savoury dishes. Not easy to obtain, but use instead of parsley, also as a garnish.

Fennel is excellent with fish dishes.

Garlic gives a pungent flavour to many soups — use sparingly. 1 small clove is generally sufficient to flavour a soup.

Mace has a slight nutmeg flavour and can be used instead.

Mint is excellent with potato, pea and lamb dishes.

Parsley is an essential ingredient both for flavouring and garnishing. Use dried parsley sparingly if fresh is not available.

Pepper — ordinary black and white is used for cooking. Cayenne pepper is VERY HOT so use carefully. Paprika pepper has a sweet taste.

Rosemary is excellent with chicken dishes.

Sage gives good flavour to many savoury dishes, particularly pork.

Sorrel makes a good soup or flavours salads.

Tarragon gives a rather hot flavour; it can be used in salads, but tarragon vinegar gives a milder taste.

Thyme is used in stuffings and as part of the flavourings for many soups.

Soups

In these modern days excellent soups can be obtained either canned or in packet form, but even so there are occasions when a home made soup is very desirable. It means you can produce a great variety of flavours, and is not difficult to make; a home made soup often enables you to 'use up' ingredients available in the larder or refrigerator.

2   RULES FOR GOOD SOUPS

1. Make sure hot soups are served really hot.
2. Try cold soups for a change in hot weather or if being followed by a hot course. You will find a number of suggestions for cold soups.
3. Taste soups before serving, and add enough seasonings etc. to 'bring out' the flavour — do not over-season, as people vary a great deal in their liking for salt etc.
4. An interesting garnish will make a great deal of difference to the appearance of a soup.

3   KEEPING A STOCKPOT

Once upon a time it was considered essential to keep a stock pot in the kitchen, and from day to day vegetables were added, and it was boiled. Obviously the reason was to have a good basis for soups, and it cannot be disputed that in many soups a good stock will improve the flavour of the soup. It is however considered quite dangerous to keep stock for a great length of time, unless stored in a refrigerator. Make the stock as freshly as possible; a pressure cooker enables you to do this quickly and easily. If it has been kept for several days, even in a refrigerator, it must be boiled well.

To make a good stock, cover the bones of beef (for a brown stock) or veal or poultry (for a white stock) with cold water, add a bay leaf, seasoning and simmer gently for several hours. Directions for making stock with a pressure cooker can be found in Recipe 89. Vegetables can be added if wished, but they cause the stock to spoil more rapidly.

The carcase of game and poultry can also be used to produce good stock. In vegetable soups however, often you will find it better NOT to use a stock, since this detracts from the natural vegetable flavour. If stock is not available, do not let this prevent your making soup; use some of the excellent yeast extract or bouillon cubes available.

4   MODERN AIDS TO SOUP MAKING

Sieving soup has always been a tiresome and slow job. The modern electric liquidiser (or blender) as illustrated means this can be done without any effort, within minutes.

Grating vegetables for soup often means sieving is unnecessary, for they become so soft and fine that the soup can be served as it is.

A pressure cooker not only produces stock for soups quickly, but is an excellent method for all soup cooking. See Recipe 89 onwards.

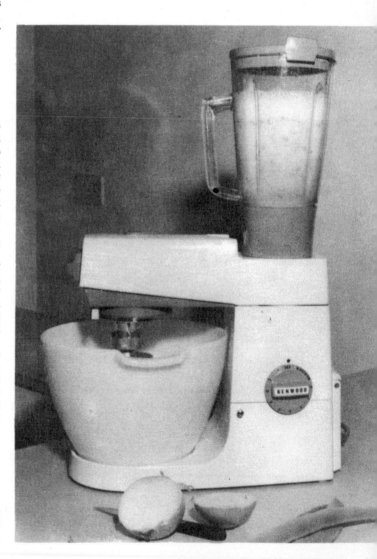

Easy-to-make Vegetable Soups

A vegetable soup is an ideal start to a meal, and an excellent way of using vegetables when they are cheap and plentiful. Do not over-cook the soups, since you retain more of the fresh vegetable flavour by fairly short cooking.

Try the thicker soups or chowders both in this Vegetable soup section and further on in the book. They are almost a 'meal' in themselves, and are ideal for snack suppers.

5   CREAM OF ARTICHOKE SOUP

1½ lb. artichokes	¼ teaspoon vinegar
1 pint water or white stock	seasoning
¼—½ pint milk	½ oz. flour
2 oz. butter	paprika pepper

Wash and peel the artichokes and, if large, cut into small pieces. Remember to keep the artichokes in cold water, with a tablespoon of lemon juice to keep them a good colour, until ready to cook them. Put into a saucepan with the water or stock, vinegar and seasoning. Simmer gently for a good 30 minutes. Rub through a sieve, then return the purée to the saucepan together with the butter. Blend the flour with the cold milk, stir into the boiling purée and continue cooking, stirring all the time, until a smooth thick sauce. Garnish with paprika pepper and serve with toast. If liked a few of the artichokes can be saved and cut into tiny pieces and then put into the soup.

6   CREAM OF ASPARAGUS SOUP

1 lb. asparagus	1 oz. butter
1 pint water or white stock	1 onion
seasoning	¼ pint thin white sauce*
	little cream

* Made with: ¼ oz. butter, ¼ oz. flour, ¼ pint milk

Cut the asparagus into small pieces. Toss in the melted butter, cook for 5 minutes. Add the water and chopped onion. Simmer steadily until the asparagus is very soft, then rub through a hair sieve. Reheat the asparagus purée and add to the hot sauce. Follow directions for Cream of Tomato Soup (Recipe 42).

7   ASPARAGUS PURÉE SOUP

This gives a much stronger flavoured soup than Recipe 6.

2 oz. butter	1½ lb. asparagus
1 oz. flour	1¼ pints water or stock
1 tiny onion	seasoning
little cream	

Heat the butter and fry the finely diced onion until soft, but not coloured. Blend in the flour and the stock and bring to the boil. Add the chopped asparagus (be careful to keep some tips intact) and simmer gently until the tips are quite tender. Remove some to use as garnish but continue cooking the rest of the asparagus until very soft. Rub through a sieve, then return to the pan, adding a little cream and extra seasoning if desired. Garnish with the asparagus tips.

8   CREAM OF BEETROOT SOUP

Ingredients as Cream of Asparagus Soup (Recipe 6), but use 1 lb. beetroot, instead of asparagus. Cut this into small pieces to speed cooking process.

Variations on this:

Beetroot and Celery Soup. Use ½ beetroot and ½ celery.
Beetroot and Onion Soup. Use 12 oz. beetroot and 2 onions.

Today it is generally considered more attractive to serve soup in cups rather than in wide soup plates. This is practical, too, because the soup keeps very much hotter in a deep cup than in a wide receptacle.

9   CAULIFLOWER SOUP

1 medium sized cauliflower	1 oz. butter
1 onion	1 oz. flour
1 pint water or white stock	¼ pint milk
seasoning	cayenne pepper

Cut up the stalks of the cauliflower and some of the flowers. Put into a pan with the chopped onion, water and seasoning and simmer gently until tender. Rub through a sieve. Make white sauce of the butter, flour and milk; add the cauliflower purée and reheat, adding a little extra milk if too thick. Meanwhile divide the rest of the flowerets of cauliflower into very small pieces. Boil in salted water until just tender. Put into the soup, and garnish with cayenne pepper.

Variations:

Cream of cauliflower soup. Use a little less water, and add cream to the soup after blending with the sauce.
Cheese and cauliflower soup. Add 2—3 oz. grated cheese to the soup and heat until melted.
Golden ball cauliflower soup. Blend the yolk of an egg with a little cream. Stir into the soup just before serving and thicken without boiling. Garnish with egg yolk, rubbed through a sieve to look like mimosa balls.

10 CELERY SOUP OR CHOWDER

8 – 10 oz. celery	2 medium sized potatoes
¼ pint milk	½ pint white stock or water
1 onion	½ oz. flour
1 oz. butter	seasoning

Chop the celery into very tiny pieces and chop or grate the onion. Cut the potatoes into small dice. Simmer together in the stock or water until tender, seasoning well. Meanwhile make a thin sauce of the butter, flour and milk, add celery mixture to this. Heat thoroughly, re-season if necessary and serve garnished with the tiny celery tips or croûtons of fried bread (Recipe 91).

11 CREAM OF CELERY SOUP

1 good sized head celery	2 oz. butter
1¼ pints stock or water	¼ pint milk
¼ pint cream or evaporated milk	seasoning, including celery salt
1 oz. flour	cayenne pepper

If you do not wish to sieve this soup, cut the celery into very tiny pieces. Simmer the celery with the water or stock until tender, sieve if wished. Meanwhile make a white sauce of the flour, butter and milk; this will be very thick, so the celery mixture or purée needs to be added, and blended very slowly into this. Re-heat, and then add the cream, taste and re-season if wished. Garnish with cayenne pepper.

Variations:

Cream of celery soup with almonds. Sprinkle blanched shredded almonds on the soup before serving; these can be browned if wished.
Chicken and celery soup. Use chicken stock, and add little diced cooked chicken before serving.
Brown celery soup. Use brown stock.
Celery and tomato soup. Either use tomato juice instead of water or add 2 or 3 tomatoes to the celery.

12 CARROT SOUP

1 lb. carrots	1 oz. butter or margarine
1 onion	1 oz. flour
1 pint stock or water	¼ pint milk
seasoning	watercress

Peel and chop the carrots and onion and simmer gently in the water or stock until tender. Rub through a sieve. Meanwhile make a sauce of the butter, flour, and milk, add the carrot mixture, reheat and season to taste. Garnish with chopped watercress.

Variations:

Cream of carrot soup. Add a little cream before serving; use slightly less water.
Carrot and rice soup. Ingredients as above, but do not sieve, but dice the carrots or onion. Add 1 oz. rice and cook with the vegetables.
See also Potato and Carrot Soup (Recipe 34).

13 SWEET CORN SOUP

3 – 4 corn cobs	1 oz. flour
1 onion	1 oz. butter
½ pint water	¼ pint milk
salt	pepper
little cream	little sherry

Remove the green leaves from the corns, and put these corn cobs (split down the centre if wished) with the onion into a pan of water and simmer steadily until the corn is soft. Strip off the cob. Make the white sauce with the butter, flour and milk, add the ½ pint water in which the corn and onion were cooked, straining this if wished. Stir the corn cobs into the sauce, and season very well. Add the cream and sherry.

If wished canned corn or cooked frozen corn can be used instead. A little chopped celery can be added instead of onion to the water.

CABBAGE SOUPS

Cabbage can be used in place of cauliflower in the Cauliflower Soups (Recipe 9), and the following is a particularly good filling winter soup.

14 BACON AND CABBAGE SOUP

4 oz. diced bacon	1 large onion
medium sized cabbage	1¼ pints good brown stock
2 skinned tomatoes	
seasoning	1 oz. dripping or butter
	1 oz. butter

Heat the butter and dripping (or all butter) and fry the chopped onion in this until golden brown, add the chopped tomatoes and bacon and cook together. Pour in the brown stock and bring to the boil, add the finely shredded cabbage and cook fairly quickly until tender. Season well. This soup can be sieved if wished, but it is not necessary if the cabbage is well shredded. Do not overcook the cabbage, so it has a 'nutty' flavour.

15 CHESTNUT SOUP

1 lb. chestnuts	¼ pint milk
1 pint water or white stock	good pinch salt, cayenne pepper and sugar (if liked)
2 oz. margarine or butter	

Split the skins of the chestnuts; cover with water and cook for 15 minutes. Peel the nuts while still hot; then return to the saucepan with the pint of water or stock. Simmer gently for 45 minutes. Rub the chestnuts through a sieve; then put the purée into the pan, together with the butter or margarine, milk and seasoning. Heat slowly, then serve with crisp pieces of toast or croûtons of bread.

16 QUICKLY PREPARED CHEESE SOUP

2 small thinly sliced onions	¼ pint white stock or water
1¼ oz. butter	6 oz. small diced Cheddar cheese
1¼ oz. plain flour	
1 pint milk	½ level teaspoon salt
	pinch cayenne pepper and grated nutmeg

Cook the onion in the butter for a few minutes, without browning. Toss in the flour and stir over a low heat for a further minute. Add the milk and stock or water gradually, and stir until boiling. Season, and simmer gently for 5 minutes. Mix in the cheese and reheat without boiling until it has melted. Serve hot with toast or fried croûtons.

17   CHICORY SOUP

about 8 — 9 oz. chicory
1 or 2 leeks
1 oz. butter or margarine
1 oz. flour

½ pint milk
squeeze lemon juice
1¼ pints water or white
    stock
seasoning

Chop the chicory into small pieces, and slice the leeks. Put into a saucepan with the water or stock and seasoning and simmer until tender. Rub through a sieve. Make a white sauce of the butter, flour and milk, add the chicory purée, and the lemon juice. Re-season to taste. This soup is improved if a good knob of butter is added just before serving.

Variation:

Cream of chicory soup. Just add a little cream before serving, and use slightly less water in cooking the chicory. See also Celery Soups (Recipe 11).

18   THICK CUCUMBER SOUP

1 medium sized cucumber
2 egg yolks
¼ pint cream
seasoning

1 good sized onion
little lemon juice
1 pint water

If all the peel is left on the cucumber this gives a bitter taste, although this can be improved if the cucumber is simmered for a few minutes in one lot of water, then this water is thrown away and a new amount of water is used. However, the very best solution seems to be to peel the cucumber completely, or to give a slightly strong flavour to keep the peel on about one-third of the cucumber. Cut the cucumber into small pieces and chop the onion. Put into a pan with the water, lemon juice and seasoning and simmer until tender. Rub through a sieve, or leave diced. Beat the egg yolks with the cream, add to the cucumber purée, and heat, without boiling. Serve garnished with croûtons of bread (Recipe 91).

Variation:

Quick Cucumber Soup. Add 3 oz. peeled and chopped cucumber to a 10 oz. can of condensed chicken soup diluted with ½ pint milk. Simmer 5 minutes, and serve hot or chilled, garnished with slices of cucumber.

19 CUCUMBER PURÉE SOUP

2 medium sized cucumbers	little celery
	1 onion
seasoning	1 oz. butter
¼ pint white stock	1 oz. flour
parsley	¼ pint milk

See Recipe 18 for remarks on peeling cucumbers. Chop the cucumber and onion and mix with the chopped celery. If celery is not obtainable chicory or celeriac could be used instead. Put into a pan with the stock and simmer until tender. Rub through a sieve. Meanwhile make a white sauce with the butter, flour and milk, add the cucumber purée and reheat. Season well. A little lemon juice or vinegar can be added when heated but do not boil again. Garnish with chopped parsley.

20 WHITE FOAM SOUP

1½ oz. butter	pinch ground mace
1 oz. flour	pepper and salt
1 quart milk	2 eggs
1 onion, chopped	4 oz. grated Cheddar
1 stick celery diced	cheese
(when available)	1 tablespoon chopped
or 1 teaspoon celery	parsley

Melt the butter, add the flour and cook gently for a minute, stirring. Mix in the milk gradually and bring to the boil, stirring. Add the onion, celery, mace and seasoning, and simmer 20—30 minutes. Cool slightly and add the grated cheese and beaten yolks. Reheat without boiling, stirring until the cheese is melted. Beat the egg whites until stiff, fold half into the soup and put the rest into the soup bowl and pour the soup over. Sprinkle with chopped parsley and serve at once.

21 LETTUCE SOUP

Use the same ingredients as for Cauliflower Soup and variations (Recipe 9), but since lettuce has less flavour than cauliflower and weighs lighter you will need a good sized lettuce. If you remove the heart from 2 lettuces and use all the outer leaves this gives the best flavour and will give a good consistency. A little sour cream can be stirred in, if wished.

22 LEEK AND POTATO SOUP

3 good sized leeks	1 lb. potatoes
1½ pints white stock or water	1½ oz. margarine or butter
¼ gill cream or evaporated milk	¼ gill milk
parsley	seasoning

Slice the leeks, using some of the green part to give a good colour, then heat the butter in the pan and cook the leeks for about 5 minutes taking care they do not discolour. Add the sliced potatoes, stock and seasoning. Cook steadily for approximately 30 minutes. Sieve, then return to the pan, adding milk and cream, and reheat without boiling. Pour into hot soup tureen and stir in a little extra butter and chopped parsley. Garnish with Duchesse potato rings. (Recipe 36.)

23 CREAMED LEEK SOUP

4 good sized leeks	2 oz. grated cheese
1½ pints white stock	1 oz. butter
seasoning	1 oz. flour
cayenne pepper	¼ pint milk
¼ pint cream or evaporated milk	

Wash and chop the leeks. If you do not desire to serve this as a smooth sieved soup, then chop the leeks very finely indeed. Put into a pan with the stock and seasoning and cook until tender. Rub through a sieve. If not sieving use only 1 pint stock. Meanwhile make a very thick white sauce of the butter, flour and milk, and gradually blend in the leeks and liquid or sieved leek purée. Bring to the boil and cook together for several minutes. Stir in the cream and reheat. Garnish with cheese and cayenne pepper.

24 LENTIL SOUP

8 oz. washed lentils	½ oz. flour
1 pint stock or water	1 oz. butter
little chopped bacon	½ pint milk
1 onion	little chopped thyme or parsley
1 carrot	seasoning

Put the lentils, bacon, chopped onion, carrots, and stock into a pan. Add seasoning and thyme and simmer gently for about 1½ hours. The lentils can be soaked overnight if wished. Add the seasoning at the very beginning of cooking. Meanwhile make a very thin sauce with the butter, flour and milk. Add the lentil purée and reheat. Season to taste. Garnish with chopped parsley.

Variations:

Lentil and celery soup. Use about 6 oz. lentils and 4 oz. chopped celery.
Lentil and tomato soup. Use 4 oz. lentils only and 8 oz. tomatoes.

25   LENTIL PURÉE

This recipe is very much as above, but use rather more bacon or add a ham bone to the stock. Do not make a sauce, but when the lentil purée has been sieved, enough top of the milk or thin cream to give the correct consistency should be added.

If lentils are used instead of dried peas in Recipe 38 you have another excellent lentil soup.

26   CHEESE SOUP

¼ onion (finely chopped)	8 oz. grated processed
2 oz. butter	Cheddar cheese
1½ oz. flour	3 carrots (finely chopped
1 pint milk	or grated)
1 pint stock	2 sticks celery or piece of
2 teaspoons salt	celeriac (finely chopped
pinch pepper	or grated)

Sauté the onion in the butter until tender. Add the flour and cook slowly for a minute, stirring well. Add the milk,

seasoning and stock gradually, stirring continuously, and bring to the boil. Add the grated cheese and stir until melted. Add carrots and celery, and cook until the vegetables are tender. Serve hot with caraway seed toast fingers.

Caraway Seed Toast Fingers

crusts from slices of bread	butter
	caraway seeds

Remove the crusts from several slices of bread, cut fairly thin. Butter one side and sprinkle with caraway seeds. Toast the buttered side to a golden brown and cut into fingers. Serve at once.

27   CREAM OF MUSHROOM SOUP

8 oz. mushrooms*	2 oz. margarine or butter
1 pint water or stock	2 oz. flour
¾ pint fresh milk	seasoning

Chop mushrooms finely unless it is desired to strain the soup. Melt margarine or butter in saucepan, fry mushrooms for 5 minutes, stirring to prevent their discolouring. Stir in the flour and cook for 3 minutes. Remove the pan from the heat and gradually add water and milk. Bring to the boil and cook until soup thickens. Season.

* The stems of mushrooms could be used if desired

28   MUSHROOM SOUP

8 oz. mushrooms	1 pint milk or milk and
dash of vinegar	chicken stock
few bacon rinds	seasoning
2 oz. butter	2 tablespoons cream or
1 oz. cornflour	top of milk
	grated nutmeg

Wash mushrooms, but leave them whole; put them with 1 pint water, a dash of vinegar and bacon rinds into a pan, bring slowly to the boil, then simmer till tender — about 10 minutes. Strain water, discard rinds, and cut mushrooms into strips. Melt butter in the pan, add cornflour and mix well, then add the milk, stir until boiling and cook for a few minutes. Stir in the mushrooms and the water in which they were cooked, bring to boiling point again, season carefully, stir in the cream just before serving and add a grating of nutmeg. Garnish with croûtons of fried bread. *Illustrated in colour picture No. 3.*

29   NETTLE SOUP

Young nettles make an excellent soup. Either wear gloves when picking them or grasp very firmly. Wash well and follow exactly the same directions as Cream of Spinach soup (Recipe 53). Garnish with chopped chives. Young nettles can also be shredded finely and added to Consommé (Recipe 55). *Illustrated in colour picture No. 4.*

30   CREAM OF ONION SOUP

Although onions have such a strong flavour when raw, they give a most delicate flavoured soup. Another Onion Soup recipe is found in Recipe 110.

4 really large onions	¼ oz. cornflour
1 pint stock or water	1 oz. grated cheese
seasoning	if desired
cayenne pepper	2 oz butter
	¼ pint milk

Cook the onions in the stock or water until tender, then either chop finely or sieve; make sure the onions are seasoned well during cooking. Make a sauce of the cornflour, butter and milk and add the chopped onions and stock or onion purée. Heat together, and re-season if necessary. Serve garnished with cayenne pepper and grated cheese.

Variations:

Leek and Onion Soup. Mix leeks and onions.
Brown Onion Soup. Use brown stock both for simmering the onions and for the sauce, so that instead of a creamy white soup you have a brown one. Add a little Worcestershire sauce and dark sherry if wished.

Potato Soups

33 QUICK POTATO CHOWDER

8 oz. peeled potatoes	2 rashers of bacon
4 oz. scraped carrots	1 onion
piece celery	1¼ pints good stock
grated cheese	seasoning
	chopped watercress

Grate all the vegetables, and cook in the stock for about 5—10 minutes only. Meanwhile dice and fry the bacon. Add to the well seasoned soup and garnish with cheese and chopped watercress. For a very thick chowder a little more potato can be used.

34 POTATO AND CARROT SOUP

Use Cream of Potato Soup (Recipe 32), but use 5 oz. potatoes and 5 oz. carrots.

35 POTATO AND GREEN PEA SOUP

4 oz. peeled potatoes	1½ pints water or stock
1 lb. peas	little mint
salt	pinch sugar
pepper	little cream

Dice the potatoes, and if the pea pods are very young do not bother to shell the peas — just chop up the pods containing the peas.

If the peas and the pods seem rather tough, then simmer the pods for a short time in the stock or water before adding the peas and diced potatoes. Simmer pods, potatoes, peas, in the stock, adding a little salt and pepper, and sprig of mint to taste. When quite tender rub through a sieve. Reheat adding pinch sugar and any extra seasoning and a little cream or knob of butter. Garnish with freshly chopped mint.

New potatoes and young peas together make a delicious summer soup.

31 JULIENNE POTATO SOUP
with Cheese Rusks

12 oz. potatoes	2 pints white stock (water
1 medium sized onion	may be used)
¼ oz. butter	1 level teaspoon salt
2 oz. bacon (optional)	pinch pepper, nutmeg and
	thyme

Cheese Rusks

4 large slices thickly	4 oz. finely grated
buttered white or	Cheddar cheese
brown bread	

Scrub and peel the potatoes and cut into match-like strips and slice the onion thinly. Heat the butter in a saucepan and brown the onion lightly. Add the potato strips, seasoning and flavouring, and pour on the boiling stock. Cook gently for 15—20 minutes. Serve hot with cheese rusks.

To make the cheese rusks: cover the buttered bread slices with the finely grated cheese, pressing down with a knife. Bake in a moderately hot oven (400°F. — Gas Mark 5) for 15—20 minutes until crisp and golden brown. Cut neatly. The soup and rusks make a nourishing meal.

32 CREAM OF POTATO SOUP

8 oz. peeled potatoes	¼ pint milk
1 pint white stock or water	little cream, or evaporated
1 large onion	milk
bay leaf	1 oz. butter
cayenne pepper	1 oz. flour
watercress	seasoning

Simmer the potatoes and onion with bay leaf in the stock until soft. Rub through a sieve. Make a white sauce of the butter, flour and milk, and add the potato purée. Stir in the cream, and a little extra butter if possible. Season well and garnish with cayenne pepper and chopped watercress. *Illustrated in colour picture No. 6.*

Variations:

Potato and Onion Soup. Use 2 large onions, chopped, and plenty of butter. Garnish if liked with very soft pieces of cooked potato. (See illustration on right.)

Quick Potato Soup. Grate the potatoes and cook for about 5 minutes until soft in ½ pint stock only. Add to the sauce and stir in cream to taste. Garnish with slices of hard-boiled egg. *Illustrated in colour picture No. 5.*

36 DUCHESSE POTATOES

Beat a good knob of butter and an egg or egg yolk into well mashed potatoes. It is advisable to sieve the potatoes so they can be piped easily. Put into a cloth bag with a large potato rose pipe and pipe into small rosettes or rings on to well greased baking trays. Brown for a few minutes in a hot oven. Excellent on most soups as a substantial garnish.

37 CREAMY POTATO CHOWDER

5 medium sized potatoes	1¾ pints milk
3 medium sized onions	salt and pepper
1 can mushroom soup	grated nutmeg
(16 oz.)	1 teaspoon made
1 oz. butter	mustard

Dice the potatoes and slice the onion. Cook the potatoes and onions in a small amount of water until tender, then rub through a sieve. Add the mushroom soup, butter, milk, salt and pepper to taste, nutmeg and mustard. Heat gently. For colour a few green peas, sliced carrot or pepper can be added. Serve hot or icy cold.

Variations:

Add a dash of angostura bitters to the soup; whip ¼ pint cream and top each serving.

Top with dabs of cottage cheese, chive flavoured. Season the chowder with a very little curry powder. Reduce the potatoes by 2, and add 2 oz. fluffy cooked rice just before serving.

See also Quick Potato Chowder, and Potato soup (Recipes 31—35).

38 DRIED PEA SOUP

8 oz dried peas	1 teaspoon sugar
2 pints bacon stock *	sprig mint
2 onions	seasoning
1 carrot	2 rashers bacon
1 turnip	

* When you have stock left from boiling a piece of bacon, try to use it in a soup like this, because the flavour is excellent. A lentil soup or a vegetable soup can be made with bacon stock too with very good results.

Soak the peas overnight in the bacon stock — put into saucepan with the vegetables, seasoning and mint and simmer gently for approximately 1¼ to 1½ hours. Either rub through a sieve or beat until very smooth. Taste and re-season. Garnish with crisp pieces of bacon.

39 PEA SOUP

When peas are very young it is possible to make this soup with the pea pods only — so using the peas as a vegetable.

Pods from 2 lb. fresh peas can be used instead of the quantity of peas and pods given in this recipe.

1¼ lb. peas (including	salt
pods)	pepper
1¼ pint water or ham	little mint
stock	small onion (if desired)
good pinch sugar	
good knob of butter	

Wash pods and shell. Put the pods and peas into the saucepan with stock, the onion, seasoning, little sprig mint and simmer until tender. Rub through a sieve; this must be done very vigorously, so only the skins of the pods are left. Return to the pan, reheat, adding a little sugar to taste and a good knob of butter. Serve garnished with a few freshly cooked peas or chopped mint or croûtons of fried bread. If the pods are very fleshy the soup may be a little thick when sieved so add a small quantity of extra stock or milk.

40 RICE SOUP

Rice may be added to many of the soups in this section to give a more substantial dish, but the following is excellent for an invalid soup for it is nutritious and full of flavour.

3 oz. rice (use either	2 oz. butter
Patna or round rice)	¼ pint milk
1 pint stock	salt
pepper	1 onion
nutmeg or bay leaf	
to flavour	

Heat the butter in the pan, and toss the rice in this for several minutes. Add stock and seasoning and cook steadily for about 20 minutes. If you wish to keep the onion in the soup it should be finely chopped, but if put in whole it can be removed when wished. The bay leaf should also be removed when serving. Add milk, reheat and season.

Variations:

Curried rice soup. Add 1 or 2 teaspoons curry powder when cooking the rice in the butter.

Bacon and rice soup. Dice 1 or 2 rashers of bacon finely and add to the rice, after being fried in the butter.

Savoury rice soup. Use a little extra butter, and after frying the rice add thinly sliced onions and tomatoes, toss in the butter, then proceed as before.

41 SORREL SOUP

Ingredients as Cream of Spinach Soup (Recipe 41), but use sorrel instead of spinach.

44   TOMATO AND RICE BROTH

1½ pints tomato juice or	2 oz. rice
8 oz. tomatoes and	salt
1 pint water	pepper
1 diced onion	1 diced carrot
little diced celery	cheese or ham to garnish
or celeriac	

If using tomatoes they should be simmered in the water or stock, then the liquid strained off. Add the rice to the boiling tomato liquid, together with the diced vegetables. Season well and cook for about 20 minutes until rice and vegetables are tender.

Serve with grated cheese if wished or topped with finely diced ham.

45   JULIANA SOUP

¼ oz. butter	1 pint milk
1 small finely chopped	¼ pint water
onion	pepper, salt and sugar
¾ oz. plain flour	to taste
3 tablespoons tomato	4 oz. grated cheese
purée	

Melt the butter and lightly fry the finely chopped onion. Mix in the flour, and cook for a minute. Add the milk, water and tomato purée, and bring to the boil stirring all the time. Season and simmer gently for 5 minutes. Add good pinch of sugar to taste and stir in the grated cheese just before serving. Reheat to melt the cheese and serve hot with fried or toasted croûtons. Cheddar or Cheshire cheese is ideal for this soup.

42   CREAM OF TOMATO SOUP

1 lb. tomatoes	bouquet garni
1 onion	salt
1 carrot	pepper
1 stick celery	¾ oz. cornflour
little fat bacon	¼—½ pint milk
1½ pints stock	pinch sugar

Slice the vegetables. Fry the bacon slowly to extract the fat, then add the vegetables and sauté for about 10 minutes. Add the stock (or water), seasoning and *bouquet garni*, bring to the boil and simmer gently until tender — about 1 hour. Remove the *bouquet garni*, rub the soup through a fine sieve, and add the cornflour, blended with the milk. Return to the pan, bring just to the boil, stirring well, and cook gently for 2—3 minutes. Re-season, add the sugar and serve with your chosen garnish.

Try a sprinkle of finely chopped white of egg, or attractively shaped croûtons, toasted golden brown, or cut shapes in white of egg.

43   TOMATO AND CELERY SOUP

1 lb. tomatoes	2 oz. butter
small head celery	1½ pints water or white
salt	stock
pinch brown sugar	pepper
	¼ oz. cornflour

Chop the tomatoes and celery into small pieces and simmer with 1 pint of the stock and seasoning until soft. Rub through a sieve, then return to the saucepan, together with the butter and the cornflour, blended with the other ½ pint water or stock. Bring to the boil, and cook until thickened, adding the sugar and extra seasoning required.

46   TOMATO AND LENTIL SOUP

1 2 oz. tomatoes.   *2 oz. lentils*
1¼ pints stock (preferably   *salt*
  bacon stock)   *pepper*
knob of butter   *bouquet garni*

Simmer the tomatoes and lentils (which can be soaked
overnight in the stock) together with the well seasoned
stock until tender. Either rub through a sieve, or if you
skin the tomatoes beforehand there is no need to sieve,
just beat the mixture well with a wooden spoon. Heat
with the butter, seasoning and herbs for about 5 — 10
minutes.

47   CREAM OF TURNIP SOUP

Ingredients and method as Cream of Potato Soup (Recipe 32) when the turnips are young and not too strong
flavoured. As they very quickly become rather strong
flavoured it is a good idea during the winter months to
use a mixture of turnips and potatoes. A pinch of grated
nutmeg gives a good flavour to this soup.

48   CREAM OF VEGETABLE SOUP

Ingredients and method as Cream of Potato Soup (Recipe 32), using a mixture of vegetables in season. Make
sure not to use too many of one vegetable, so the soup is
flavoured by the mixture.

  Garnish with fried croûtons of bread, chopped parsley,
or for a more substantial soup top with toast and grated
cheese and brown under a moderate grill.

49   QUICK VEGETABLE SOUP

approximately 1¼ lb.   *1¼ pints stock or water,*
  mixed vegetables   *with bouillon cube*
chopped parsley   *grated cheese*
seasoning

Peel and grate the vegetables on a coarse grater. Bring
the stock or water and bouillon cube to the boil, add the
vegetables and seasoning and cook rapidly for about
5 — 8 minutes until the vegetables are just tender. Pour
into hot soup cups and sprinkle with lots of grated cheese
and parsley.

  Do choose a good mixture of vegetables for an interesting flavour.

50 THICK VEGETABLE BROTH

1¼ lb. mixed vegetables	1 oz. rice or pearl barley
chopped parsley	1¼ pints stock or water
seasoning	with a bouillon cube
	grated cheese

Peel and cut the vegetables into small dice or grate them very coarsely. If using pearl barley blanch this by putting into cold water, bringing to the boil, and cooking for 1 minute. Strain, then cook in boiling salted water until tender. If using rice cook in boiling salted water until soft. Meanwhile put the vegetables and stock into pan and cook until tender; this will vary according to how large the pieces, but will take from 10 — 20 minutes. Add the barley or rice and reheat then serve garnished with chopped parsley and cheese.

51 PARTY CHOWDER

1 rasher bacon	2 oz. rolled oats
1¼ oz. butter	2 pints stock
8 oz. carrots	2 tablespoons dried onion
8 oz. skinned tomatoes	or 2 large onions
small can peas	salt
2 tablespoons cream	pepper
grated cheese	

Dice or slice the carrots thinly, and chop the onions and tomatoes. Melt the butter in a saucepan, and lightly fry the oats until golden brown. Gradually add the stock, and bring to the boil, stirring all the time. Add carrots, diced bacon, onions, tomatoes and seasoning and simmer for 40 minutes. Add peas and simmer for a further 10 minutes. Sieve if wished. Stir in the cream and serve the soup sprinkled with grated cheese.

52 SPRING SOUP

12 small spring onions	½ small lettuce (or young
few small young carrots	nettle leaves)
2 teaspoons flour	¼ pint milk
1¼ pints stock or water	1 egg
seasoning	2 oz. butter or oil

Slice the onions and shred the lettuce or nettle leaves. Heat half the butter in a saucepan and fry the lettuce,

half the onions and all the carrots for a few minutes. Add the stock and simmer gently for 30 minutes. Rub through a sieve, then return to the pan, blending the flour with the milk; stir in the flour and milk, bring to the boil and cook until slightly thickened. Little thickening is used in this recipe. Season well. Meanwhile heat the rest of the butter or oil and fry the remainder of the onions. Blend a beaten egg into the soup, and cook WITHOUT BOILING for a few minutes. Garnish with the fried onion.

53 CREAMED SPINACH SOUP

1 lb. spinach or 1 small	1 oz. cornflour
packet frozen spinach	1¼ pints milk
1 oz. butter	2 egg yolks
1 small onion — sliced	3 tablespoons cream
salt	nutmeg
pepper	

Cook and sieve the spinach. Heat the butter in a saucepan and sauté the onion until tender, but not brown. Add the cornflour, mix well and cook for a few minutes. Add the milk, stir till boiling and boil for 3 minutes. Strain the sauce on to the spinach, then return to the heat.

Mix the egg yolks and cream, add a little of the soup, then return all to the saucepan. Add seasonings, and reheat gently before serving, for several minutes. Do NOT ALLOW TO BOIL. Garnish with croûtons of fried bread. *Illustrated in colour picture No. 9.*

54 WATERCRESS SOUP

2 pints milk	8 oz. watercress (leaves
2 oz. margarine	only)
2 oz. flour	1 tablespoon lemon juice
seasoning	1 egg

Heat the margarine in a large saucepan, stir in the flour, and cook steadily for several minutes. Remove from the heat, add the cold milk. Return to the heat, stirring all the time. When the mixture has thickened, add chopped watercress and seasoning, then draw to one side for 1 minute. Whisk in beaten egg and lemon juice. Serve at once.

3   MUSHROOM SOUP (Recipe 28)

4   NETTLE SOUP (Recipe 29)

5   **LOBSTER AND ASPARAGUS BISQUE** (Recipe 83)
QUICK POTATO SOUP (Recipe 32)
CONSOMMÉ (Recipe 55)
JELLIED CONSOMMÉ (Recipe 95)

Meat Soups

In this section are a variety of meat soups, from clear consommé to really thick broths. A good stock is essential for consommé and for many of the recipes, so it is worth while reading Recipe 92 on how to obtain this. When it is not possible to make stock you will find water with a yeast extract or meat extract or a good bouillon cube a useful substitute.

The bones of poultry or game can be used to make delicious soups — for a special occasion try the famous hare soup (Recipe 70) or devilled rabbit soup Recipe 77). You will find recipes for many other traditional soups — mock turtle (which is made from calf's head), oxtail, kidney soup and Scotch broth. All these make a very good first course for a cold meal.

55 CONSOMMÉ

12 oz. shin of beef	1 carrot
2 pints good stock	small piece celery
seasoning	sprig parsley
1 onion	bay leaf

Cut the meat into small pieces and put them into the saucepan together with the other ingredients. Simmer very gently for 1 hour, then strain through several thicknesses of muslin. Add a dessertspoon sherry if desired. To clear a consommé put in a stiffly beaten egg white and clean egg shell and gently simmer again for 20 minutes, then re-strain. *Illustrated in colour picture No. 5.*

56 CONSOMMÉ JULIENNE

To the above quantity allow:

1 good sized carrot	1 leek or onion
½ medium-sized turnip	small piece cabbage
1 oz. margarine	

Cut the vegetables into thin pieces about the size and thickness of a matchstick. Melt a good oz. margarine in a saucepan and toss the vegetables in this until just turning brown. Add about ½ gill of the consommé and cook gently until quite tender. Take off any fat and add to the consommé, reheating gently.

57 CONSOMMÉ CELESTINE

consommé (Recipe 55)	thin pancake batter
	oil or fat for frying

Make the pancakes in the usual way, then cut into wafer thin strips. Heat in the consommé.

58 CONSOMMÉ CHASSEUR

consommé (Recipe 55)	about ¼ teacup very finely
little port wine	diced cooked game or
	poultry

Heat the diced game in the consommé. When very hot add port wine.

59 BANQUET CONSOMMÉ

To the quantity of consommé given add julienne of smoked salmon.

60 CONSOMMÉ JARDINIÈRE

Use the same vegetables as in the previous recipe, but this time cut them either into small cubes or, using a vegetable cutter, shape into tiny rounds the size of a pea. Simmer in the consommé for a good 15 minutes.

61 CONSOMMÉ AU MACARONI

To the quantity of consommé given add 2 tablespoons quick cooking macaroni (or spaghetti). Cook 5 — 7 minutes in the consommé, then add a little finely chopped parsley.

62 CONSOMMÉ ROYALE

In this soup the garnish is made by the following custard: Put the yolks of 1 or 2 eggs into basin, whisk lightly, then add 1 whole egg and ½ gill stock or milk. Mix together and season well. Cover with greased paper and steam for 20 — 30 minutes. When quite cold and firm cut into small fancy shapes.

63 CONSOMMÉ AU VERMICELLI

To the quantity of consommé given add 2 tablespoons vermicelli. Cook gently for 7 minutes, than serve.

SOUP GARNISHES. Fried onion rings, croûtons, chopped parsley, grated cheese are all suitable garnishes for soups. See Recipes 129, 130 for more ideas for garnishes

64   CHICKEN SOUP

bones of 1 chicken	seasoning
1 teacup cooked chicken meat	1 tablespoon cornflour
¼ pint milk	2 pints chicken stock *
1 oz. butter	

* You will obtain this chicken stock from boiling a chicken, but if you have roasted the chicken, then it is suggested you use a chicken bouillon cube dissolved in water

Simmer the carcase in the stock for an hour, then strain. Add the cooked chicken meat and milk and cook for a further 15 minutes, then rub through sieve. Blend with cornflour, add butter, seasoning. Cook for 10 minutes.

65   CREAM OF CHICKEN SOUP

1 small boiling fowl	2 oz. butter
water to cover	2 oz. flour or 1 oz. cornflour
bouquet garni	
2 egg yolks	1 pint milk
seasoning	¼ pint cream or evaporated milk

Cut up the fowl if wished or use whole, then cover with cold water, add *bouquet garni* of herbs, seasoning and a few vegetables if wished (1 carrot, 1 onion, piece of celery). Do not use too many vegetables, otherwise the delicate flavour of the chicken will be lost. Simmer for 2 — 3 hours until tender. Take all the meat from the bones and rub through a sieve. Add to the stock to give a smooth thick mixture. Meanwhile make a sauce of the butter, flour, and milk. When thick and creamy add to the chicken mixture and reheat gently. Beat the egg yolks with the cream and add to the soup, then cook gently until thickened again; this takes about 3 minutes. Do NOT BOIL. This soup makes a large quantity, enough for about 12 — 18 portions, so is only suitable for large parties. It can however be adjusted as below.

Variations:

Economical Cream of Chicken Soup. Use the chicken soup recipe 64, using a little less stock, and add 2—3 tablespoon cream.

Chicken and Vegetable Soup. Use Recipe 64 or 65 but add a good mixture of vegetables to the chicken or chicken carcase when simmering. These should be added half way through cooking, so they retain as much colour and flavour as possible.

66   CHICKEN BROTH

approx. 2 pints stock from cooking chicken	1 oz. rice or pearl barley

Use the vegetables already cooked with the chicken plus about 1 teacup fresh finely-diced vegetables — or if preferred strain away the vegetables and use 2 or 3 teacups freshly diced vegetables. A really filling soup

If using pearl barley blanch this first by putting into cold water, then bring the water to the boil and strain. Add the blanched barley or rice to the stock and the vegetables and cook steadily for 15 minutes. Add tiny pieces of chicken and continue heating for about 10 minutes. Add seasoning, well tasting first, then pour into a hot dish. Garnish with the parsley and croûtons of fried bread. *Illustrated in colour picture No. 33.*

67   TURKEY SOUPS

Any of the recipes for Chicken soups can be used with turkey, and the bones of turkey make an excellent stock for this purpose. Use all the skin of the turkey after Christmas in the stock, for this provides much of the flavour. Use small pieces of stuffing to garnish the soup. *Chestnut and Turkey Soup* is a rather unusual mixture. Proceed as for Chicken Soup (Recipe 64) using some of the bones of the turkey. Instead of the chicken meat in Recipe 64 simmer about 4 oz. shelled chestnuts. Sieve and proceed as before.

68 GIBLET SOUP

giblets of poultry	2 oz. butter or poultry fat
1¼ — 2¼ pints water or	1 small onion
poultry stock*	1 tablespoon flour
bay leaf	parsley

* The amount of liquid depends on the size of the giblets. Large turkey or goose giblets need the larger amount of water, and you may care to increase the amount of onion

Heat the butter and toss the sliced onion in this. Work in the flour and cook gently for several minutes. Add the stock and giblets and simmer until the soup is cooked and the giblets really tender, putting in a bay leaf and sprig of parsley. Take the giblets out of the stock, rub through a sieve, or chop very finely indeed, return to the soup and reheat. A little sherry or port wine is excellent in this soup. Remove bay leaf and parsley before serving, and garnish with finely chopped parsley and croûtons.

69 GAME SOUP

Ingredients as Hare Soup (Recipe 70) but use the bones of the game, the liver etc. If using just the carcase of 1 bird halve the quantitites of water or stock etc.

70 HARE SOUP

bones of the hare	head and any other parts
2 pints water or stock	of flesh such as liver not
2 onions	being used in main dish.
2 bay leaves	Blood of hare can also be
2 small carrots	added to give richness of
piece of turnip	flavour
bouquet garni	¼ gill port wine or
1 oz. flour	Madeira (not essential)
	pinch sugar with seasoning
	2 oz. dripping, margarine
	or butter

Put the bones, meat, diced vegetables, herbs and blood into pan with the water or stock. Bring to the boil and continue cooking gently for 1½ hours. Strain carefully, and if any meat is left on the bones this should be sieved, minced or pounded until very fine and returned to the soup. Blend the flour with a little of the soup, add to the remainder, together with the margarine, butter or dripping. Bring slowly to the boil and cook until thickened, season then simmer for about 10 minutes. Lastly stir in the port wine. The butter etc. could be omitted if wished.

Variations:

Rabbit Soup. As above, but use rabbit instead of hare.
Creamed Rabbit or Hare Soup. Use 1½ pints stock, then make a white sauce with the flour, butter and ½ pint milk. Blend the hare stock etc. into this.

71 LIVER SOUP

8 oz. liver (can be ox	2 skinned tomatoes
liver)	2 oz. dripping or butter
1 onion	2 pints stock or water
1 oz. flour	seasoning
¼ pint thin cream or milk	

Cut the liver into *small* pieces, and fry for about 3 minutes in the dripping or butter. Take care it does not become hard on the outside. Add stock, seasoning, finely chopped onion and finely chopped tomatoes. Simmer gently for 30 — 45 minutes. Blend the flour with the milk or cream, stir into the soup and thicken slowly. Re-season if wished. If desired the liver can be sieved after cooking, but if finely chopped this is not necessary.

72 LIVER AND MUSHROOM SOUP

Use ingredients as Liver Soup (Recipe 71), but omit the tomatoes and use 4 oz. finely chopped mushrooms.

Variations:

Liver and Celery Soup. Omit tomatoes and onions and use a small head celery. This soup is better sieved.
Liver and Vegetable Soup. Make the Liver Soup (Recipe 71), but add 2 teacups cooked diced vegetables just before serving.

73 MOCK TURTLE SOUP

small calf's head	bouquet garni
water	seasoning
sherry or Madeira	

Wash the calf's head, split down the centre, remove brains if wished to use for a separate dish (also the tongue can be taken out). Cover with cold water, bring to the boil, throw away the water and cover with fresh water, add seasoning and herbs and simmer gently until tender — this takes 2 — 3 hours. Strain off the stock, and put into a pan. Cut the meat from the head. Clear the stock as described in Consommé (Recipe 55), add the diced meat and heat gently then put in sherry or Madeira just before serving.

This makes enough for about 8 — 10 people.

74 MULLIGATAWNY SOUP

2 pints stock*	2 onions
1 apple	1 oz. sultanas
2 oz. fat or dripping	1 tablespoon curry powder
1 tablespoon chutney	1 oz. flour
large carrot	seasoning
pinch sugar	little lemon juice or
	vinegar

* Best stock for this is made by simmering lamb or mutton bones or a small lamb's head

Chop the apple and vegetables into tiny pieces, and toss in the hot dripping, then work in the flour and curry powder. Add the stock, bring to the boil and cook until thickened. Add the other ingredients and cook together for about 45 minutes — 1 hour. Rub through a sieve, return to the pan and taste. Re-season if necessary or add little extra sugar or lemon juice.

75   KIDNEY SOUP

2 pints stock or water	8 oz. kidney (ox kidney
parsley	can be used)*
1 small onion	2 oz. butter
little port wine or	1 oz. flour
Burgundy	

* If using lambs' kidneys the cooking time will be 30 minutes only, so reduce the amount of stock to 1¼ — 1½ pints

Chop the kidney very finely, and fry with the finely chopped onion in the hot butter for a minute or two. Make sure not to harden the outside of the meat. Blend in the flour, and gradually add the stock. Bring to the boil, stir until smooth then simmer gently, adding seasoning and a spring of parsley, for about 1½ hours. Remove the parsley, add port wine and serve.

Variations:

Clear kidney soup. Recipe as above, but omit the flour and when kidney is cooked strain, return to pan adding the port wine.
With poached eggs. Put a poached egg into each hot plate or soup cup, then pour over the very hot soup.

Heat the fat and fry the chopped onion in this for a few minutes. Add diced bacon and apple and cook for a further few minutes, then work in the curry powder and flour. Add the stock, bring to the boil, and stir until smooth. Put in the rabbit carcase, head and other ingredients and cook steadily for 1½ — 2 hours. Either rub through a sieve or strain the soup for a clearer soup, reheat and serve.

Other methods of making rabbit soup at end of Recipe 70.

76   OX-TAIL SOUP

1 small ox-tail	2 oz. flour
1 small turnip	2 oz. cooking fat or
3 medium carrots	margarine
1 large onion	good pinch of mixed herbs
3 pints stock or water	salt, pepper

Soak the cut up ox-tail for an hour or so — throw away the water. Heat the fat and fry the sliced vegetables for about 5 minutes. Add the stock, ox-tail, pinch of herbs and plenty of seasoning and simmer gently for about 3 hours. Blend the flour with a teacup cold stock or water and stir this into the soup. Bring to the boil and cook for about 10 minutes. Take out the pieces of ox-tail, cut the meat from the bones, return to the soup and reheat. There is a fair amount of fat on this soup, so it is quite a good idea to make it the day before — allow it to cool and then take the fat from the top.

78   SCOTCH BROTH

1 oz. pearl barley	2 pints water
3 oz. sliced leeks or onion	salt and pepper
8 oz. stewing beef or	8 oz. diced carrot
mutton	8 oz. diced swede
2 oz. sliced cabbage	
1 tablespoon chopped	
parsley	

Blanch the barley by putting into cold water, bringing to the boil, then pouring the water away. Put the barley, diced beef and water into a pan, bring to the boil, skim, and simmer gently for 1 hour. Add the prepared vegetables, except the cabbage, plenty of seasoning and cook for a further 1½ hours. Add the cabbage and allow another 15 minutes cooking. Skim off any superfluous fat from the broth, pour into hot dish or soup cups and garnish with the parsley. If desired the meat can be left in one piece and removed from the soup and used for a separate dish.

77   DEVILLED RABBIT SOUP

bones from rabbit carcase	head and liver of rabbit
1 apple	2 onions
2 rashers of bacon	2 teaspoons curry powder
1 oz. fat	1 oz. flour
2 pints water or stock	bouquet garni
	little chutney

79   SHEEP'S HEAD BROTH

Ingredients as for Scotch Broth, but use a small sheep's head instead of the stewing beef or mutton. At the end of the cooking time the head can be removed and used as a separate dish or all the meat can be removed from the head, diced finely, then added to the broth. Other ingredients as the Scotch Broth (Recipe 78).

Fish Soups

A good soup can be made with most fish, and this makes an excellent start to a meal if a meat course is to follow. Many fish soups can be given to invalids. Do not overcook fish, particularly the shell variety.

80   WHITE FISH SOUPS

12 oz. white fish (plaice
*   cod, whiting, fresh*
*   haddock etc.)*
seasoning
small sprig parsley or
*   dill or fennel to flavour*

¾ pint water
small piece of onion
2 oz. butter
1 oz. flour
¾ pint milk

Put the fish, cut into pieces, the water, onion, seasoning and herb or herbs into a pan and simmer gently until the fish is just cooked. Rub through a sieve. Meanwhile make a sauce of the butter, flour and milk, add the fish purée and reheat, adding extra seasoning. Garnish with chopped bacon snippets, chopped parsley, chopped dill as desired.

Variations:

Fish and potato soup. Cook 2 potatoes with the fish, rub through a sieve. Omit the flour and just add milk and butter and reheat.
Cream of fish soup. Add little cream just before serving, and use slightly less water in cooking the fish.
Golden fish soup. Use slightly less milk in the sauce. Blend the yolks of 2 eggs with ½ teacup milk or thin cream, add to the fish soup and cook gently, without boiling, for several minutes.

81   FISH CHOWDER

1 lb. fresh haddock or
*   whiting or cod*
4—5 medium sized
*   potatoes*
2 pints fish stock or water
seasoning

1 large onion
1 large can evaporated
*   milk*
2 oz. butter
chopped parsley or
*   watercress*

Wash haddock, cut into small pieces. Peel and quarter potatoes, boil for 5 minutes, in enough water to cover. Add onion and fish. Cook until fish is tender — this takes about 20 minutes. Add evaporated milk, stock or water and butter, season to taste. Heat through. Garnish with finely chopped parsley or watercress and serve.

82   LOBSTER BISQUE

Thick soup for parties

½ large lobster or small
*   lobster*
2 oz. margarine or butter
1 oz. flour
1 pint water or fish stock

2 tablespoons cream
½ pint milk
1 oz. flour
1 teaspoon lemon juice
seasoning, including
*   paprika pepper*

Remove the flesh from the lobster and cut into small pieces. Save a few of the pieces for a garnish. Put the shell — well washed and crushed — into a large saucepan. Cover with the water or stock, add the lemon juice and simmer gently for a good 30 minutes. Strain carefully through a fine sieve and return to the pan together with lobster meat. Blend the flour with the milk and stir this into the soup together with the margarine or butter. Bring slowly to the boil and cook, stirring all the time until thickened. Add the cream, reheat and serve. Garnish with paprika pepper and the whole pieces of lobster.

83   LOBSTER AND ASPARAGUS BISQUE

Use Recipe 82 but instead of all fish stock use partly asparagus stock. Garnish with asparagus tips and pieces of lobster. *Illustrated in colour picture No. 5.*

84 LOBSTER CHOWDER

1 — 2 rashers bacon	1¼ teacups milk or
1 teaspoon finely chopped	evaporated milk
onion	1 pint water
1 medium sized diced	good pinch sugar
potato	1¼ oz. flour
1 small lobster	salt, pepper

Remove the flesh from the lobster. Put the shell into pan with 1 pint water and simmer gently for about 15 minutes. Strain, and add enough water to make up to 1 pint again. Take the rind from the bacon and cut into narrow strips. Put into a pan and fry lightly, add the onion and flour and cook gently — without colouring. Gradually add the lobster stock, stirring all the time. When the sauce has come to the boil and thickened, add lobster, cut into small pieces, and the rest of the ingredients. Either reduce heat under pan or put in double saucepan and cook until a thick creamy mixture. Serve with crisp fingers of toast.

85 MUSSEL SOUP

2 pints mussels	2 oz. rice
1 finely chopped onion	2 tablespoons finely
1 large skinned chopped	chopped celery
tomato	1¼ pints water
small bunch parsley	squeeze lemon juice or
seasoning	little vinegar

Scrub mussels well, discarding any that are open and will not close when sharply tapped. Put into a large saucepan with onion, celery, parsley and seasoning and heat slowly until mussels open. Remove mussels from liquid, take off shells. Meanwhile reheat liquid, add rice and cook until tender with chopped tomato and seasoning. Remove sprig of parsley, add mussels and lemon juice or vinegar, and re-heat gently. Garnish with chopped parsley. Always remove the 'beard', i.e. the rather stringy part, from mussels.

86 CREAM OF MUSSEL SOUP

2 pints mussels	2 oz. butter
1 onion	2 oz. flour
¼ pint water	1 pint milk
seasoning and bunch	little white wine if liked
parsley	

Prepare mussels and inspect them carefully, as described in Recipe 85, then put into a pan with onion, sprig parsley, water (slightly less water if adding white wine) and seasoning. Heat gently until mussels open. Take off shells and be careful to remove 'beard', i.e. the rather stringy part, from mussels. Meanwhile make a white sauce of the butter, flour and milk. Strain mussel liquid into this, add white wine, and heat. Put in mussels, heat gently and serve garnished with chopped parsley.

87 TUNA CHOWDER

7 oz. can tuna fish	12 oz. cooked vegetables
¾ pint white sauce or	such as green peas,
10 oz. can of tomato	sliced carrots, cut
or mushroom soup	celery, sliced onion
3 hard-boiled eggs	lemon
pepper	4 oz. short crust pastry
salt	(see Recipe 485)
	milk for glazing

Combine flaked tuna, sauce or soup, vegetables, sliced eggs. Season to taste with pepper, salt and lemon juice. Turn into pie dish, top with pastry. Slit or prick steam holes; decorate pie in the savoury tradition, if liked, with pastry leaves or other dainty fancy shapes. Brush with milk. Bake in centre of hot oven (450° F. — Gas Mark 7) for 10 minutes; reduce heat, bake for a further 10—15 minutes. Serve hot from oven.

Shell Fish Soups

Most shell fish can be made into soups, for example prawns shrimps or crab can be used in the Lobster Bisque and Chowder (Recipes 82—84).
Shell fish can also be used in the white fish recipes (80), but do not cook the fish (unless using the uncooked frozen scampi) since overcooking will make it tough.
The following is a good basic creamy shell fish soup:

88 CREAMED SHELL FISH SOUP

8 oz. prawns or shrimps	2 oz. butter
(weight when peeled)	2 oz. flour
¼ pint water	1 pint milk
little cream	seasoning

If using fresh shrimps or prawns simmer the shells in the water to obtain good flavoured stock. If using ready prepared or frozen fish, add a few drops anchovy essence to the water. If using uncooked frozen scampi simmer gently in the water for about 5 minutes, then strain off the liquid. Chop the shrimps or prawns into small pieces, make the white sauce of butter, flour and milk, add the fish stock, together with 2 or 3 drops cochineal if wished to give a pale pink colour. Add the shell fish and cream, taste and season as necessary and heat gently.

Pressure Cookers for Soups

Soup making, which normally takes a fairly long cooking time, can be done in a matter of minutes in a pressure cooker. In addition bone stock can be prepared quickly and easily, and you will extract the very maximum flavour from the bones. You will find that pressure cooking does not spoil the flavour of the soups, in fact there tends to be an improvement in the flavour.

Certain things are very important to remember:

1. Make sure the cooker is never more than half filled when making soups in your pressure cooker.
2. Allow pressure to drop at room temperature, and use 15 lb. pressure.
3. Reduce the amount of liquid in the soups — for soups that normally take a long time in cooking you will find you need half the normal quantity of liquid only.
4. Do not over-season ingredients when pressure cooking soups; you retain more of the natural mineral salts from the vegetables.

89 MAKING STOCK IN A PRESSURE COOKER

The following gives a good beef stock, but follow directions for other stocks in Recipe 92.

2 lb. bones, large marrow bones if possible	1 carrot
	1 turnip
2 pints water	1 onion
	1 teaspoon salt

Break the bones and put into the pressure cooker with the other ingredients. Bring slowly to the boil, and remove the scum from the top. Fix the lid and bring steadily to pressure. Reduce the heat and cook for 45 minutes. Allow pressure to return to normal before removing lid. When the stock is very cold remove any fat from top. Do not add potatoes or other green vegetables, to this stock, as it will then not keep.

90 PRESSURE COOKED SOUPS

If you wish to adapt the recipes in this section for cooking in your pressure pan, the following will be a guide to some of the soups.

Cream of Artichoke Soup (Recipe 5).	Use ¾ pint liquid. Cook for 10 minutes at pressure
Cream of Asparagus Soup (Recipe 6)	Use ¾ pint liquid. Cook for 10 minutes at pressure or less if very small and tender.
Asparagus Purée Soup (Recipe 7)	Use 1 pint liquid. Cook for 10 minutes at pressure.
Cream of Beetroot Soup (Recipe 8)	Use 1 pint liquid. Cook for 10 minutes at pressure.
Cauliflower Soup (Recipe 9)	Use ¾ pint liquid. Cook for 5 minutes at pressure.

As you will see the vegetable soups take a few minutes only. Give just a little longer than you would give to cook the vegetable when fresh in your pressure cooker. On the whole reduce the liquid by 25%. After softening the vegetables allow pressure to drop and then treat the pressure cooker like an ordinary pan.

Consommé (Recipe 55)	Use just over 1¼ pints liquid. Cook for 25—30 minutes at pressure.
Chicken Soup (Recipe 64)	Use about 1 pint stock. Cook for 25—30 minutes at pressure.

Meat and poultry soups need less than half the ordinary cooking time, and nearly 50% less liquid. You will also find the meat extra tender and easy to sieve if desired.

The long cooking soups — lentils, oxtail, kidney etc. — are all ideal for pressure cooking.

The way a soup, like any other dish, is presented makes a great deal of difference to its appeal. Try to work out colourful garnishes that make the soup *look* appetising as well as taste good.

In the picture you will see some easy garnishes.

ALMONDS. An unusual but very delicious garnish on creamy soups — excellent with chicken soup. To give colour they should be browned lightly.

BREADCRUMBS. Rather coarse breadcrumbs, fried until golden brown; excellent with most soups, particularly vegetable soup.

CHEESE. Grated cheese can be served with most soups, particularly onion and vegetable soups. Cream cheese is delicious with Borshch and some of the cold soups.

CONSOMMÉ GARNISHES. These will be found under the individual recipes — the choice of garnish gives the name to the consommé.

CHEESE BALLS. Mix 2 oz. grated cheese (preferably Parmesan) with 2 stiffly beaten egg whites and few fine breadcrumbs. Fry in deep fat until crisp and golden brown (this takes a very few minutes only).

CROÛTONS. Cut bread into really small dice, or other shapes. Either toast first or fry in hot fat until crisp and golden brown, then drain on kitchen roll. Serve on top of the soup or in small dishes, so every one may help themselves.

EGG. Both the yolk and the white of hard-boiled egg make attractive garnishes — use the white on dark coloured soups and the yolk on tomato or other soups. You can rub the yolk through a sieve to look like mimosa balls or chop either white or yolk very finely.

HERBS. These can be sprinkled on top of the soup as well as being cooked with it to give flavour.

SAVOURY DUMPLINGS. Dumplings the size of a tiny nut can be put on the soup. Add chopped herbs or parsley to the mixture before cooking.

ONION OR CHIVES. Either chopped and fried onions or chopped chives give both flavour and colour to soups. In the picture chopped chives garnish a tomato soup.

PASTRY. Pastry rings can be baked round the edge of the dishes (see picture) or in tiny shapes.

POTATOES. These can be mashed (see Duchesse Potatoes, Recipe 36) then piped or made into attractive shapes to make the soups more substantial, and help to thicken the soup.

MEAT OR FISH BALLS. These are excellent in clear or vegetable soups. Mix equal quantities of flaked fish or minced meat and fine crumbs, season well and bind with egg. Fry until crisp and golden brown.

FORCEMEAT BALLS. Made from stuffing and baked, these are excellent with game soups.

TO SERVE WITH SOUPS

MELBA TOAST. Cut wafer thin slices of bread, put on to baking trays and crisp in the oven.

CHEESE STRAWS. Hot cheese straws are particularly good with vegetable soups. See Recipes 361, 362.

FRENCH TOAST. Butter slices of bread and toast on the buttered side under the grill. Cut into fingers.

92   **STOCKS FOR SOUPS**

You will find details of making stock in Recipe 3, and under Consommé (Recipe 55) and also in Recipe 89 (making stock in a pressure cooker).

Recipe 89 can be used for making stock in a saucepan, but due to the much longer cooking time use 3½—4 pints water and simmer for about 3 hours.

BROWN STOCKS are those made from beef bones, mutton and game, and they should only be used for meat soups unless the recipe specifically states to the contrary.

WHITE STOCKS are made from poultry bones (do not include any giblets or the body of the bird), and from veal. Use for vegetable soups etc.

FISH STOCKS are made from the bones and skin of fish, or the shells of fish. This gives a very good flavour to fish soups.

VEGETABLE STOCKS are made from boiling vegetables and should be used for many vegetable soups, although in some cases, where the vegetable has not a very strong flavour, additional 'body' is given to the soup by using a white meat stock.

It must be stressed again, as stated in Recipe 3, that a stock pot should not be left in a warm kitchen. The stock must either be used soon after making, or kept in a refrigerator. Potatoes and green vegetables are not good things to add to stock, since they help it to deteriorate

93   CORRECTING FAULTS IN SOUP

If the soup is too salt, either add a little milk or chop one or two potatoes, add to the soup, allow to simmer and then remove potatoes before serving.

If the soup has become slightly burned you can disguise this by adding a little curry powder — if badly burned of course nothing can be done. If the soup is slightly lumpy when being cooked whisk very hard; if the lumps do not come out it must be sieved.

If soup curdles when an egg is added it means it was too hot, or had been allowed to boil with the egg in. Whisk very sharply.

6 CREAM OF POTATO SOUP WITH POTATO SALAD (Recipe 32)

7   **CHINESE CUCUMBER SOUP** (Recipe 112)

8   **SWISS SPINACH FLAN** (Recipe 276)

9   **CREAMED SPINACH SOUP (Recipe 53)**

10   CREAM OF ONION SOUP (Recipe 30)

Summer Soups and Fruit Soups

In summer a cold soup or a fruit soup makes a very pleasant start to a meal. The fruit soups in particular are most refreshing and while they may appear an unusual taste to some people they will be found very popular.

If making jellied soups take care not to make the soup TOO STIFF; it should be only a lightly set jelly. In the same way if icing soups remember there is a large water content, and they will become very hard indeed if left too long in the freezing compartment.

94 CREAM OF APPLE SOUP

½ pint white sauce	water
(Recipe 241)	sugar
seasoning	juice 1 lemon
1¼ lb. apples, cut finely	1 glass cider

Make the white sauce and keep hot. Simmer the apples with water to cover, sugar to taste and lemon juice. Sieve the apple mixture, add to hot sauce, with 1 glass of cider. Whisk together and serve at once.

95 JELLIED CONSOMMÉ

12 oz. shin of beef	1 carrot
2 pints good stock	small piece celery
seasoning	sprig parsley
1 onion	bay leaf

Make Consommé as Recipe 55 and allow to cool, when it will set into a light jelly. If the weather is hot and you have no refrigerator, dissolve 2 *level* teaspoons powdered gelatine in consommé. Beat lightly before putting into soup cups. Garnish with slices of cucumber or lemon or smoked salmon. *Illustrated in colour picture No. 5.*

96 ICED CHERRY SOUP

1¼ lb. cherries or can of	sugar to taste
cherries	few whole cherries
juice 1 lemon	mint
water	

Cover fruit with water. Simmer gently, adding sugar to taste, and lemon juice. Rub through sieve, pour into freezing trays to lightly freeze. Serve in soup cups decorated with whole cherries and mint leaves.

Variations:

Other fruits can be used instead. Try:
Cherry plums — use the small rather 'sharp' small plums known as cherry plums. A very little white wine added to the mixture gives an excellent flavour.
Crabapple soup is made like the Iced Cherry soup. Add a little cider if wished and garnish with wedges of lemon.
Mixed soft fruits — red currants and raspberries can be used.

97 ICED CUCUMBER SOUP

1 medium sized cucumber	¼ gill milk or
1 small chopped onion	evaporated milk
½ oz. butter	seasoning
½ pint stock	lemon

Cut cucumber into pieces — leaving on some of the peel. Fry onion in butter, add cucumber, half the stock, seasoning and simmer gently for about 15 minutes. Put through sieve or into electric blender to make purée. Add milk and rest of stock, and when cold pour into freezing tray and leave until lightly frosted. Serve in soup cups garnished with lemon.

98 ICED TOMATO SOUP

1½ lb. tomatoes	1 small chopped onion
1 pint water or white stock	few drops Worcestershire
¼ small beetroot,	sauce
preferably uncooked	1 teaspon vinegar or
small pieces of celery	lemon juice
	seasoning
	2 bay leaves

Make the soup as directed in Recipe 103, but when ready pour into freezing tray or refrigerator and leave for a short time, until slightly iced. Serve garnished with lemon.

99 JELLIED TOMATO CONSOMMÉ

about 1¼ pints tomato juice (canned or bottled)	1 tablespoon finely chopped onion or chives
good pinch celery salt	seasoning
1 bouillon cube	1 level tablespoon powdered gelatine
	¼ pint water or white stock

To garnish :

mint	small wedges of lemon

Dissolve the bouillon cube in the water or stock, add to the tomato juice, and simmer with the onion for about 5—10 minutes. Pour over the powdered gelatine, which can be softened in tablespoon cold water, stir until thoroughly dissolved. Season well. Allow to cool, and just begin to stiffen, then whisk lightly with a fork and pile into very cold soup cups. Garnish with sprigs of mint and serve with lemon.

100 COLD MUSHROOM SOUP

1 pint white stock	2 tablespoons cream
¼ pint milk	seasoning
8 oz. mushrooms	1 tablespoon cornflour
1 tablespoon finely chopped chives or spring onion	little chopped parsley

Chop the mushrooms very finely, and simmer together with the chives in the white stock for about 10 minutes only. Blend the cornflour with the milk, add to the soup and cook until thickened. Taste and season well. When quite cold, stir in the cream. Put into 4 soup cups, and garnish with parsley.

101 CHILLED SUMMER CHOWDER

1 large onion	¼ pint milk
1 oz. butter or margarine	seasoning to taste
1 pint stock (a bouillon cube or bottled extract can be used)	¼ pint double cream or yoghurt or top of milk
2 oz. fine semolina	chopped chives or parsley

Peel and slice onion very thinly then cook the onion slowly in the butter till pale gold. Add stock, sprinkle in semolina, then continue cooking, stirring, until mixture thickens. Cover pan and simmer gently about 30 minutes or till onion is tender. Remove from heat, stir in milk then add seasoning to taste. Rub through a sieve so that mixture is like a smooth purée, leave till cold then blend in the cream or yoghourt. Pour into soup bowls and chill. Before serving, sprinkle with chives or parsley. (Illustrated opposite.)

102 COLD MULLIGATAWNY SOUP

Use the ingredients and method of making Mulligatawny Soup as described in Recipe 74. Make the soup a little more liquid, and if wished increase the amount of curry powder slightly. Serve very cold garnished with tiny pieces of raw cauliflower.

103 CLEAR TOMATO SOUP

1¼ lb. tomatoes	1 small chopped onion
1 pint water or white stock	few drops Worcestershire sauce
¼ small beetroot, preferably uncooked	1 teaspoon vinegar or lemon juice
small piece of celery	seasoning
	2 bay leaves

Put the ingredients all together in a large saucepan and cook gently until the tomatoes are very soft. This should take about 25 minutes. Remove the beetroot and bay leaves; then rub first through a sieve and finally strain through muslin. Reheat or serve cold.

If a slightly thickened soup is desired it will only be necessary to rub through the sieve, without straining afterwards.

104 GAZPACHO (1)

1 medium sized cucumber	1 lb. tomatoes
1 or 2 cloves of garlic	1 small capsicum (green pepper)
seasoning	1 onion or several spring onions
little olive oil	lemon juice or white wine vinegar
water	

Put the water into the refrigerator to become very cold. Skin the tomatoes if wished, as this helps to sieve the mixture, and if using an electric blender or liquidiser gives a smooth mixture. Peel the cucumber and cut into very small dice. Save a little cucumber as a garnish. Chop the tomatoes, onion, garlic, add to the cucumber and either pound until smooth or rub through a sieve; the capsicum can also be sieved or chopped very finely. Remove all the seeds and core of this. If using an electric liquidiser you will need to add a little water so none of the thick mixture is wasted. Put the purée into basin, then gradually beat in seasoning, olive oil, and enough cold water to give a flowing consistency. Taste and re-season and add lemon juice. Serve garnished with the cucumber. This soup must be very cold so put in the refrigerator until ready to serve and serve in ice cold soup cups.

Gazpacho is a Spanish speciality, and there are many ways of making this refreshing cold soup. Another, very quick method will be found in Recipe 125.

105   VICHYSSOISE (1)

To serve cold

You will find slight modifications on this recipe under Recipe 121, since that recipe gives a better result when served hot.

8 medium sized leeks	*2 tablespoons chopped*
1¼ pints chicken stock	* chives**
2 medium sized potatoes	*1 tablespoon chopped*
¼ pint cream	* parsley*
	seasoning
	2 oz. butter

* *If chives are not obtainable use the green tops of spring onions*

Heat the butter and toss the chopped leeks in this until pale golden colour, do not allow them to brown. Add the stock, the chopped peeled potatoes, half the chopped chives and all the parsley. Season well and simmer gently for 30 minutes. Rub through a fine sieve, then gradually add the cream when the purée is cool. Taste when quite cold and add seasoning as wished. Serve very cold topped with the chopped chives.

106   VEGETABLE CREAM

Use ingredients as Vichyssoise, but instead of the leeks use a mixture of young vegetables — carrots, small piece of turnip, French or broad beans and a tomato.

Soups from Abroad

107   BOUILLABAISSE

You must use a wide mixture of fish for this French soup.

approx. 1¼ lb white fish	*good pinch saffron*
* — use if possible*	* powder*
a mixture consisting of	*2 teaspoons salt*
sole or plaice, red	*pepper to taste*
mullet, eel, hake, John	*1¼ pints water*
Dory	*¼ pint white wine*
1 small lobster or few	*½ gill olive oil or 3 oz.*
prawns	*butter*
1 large onion	*2 tomatoes*
1 or 2 cloves of garlic	*bay leaf*
chopped parsley	

Heat the oil or butter in a large saucepan, then fry the sliced onion, crushed garlic and sliced tomatoes until soft. Put in all the other ingredients except the shell fish and wine, cutting the fish into small pieces. Simmer for 15—20 minutes. Take out the bay leaf and add the chopped lobster meat or prawns and heat for a further 5 minutes. Add wine and reheat. Pour into hot dish or soup plates and garnish with chopped parsley. Serve with toast or French bread.

Note. The amount of liquid can be adjusted — for a thinner soup use 2 pints water, for a very thick soup, almost like a stew, use about ¾—1 pint water only.

108 BORSHCH

1 large raw beetroot or use slightly more cooked beetroot	2 or 3 tomatoes
1 carrot	2 pints water or stock*
1 onion	seasoning
little sour cream or cream cheese	clove garlic
	little chopped celery
	vinegar

* Use only 1¼ pints water or stock with cooked beetroot

Grate the beetroot and put into pan with the grated or chopped carrot and onion, tomatoes, crushed garlic and celery. Add the stock. Simmer for 1½ hours with raw beetroot or about 40 minutes with cooked beetroot. Season and add little vinegar. Top with sour cream or cream cheese before serving.

Variations:

This soup can be jellied. Dissolve about 1 level tablespoon powdered gelatine in the soup when cooked. Allow to cool, but not set, then stir in sour cream. Serve in soup cups topped with cream cheese.
Cranberries make a delicious addition to the soup. Use about 6 oz. instead of carrot, onion and celery.

109 CELERIAC SOUP

This root vegetable, which looks rather like a darkish turnip, but has the delicious flavour of the base of celery, can be used in place of celery in Recipes 10 and 11. If cut into small pieces it will become very soft when cooked, so is easy to sieve, or it can be mashed with a fork or potato masher, then used as a purée.

110 FRENCH ONION SOUP WITH CHEESE

1¼ lb. onions	salt and pepper
2 oz. butter	slices of French bread
1¼ pints stock or water	grated Cheddar cheese

Slice the onions thinly and cook gently in the butter until brown, taking 30 minutes. Add the stock or water, season well and cook gently for another 30 minutes. Put slices of bread into the bottom of the soup tureen, pour over the soup and sprinkle on plenty of grated Cheddar cheese. Put into a hot oven or under the grill to brown.

111 DUTCH MIMOSA SOUP

Ingredients as Onion Soup (Recipe 30) but when the soup is put into dishes cover the top with balls of cheese made by rubbing a soft Dutch Edam cheese through a coarse sieve. Garnish with sprigs of parsley.

112 CHINESE CUCUMBER SOUP

1 medium sized cucumber	1 dessertspoon cornflour
8 oz. pork or chicken (cooked)	1¼ pints white stock
	salt and pepper
1 — 2 tablespoons soy sauce	little sherry if wished

Save several slices of cucumber for garnish, and leave the skin or part of the skin on this. Peel the rest of the cucumber and cut into wafer thin slices, then dice if wished. Cut the meat into tiny pieces. Blend the cornflour with some of the cold stock. Bring the rest of the stock to the boil, pour over the cornflour, return to the pan and cook until thickened. Add cucumber, chicken or pork, soy sauce and salt and pepper. Heat gently for about 5 minutes. If wished you can use uncooked pork or chicken, and if cut very thinly then diced finely it will cook very quickly — it must of course be good quality. Add sherry just before serving, and garnish with cucumber slices. *Illustrated in colour picture No. 7.*

Making tiny dumplings for goulash soup

113   DUTCH BEAN BROTH

3 oz. butter or haricot beans	2 pints water
3 onions	seasoning
knob of butter	little cream or sour cream

Soak the beans overnight in the water, then cook until tender with the onions. Rub through a sieve if wished. If you do not wish to sieve them chop the onions finely. Season well, and add knob of butter and cream. Garnish with croûtons of fried bread.

114   ITALIAN BREAD SOUP

2 oz. breadcrumbs	1¼ pints white stock
3 eggs or egg yolks	knob of butter
bay leaf	grated Parmesan cheese

Bring 1 pint of the stock to the boil, add the crumbs, seasoning and approximately 2 oz. grated cheese (less if wished). Simmer for a few minutes with the bay leaf. Remove bay leave. Blend the eggs with the ½ pint stock, add to soup and cook gently without boiling, stir in butter.

115   FRENCH PEASANT SOUP

2 pints good stock or use water and bouillon cube	pepper
1 lb. mixed root vegetables	2 oz. stale breadcrumbs
salt	2 oz. grated cheese
	2 tablespoons chopped parsley

Bring the stock or water to the boil, then add bouillon cube, and the diced vegetables. Cook until really tender, adding seasoning to taste. Stir in the crumbs and cheese and parsley and serve at once. A small piece of fat bacon can be cooked with the vegetables, then the bacon diced and returned to the soup.

116   GERMAN BEER SOUP

1½ pints light ale or mild beer	6 lemon slices
1 or 2 cloves	pinch powdered cinnamon
¼ pint cream, milk or evaporated milk	3 eggs or egg yolks
	good pinch sugar

Simmer beer with the sliced lemon, cloves, cinnamon and good pinch sugar. Beat the eggs and cream together, in a rather large basin, then strain the beer mixture over the egg mixture, whisking hard. Serve at once.

117   HUNGARIAN GOULASH SOUP

4 oz. beef or veal	2 medium sized potatoes
4 oz. pork or use all beef or all veal	2 large tomatoes
2 large onions	½ — 1 level tablespoon paprika pepper (this is the sweet red pepper)
salt	1¼ pints stock or water
pepper	

Cut the meat into very tiny pieces, and put into a pan with the chopped onion and tomatoes, seasoning including the paprika pepper. Simmer gently for about 1 hour, then add the diced potatoes and continue cooking for a further 25—30 minutes. Serve garnished with tiny dumplings.

118 GERMAN SOUR CHERRY SOUP

1¼ lb. black or ripe red
   cherries
little sugar
1 pint water

approximately ¼ pint red
   wine
1 oz. flour
1¼ oz. butter

Simmer the cherries in the water, adding little sugar. Blend the wine with the flour, add to the soup, bring slowly to the boil, stirring until very smooth. Add the butter and blend carefully with the soup. Taste and if necessary add a little more sugar, but this soup must be fairly sharp. Serve with crusty bread.

119 TOMATO SOUP WITH CHEESE

Make either of the tomato soups (Recipes 42 or 43) and top with a thick layer of grated Dutch Edam or Gouda cheese. A little sour cream can be stirred in just before serving and topping with cheese.

120 ITALIAN MINESTRONE SOUP (1)

3 oz. haricot beans
1½ pints water or white
   stock
1 tablespoon chopped
   parsley
1 large onion
2 tablespoons chopped
   celery
2 oz. macaroni
2 tablespoons olive oil

1 clove garlic
1 — 2 oz. diced bacon
seasoning
8 oz. tomatoes (bottled
   or fresh)
8 oz. finely shredded
   cabbage
grated Parmesan cheese
1 large diced carrot

Soak the haricot beans overnight in the water. Chop the onion finely and toss in the hot oil, together with the crushed garlic and bacon. Add the haricot beans and water and simmer gently for about 1½ hours. Put in the rest of the vegetables, with the exception of the cabbage and cook for a further 20 minutes, adding a little more water if necessary. Add the cabbage and the macaroni and cook until both are just tender. Taste and re-season

if necessary. Serve with chopped parsley and topped with the cheese.

Note. A little red wine can be used in this recipe; put this in with the vegetables.

121 VICHYSSOISE (2)

This recipe has a slightly stronger flavour than Recipe 105, and is therefore more suitable for serving hot.

8 medium sized leeks
1½ pints chicken stock
2 good sized onions
¼ pint cream or milk

1 tablespoon chopped
   parsley
seasoning
2 oz. butter
2 eggs or egg yolks

Heat the butter, and fry the chopped onions and leek in this until golden but not brown. Add stock, chopped potatoes, and the parsley. Simmer for ½ hour, rub through a sieve and return to pan. Blend the eggs with the cream, add to the soup and cook WITHOUT BOILING for a few minutes. Re-season if wished. Top with chopped parsley or chopped chives.

122 SOUR HOT SOUP

4 oz. lean pork
1¼ oz. beancurd*
3 dried mushrooms**
1 pint stock
1 tablespoon vinegar

pepper and salt to taste
pinch monosodium
   glutamate***
2 level teaspoons
   cornflour
1 tablespoon sherry

* Available at shops specialising in Chinese or other Oriental foods
** 6 fresh mushrooms could be used
*** Monosodium glutamate (Chinese taste powder) is on sale in many food shops and supermarkets. Ask for 'Ac'cent'

Cut the pork in fine slivers and break the beancurd into small pieces. Bring the stock to the boil, add the pork, beancurd and dried mushrooms and simmer gently about 15 — 20 minutes (or until the pork is tender). Stir in the seasonings and the vinegar. Mix the cornflour smoothly with a little cold water, add to the soup and boil for 3 minutes, stirring constantly. Before serving add the sherry.

Using Ready-prepared Soups

123

It is easy to purchase a great variety of ready prepared soups today — both in packets and canned. These are produced from very fine ingredients and give an excellent flavour. If however more individual results are desired, the ready prepared soups can be a good base, and additional flavourings etc. put in.

Bouillon cubes are not only excellent flavourings for stock but also for consommé. Add a little sherry and individual garnishes.

Creamed Soups — asparagus, celery, etc., are improved by diluting with a little cream or top of the milk, and can be used for base of creamed vegetable soups, by adding few extra fresh or frozen vegetables.

Green pea soup can be given extra flavour by simmering a little chopped mint and bacon in this.

Chicken soups can be used in a variety of ways. Add diced cucumber and simmer until tender, or mixed diced vegetables to a chicken noodle soup and produce a quick Minestrone

Mushroom and tomato soups mixed are very good.

Frozen vegetables also make soup making easy — use frozen spinach purée for soups, and the ready prepared Macedoine and mixed vegetables.

124   TOMATO CRAB BISQUE

10-oz. can condensed
tomato soup
½ pint milk
1 teaspoon chopped onion
or chives
pinch salt
pinch marjoram
small can flaked crab meat
½ pint light cream or
evaporated milk

Combine the first five ingredients, and heat thoroughly. Slowly stir in the crab meat and the cream. Serve hot.

125   GAZPACHO (2)

10-oz. can condensed
tomato soup
1¼ oz. chopped green
pepper
3 oz. chopped peeled
cucumber
2 oz. grated carrot
1 tablespoon malt vinegar
1 teaspoon chopped onion
seasoning

Beat tomato soup well in a bowl then combine all ingredients. Chill thoroughly and serve.

126   PINK CHIFFON CONSOMMÉ

Top left hand corner of picture opposite

Whisk 1 white of egg to a light froth, and colour pale pink with a few drops of cochineal. Put a blob into four shallow soup cups. Divide 1¼ pints boiling beef or chicken bouillon between the cups, pouring carefully over the whisked egg white.

127   MINESTRONE

In blue soup cup

4 medium sized potatoes	1 carrot
1 onion	8 oz. cabbage
1 clove garlic	2 stalks celery
½ pint measure cooked	2 pints water
dried beans and peas	2 bouillon cubes (beef
chopped parsley	or chicken)
2 tablespoons olive oil	grated Parmesan cheese
	8 oz. short cut macaroni

Cut up the vegetables and toss in the hot oil for 2 minutes, add the liquid and bouillon cubes, and simmer for 30 minutes. Add the macaroni and cook for a further 10 minutes. Serve sprinkled with parsley and with Parmesan cheese.

128   QUICK BORSHCH

In petite marmite cup to right of picture

1 lb. grated or minced	1 chicken or beef bouillon
cooked beetroot	cube
2 pints water	4 oz. can cream
	grated lemon rind

Cook the beetroot in the water until soft, sieve and reheat with the bouillon cube. Add the cream and lemon rind before serving. Save a little cream to put on top of the soup. If serving chilled stir all the cream into soup before serving.

129   TO GARNISH READY PREPARED SOUPS

1. Dark blue soup cup shows mushroom soup garnished with savoury pastry confetti. To make this add 1 rounded dessertspoon onion or tomato powder to 4 oz. flour. Rub in 2 oz. fat, and bind with a tablespoon water. Roll out, cut into small attractive shapes, and bake for 10—12 minutes in a hot oven (450°F. — Gas Mark 7). Put on the soup just before serving.
2. Red *petite marmite* contains Cream of Onion soup, garnished with sieved egg yolk.
3. Turquoise *petite marmite* contains French Fried Onion Soup garnished with toasted cheese. Put the soup into the hot cups and either put a thick slice of cheese on top or a round of bread or toast covered with plenty of grated cheese. Toast under a hot grill for a minute.
4. The yellow soup cups contain Green Pea and Ham Soup garnished with sprigs of mint and cream.

130   MORE GARNISHES FOR SOUPS

Shown in the top right-hand corner of the picture

Cheese straws — Recipe 363. The mixture made into straws and rings.
Popcorn sprinkled with paprika pepper.

Pigs in blankets

Cheese pastry as used	tiny cocktail or
in Recipe 363	Frankfurter sausages

Roll the pastry to an oblong nearly as wide as two of the sausages. Cut in half lengthways, then into 6 pieces. Wrap the pastry round the sausages, enclosing two in each piece of pastry, so the ends are showing. Damp and seal edges and bake, join side down on greased tin, just above centre of a hot oven (450°F. — Gas Mark 7).
Serve with any soup — or as an hors d'oeuvre, or a cocktail savoury.

Using Ready-prepared Soups

11　SOUPS FOR SPECIAL OCCASIONS (all recipes on facing page)

12   MIXED HORS D'OEUVRE (Recipe 132)

Hors d'oeuvre

131 · *The first course of the meal should not be too filling, as it is meant to tempt the appetite in readiness for the main course to follow. Many of the recipes for savoury dishes can be adapted to serve as hot hors d'oeuvre. If planning a party with little help you will find it a good idea to have a cold hors d'oeuvre if the main course to follow is a hot dish. On the other hand if you are planning a main dish of cold poultry or meat with salad, then a simple hot hors d'oeuvre makes a good beginning to the meal.*

132 MIXED HORS D'OEUVRE
made in minutes

On the opposite page you see a really impressive selection of dishes to serve as an hors d'oeuvre — all of which can be assembled very quickly. It is wise to have a reasonably well stocked store cupboard so that you can produce a variety of dishes like this in the shortest possible time.

In the picture are:

Top right hand dish — Ham rolls, i.e. thin slices of ham (canned can be used) rolled or filled with cream cheese or mixed vegetables in mayonnaise, rolled, served with spring onions, tomatoes, slices of cucumber and olive.

Top left hand corner — Rollmop herrings (Recipe 163) or these can be bought ready prepared in jars. Potato salad and Russian salad — can be made by mixing diced cooked potatoes with mayonnaise, chopped parsley, grated onion — and mixing diced cooked vegetables with mayonnaise. Can also be purchased in cans, as a very useful standby in the cupboard.

In the foreground — a dish of potato puffs (can be bought ready prepared) and a most colourful Spanish Salad made by mixing fresh or canned capsicums (red peppers), pickled cauliflower, canned celery hearts (or fresh celery), strips of canned carrots and turnip, gherkins, pickled olives or walnuts. Toss in French dressing.

The very large dish is made up of ready prepared ingredients: Piccallili in the centre, cocktail onions, gherkins, green and stuffed olives, and pickled walnuts.

Completing the picture are shredded white cabbage (or sauerkraut can be used), sliced cucumber, tossed in white vinegar, and chopped parsley.

For those people who prefer a fruit hors d'oeuvre in the background are tumblers and a jug of canned orange juice.

133 MIXED HORS D'OEUVRE

In Recipe 132 you will find directions for making the hors d'oeuvre in the picture opposite, but there are many other ingredients that can be used to provide a delicious and easy to make hors d'oeuvre.

Try to have as good a variety of colour and flavour as possible.

Ideally this should consist of:

Something with a fish flavour: Sardines, anchovies, rollmop herrings, mussels, prawns, smoked salmon, fresh salmon, fish salads of any kind, cod's roe, cooked roes. Dress the fish with mayonnaise or oil and vinegar and garnish it with chopped parsley etc.

Salads: Potato, Russian, tomato, sliced cucumber, corn on the cob, lettuce, watercress, celery, rice mixtures etc. The salad should be mixed with mayonnaise or French dressing.

Meat: Diced salami, chopped sausages, small cubes or rolls of ham, tongue, chicken; these to be mixed with some dressing.

Eggs: Sliced hard-boiled, hard-boiled and stuffed (see Recipes 176 onwards) mixed with anchovies or the yolks mixed with anchovy essence etc.

In addition use some of the ready prepared savoury ingredients which are such a good standby in the cupboard — pickled gherkins, cocktail onions, olives, pickled walnuts etc.

Many of the recipes in this book can be divided into tiny portions and served as part of an hors d'oeuvre.

134 SMOKED SALMON

When buying smoked salmon make sure it is not dry, but pleasantly moist and 'oily'. Serve with thin brown bread and butter, and accompanied by cayenne or paprika pepper. Garnish with thick wedges of lemon. Allow a good 2 oz. per person as an hors d'oeuvre.

135 SMOKED SALMON ROLLS

Roll thin slices of smoked salmon round canned or freshly cooked asparagus tips. Garnish with lettuce and wedges of lemon. Serve with brown bread and butter and accompanied by cayenne or paprika pepper.

136 SMOKED SALMON AND SPINACH

An unusual but delicious combination is to serve a slice of smoked salmon with hot creamed spinach. This can be arranged in wafer thin pastry cases, if desired.

137 SMOKED EEL

Smoked eel is becoming a popular hors d'oeuvre. You buy it already smoked. Cut into convenient lengths and skin (if wished) as this is very tough. Serve with horse-radish sauce (Recipe 253), cayenne or paprika pepper, a slice of lemon and brown bread and butter.

138 SMOKED TROUT

Serve as Smoked Eel (Recipe 137).

139 POTTED SHRIMPS

These can be bought very easily and are simply turned on to a bed of lettuce and garnished with lemon. Serve with red pepper and brown bread and butter. If frozen they should be allowed to defrost but not become too soft.

140 TO MAKE POTTED SHRIMPS

To each pint of peeled shrimps (or prawns) allow approximately 2 oz. butter, a good pinch grated nutmeg and pepper. Put shrimps in a basin or in small containers. Heat the butter and flavourings. Pour over the shrimps and allow to set.

141 PRAWN COCKTAIL

picked prawns or shrimps	*lettuce*
lemon	*cocktail sauce*
	(Recipe 142)

Shred the lettuce very finely, so it can be eaten with a spoon or small fork. Top with the prawns (or shrimps) and cover with the sauce. Garnish with lemon. Serve as cold as possible.

Arrange in glasses or flat small dishes.

142 COCKTAIL SAUCE

3 tablespoons thick
   mayonnaise
1 tablespoon tomato
   ketchup or thick
   tomato purée
1 tablespoon Worcester-
   shire sauce

2 tablespoons full cream
   evaporated milk
seasoning
little celery salt
   (or chopped celery)
little finely chopped onion
   (if desired)

Mix all the ingredients together, taste and add a little lemon juice.

143 LOBSTER COCKTAIL

lobster
lemon

lettuce
cocktail sauce
   (Recipe 142)

Remove all the lobster meat from the shells. Shred the lettuce finely and arrange in glasses or flat small dishes. Put the lobster meat on top and cover with the cocktail sauce. Garnish with lemon and some of the tiny lobster claws.

144 CRAB COCKTAIL

crab
lemon

lettuce
cocktail sauce
   (Recipe 142)

Remove all the crab meat from the shell and claws. Keep light and dark meat separately. Shred the lettuce and arrange in glasses or on small flat dishes and put the crab meat on top keeping the dark to one side and the light the other. Cover with the cocktail sauce and garnish with lemon.

145 OYSTERS

Get the fishmonger to open these for you. Serve on one half of the shell, with paprika or cayenne pepper, slices of lemon and brown bread and butter. Some people like a little vinegar with them.

146 BUCKLING

These smoked herrings make an economical and excellent hors d'oeuvre. Serve with wedges of lemon, horseradish sauce and brown bread and butter. Garnish with crisp lettuce.

Meat Hors d'oeuvre

147   SALAMI

The variety of salami available now means you can serve several different kinds if wished as an hors d'oeuvre or part of a mixed hors d'oeuvre. Arrange on crisp lettuce and serve with mustard and a tomato salad. Salami tends to dry quickly, so it should be purchased when very fresh.

148   FRU ANDERSEN'S DANISH LIVER PÂTÉ

8 oz. very fat bacon   1 lb. liver
4 oz. streaky bacon

Sauce

1 oz. butter   ¼ pint milk
2 oz. flour

Flavouring

½ teaspoon sugar   1 teaspoon ginger
2 teaspoons salt   2 eggs well mixed
pinch black pepper   ¼ pint cream
1 teaspoon cinnamon

Heat butter, stir in flour, cook for 1 minute. Gradually add milk. Bring to boil. Cook until thickened. Stir in the very fat bacon and liver, which should be minced 2 or 3 times to make it very smooth. Add all flavourings, the eggs and cream. Press the mixture firmly into a greased shallow fire-proof dish. Arrange the streaky bacon rashers across the top. Stand in a water bath (another dish of cold water) and cook for 45 minutes in the centre of a very moderate oven (350°F. — Gas Mark 3).

149   BACON AND LIVER PÂTÉ

1¼ lb. pig's liver   6 fillets anchovies
8 oz. green (unsmoked)   (tinned)
    bacon   1 breakfast cup
1 clove garlic or 1 shallot   breadcrumbs

¼ teaspoon black pepper   1 whole egg
¼ teaspoon salt   1 egg yolk
    1 bay leaf

To line tin or mould: 6 oz. very thinly cut streaky bacon

Put half the liver into water to cover and simmer until just firm. Put both the cooked and uncooked liver and unsmoked bacon, garlic and anchovies through mincer twice. Add seasonings and breadcrumbs and beaten eggs. Mix very thoroughly. (If a more pronounced onion flavour is liked, add 1 tablespoon grated onion.) Lay the bay leaf at the bottom of a straight sided mould or cake tin and line the mould with the thin streaky bacon. Fill with pâté mixture and arrange one or two more thin rashers neatly over the top. Cover with a piece of grease-proof paper, without tying it down, and place in a container of very hot water reaching at least an inch up the sides of the mould. Place in centre of a moderate oven (375°F. — Gas Mark 4) for about 1½ hours, removing the paper after 30 minutes. Remove dish from oven and put a weighted plate on top of pâté. Leave until cold, then turn out on a board to set well. *Illustrated in colour frontispiece also.*

150   DEVILLED SAUSAGE

Cut cooked sausages or better still frankfurter sausages into thin slices. Make a dressing by mixing together equal quantities of chutney and mayonnaise, adding a few drops Worcestershire sauce and lemon juice. Toss the sausages in this and serve on a bed of lettuce. You will need about 2 tablespoons chutney, etc. to dress 4—5 slices sausages.

151   POTTED MEAT

Cook the meat very carefully by roasting or steaming. Put it 2 or 3 times through a mincer, making sure you have a good distribution of fat and lean and adding a pinch of salt. Pour into jars and top with melted butter. If wished, add a little stock to give a more moist texture.

Easy Cold Hors d'oeuvre of all kinds

152 **CAVIARE**

This may certainly be called an easy hors d'oeuvre, since it needs no preparation, but it is a very expensive one. Serve with hot toast and butter. Although expensive many people do not like the flavour of caviare (sturgeon's roe), so make certain it will be popular before serving. Turkish caviare is now being sold; while not plentiful, it is good and inexpensive.

153 **EGG SALADS**

Eggs in most forms make good salads and a good hors d'oeuvre.

Hard-boiled eggs can be coated with mayonnaise or use Cocktail sauce (Recipe 142). Garnish with anchovy fillets or red pepper. Slice hard-boiled eggs and arrange a slice of egg, slice of cucumber and slice of tomato in strips on the dish.

Poached eggs can be set in aspic jelly and served on a bed of salad. The egg should be firmer than usual, allowed to cool, then put into the liquid, cold aspic jelly.

Scrambled eggs mixed with chopped prawns or grated cheese or diced chicken and enough mayonnaise to give a rather soft mixture can look and taste appetising. Put the egg on crisp lettuce and garnish with rings of tomato and cucumber.

154 **FISH SALADS**

Shell, white fish and oily fish can be used in salads for hors d'oeuvre. Arrange the fish on a bed of lettuce and garnish with lemon, mayonnaise etc. Cut cooked white fish into neat pieces of large flakes.

Mock smoked salmon salad is made by taking the meat from uncooked kippers, seasoning this well, and moistening with a little oil and vinegar. Leave for several hours, then arrange on lettuce, serve, with lemon, tomato and red pepper.

155 **MEAT SALADS**

Light meat salads could be served as hors d'oeuvre, although this must depend on whether a meat course is following.

Choose meats like salami, liver pâtés and other types of pâté, tongue or ham. Dice finely and serve on a bed of lettuce or cut into very thin slices.

CHEESE HORS D'OEUVRE

156 **Stuffed Prunes**

Wash and soak the prunes overnight. Remove the stone. Fill the cavity with a little chutney and pipe a little seasoned and softened cream cheese on top.

157 **Blue Cheese Spread**

Mash a little of any blue cheese with a little cream and serve neatly piled on tiny cheese biscuits, or toasted croûtons.

158 **Cheese and Shrimp Canapés**

Cream a little butter with twice as much grated Cheddar cheese — add some cut up shrimps and a little lemon juice, cayenne pepper and salt. Spread liberally over small rounds of toast and garnish with a whole shrimp.

159 **Open Cheese Sandwiches**

Cut several Processed Cheese slices across diagonally into four. Garnish attractively with strips of anchovy, slices of stuffed olives, gherkin fans and capers.

160 **Leicestershire Spread**

Grate or crumble about 4 oz. of Leicestershire cheese and add this to about 1 oz. of creamed butter. Season and add a few chopped chives if liked. Use to make tiny colourful sandwiches or as a canapé spread.

161 ANCHOVY SARDINES

Use sardines in oil and drain them carefully. Make an anchovy butter by mixing together 2 oz. margarine and 1—2 teaspoons anchovy essence (taste as you add the anchovy essence to make certain it is not too salt). Pipe this butter on to the sardines either in small roses or fine lines. Serve with watercress.

162 STUFFED HERRING FILLETS

Bone fresh herrings and divide into fillets. Make a stuffing as follows (quantities enough for 8 fillets). Cream 1 oz. margarine until soft. Add 2 teaspoons chopped parsley, ½ teacup chopped shrimps, 1 teaspoon lemon juice. Put on to the fillets and roll tightly. Cook in the oven in a very little margarine. Drain and dress with oil and vinegar. Serve with strips of beetroot.

163 ROLLMOP HERRINGS

herrings	1 pint malt vinegar
8 oz. kitchen salt	1 tablespoon pickling
1 pint water	spices
bay leaves	onion
	gherkins

Use large herrings and clean them, take out roe, backbone and cut off their heads. If fish are very large they can be divided into 2 fillets, they are then easier to roll.

Make a brine of 8 oz. kitchen salt and 1 pint water. Soak herrings for 2 hours in the brine if filleted, twice as long if whole. Lift out of the brine and put into large shallow dish. Cover with pure malt vinegar and leave for several hours. When ready take out the fish, lay flat on table, then roll each fish or fillet round small tablespoon very finely shredded onion.

The fish will keep more firmly rolled if secured into position with tiny tooth pick or cocktail stick. Put into jars with bay leaves, gherkins and cover with the cold spiced vinegar. To make vinegar boil together 1 pint vinegar with 1 tablespoon pickling spices for 15 minutes. Herrings should be covered thoroughly and stored in a cool dry place. They will keep for 21—28 days.

164 STUFFED FISH ROLLS

Cut small fillets of white fish (sole, whiting, plaice, codling) through the centre — so giving long narrow strips. Spread these with either anchovy paste — pounded anchovies or mashed, cooked or tinned salmon. Roll tightly and cook very slowly in a small quantity of white wine or well seasoned vinegar and water. Drain thoroughly, then dress with oil and vinegar. Garnish with small lettuce leaves.

165 COD'S ROE

This is so often neglected as a savoury dish, but is delicious served either with crisp bacon or grilled mushrooms and tomatoes. If you buy the raw cod's roe, steam it — this can be done the day before — slice, roll in seasoned flour and fry until just crisp and brown.

166 CURRIED EGGS

Hard-boil eggs and cut into halves. Remove yolk and mash it thoroughly. Melt a little margarine in a pan work in curry powder (1 teaspoon to each 2 eggs). Cook for 1 minute, then add small quantity of chutney and the egg yolk. Pile back into whites and serve on a bed of watercress.

167 JELLIED HORS D'OEUVRE

1 can mixed vegetable juices
½ oz. gelatine
¼ medium-sized cucumber
2 hard-boiled eggs

2 teaspoons sweet chutney
1 teaspoon Worcestershire sauce
8 drops tabasco sauce

Pour half can of vegetable juices on to gelatine to soften. Heat remaining juice in small pan, pour on to gelatine and stir well until gelatine has dissolved. Place a slice of cucumber or hard-boiled egg in bottom of six damp dariole moulds and set in place with a teaspoonful of the jellied vegetable mixture. Chop remaining egg and skinned cucumber, mix into rest of jellied vegetable with chutney, Worcestershire sauce and tabasco. Stir well. When cucumber and egg slices have set, finally spoon in the mixture and leave to set. Chill if possible. Serve with salad ingredients.

168 SHRIMP AND TOMATO SHAPES

½ can (¼ pint) tomato juice

2 teaspoons lemon juice
2 or 3 minced gherkins

¾ oz. gelatine
dash Worcestershire sauce
½ pint picked shrimps (fresh, frozen or tinned)

lettuce or endive
onions
seasonings

Soften gelatine in 3 tablespoons cold water, then dissolve over heat by standing basin over boiling water. Stir in half the tomato juice and mix until gelatine is dissolved. Cool down with remaining tomato juice and add flavourings and seasonings to taste. Stir in shrimps last. When mixture shows signs of thickening, spoon into prepared individual moulds. When required, turn out shapes on to a lettuce or endive-lined dish, garnishing with silver onions or stuffed olives.

169 PICKLED HERRING

3 medium or 2 large herrings
1 large onion
1 tablespoon brown sugar
1 teaspoon mixed whole spice
6 thin slices lemon

1 cup vinegar
¼ cup water
3 bay leaves
12 peppercorns
2 tablespoons sour cream (optional)

Clean herrings, do not remove skin. Slice onion. Place whole herrings or sections into a quart jar. Add onion. Bring to a quick boil the vinegar, water, sugar and cool until lukewarm. Add liquid to jar with bay leaves, spices, lemon slices. Add sour cream and stir in lightly, or shake jar to distribute. Cover and let stand 24 hours before serving.

170 TUNA CHAUDFROID

1 level dessertspoon	1 teaspoon lemon juice
powdered gelatine	¼ pint mayonnaise
3 tablespoons boiling	(Recipe 186)
water	2 cans (4¼ oz.) tuna
	fillets

To garnish:

stuffed olives, gherkins	radishes
or chives	tomato
sliced cucumber	lettuce

Dissolve the gelatine in the boiling water. Add the lemon juice and when cool stir into the mayonnaise. Arrange the fillets on a wire tray, with a plate underneath to catch any 'drips'. Use the sauce when cold, but before it sets, and spoon carefully over the fillets. Allow to set. Decorate with small pieces of sliced olive, gherkins or chives, dipped in the sauce. Arrange on lettuce and garnish with cucumber etc.

171 FISH CHAUDFROID

Ingredients as for Tuna Chaudfroid (Recipe 170), but use cooked fillets of fish instead of tuna.

172 CHICKEN CHAUDFROID

Ingredients as for Tuna Chaudfroid (Recipe 170), but use cooked boned pieces of chicken instead of tuna.

173 CREAMED SALT COD PROVENÇALE

1 lb. salt codfish *	4 tablespoons corn oil
1 small clove garlic	lemon juice

* If using fresh cod do not soak

⅜ pint milk	salt and pepper to taste
2 tablespoons cornflour	bay leaf

Soak the fish in cold water overnight. Put the fillets in a pan, cover with cold water and add a bay leaf if liked. Bring the water to the boil and simmer very gently for 10 — 15 minutes. Drain thoroughly and remove any bones and skin. Break the fish into flakes and pound with a small clove of garlic in a mortar or earthenware bowl. Put into a pan and warm slightly over low heat. Work oil into the paste drop by drop, blending well all the time with a wooden spoon. Mix the cornflour to a smooth paste with a little of the cold milk, bring the rest to the boil and stir in the cornflour. Cook for a few minutes. Gradually mix the cornflour cream into the fish mixture, stirring vigorously, with a wooden spoon. Season carefully and add 1 — 2 teaspoons of lemon juice. The mixture should be creamy and very smooth. Serve hot with toasted French bread. *Illustrated in colour picture No. 19.*

174 SAVOURY MUSHROOMS

Choose tiny mushrooms — skin them, remove the stalks but keep these. Cook the mushrooms gently in a mixture of well-seasoned vinegar and water — or better still white wine. Drain them carefully. When cold pipe large rosettes of demi-sel or other soft cheese in the middle. Stand the stalks on top and dust with cayenne pepper.

175 HAM ROLLS

Cut slices of ham into small strips — measuring about 2 inches by 1 inch. Make a spread of cream cheese, chopped gherkins, chopped parsley, capers — or cream cheese, horseradish cream, finely chopped parsley. Put the spread on the pieces of ham and roll tightly. Serve with thinly sliced tomatoes.

Stuffed Eggs

176   STUFFED EGGS ON HAM

4 good sized hard-boiled
  eggs
mayonnaise
chopped parsley
seasoning

8 pieces of cooked
  ham size of eggs
chopped gherkin
little extra ham

Halve the eggs, remove the yolks, put into a basin and mash well. Add mayonnaise, chopped parsley, gherkin, seasoning, and any tiny pieces of chopped ham if desired, pile back into white cases. Stand on pieces of ham. If wished they can be put on to crisp toast or thinly sliced bread and butter, or bread and mustard butter (i. e. butter flavoured with a little made mustard). *Illustrated in colour frontispiece.*

177   ASPARAGUS EGGS

8 small stalks of cooked
  or canned asparagus
4 good sized hard-boiled
  eggs

mayonnaise
seasoning
lettuce
little extra ham

Cut the tips off the asparagus, and chop the well strained stalks finely. Halve the eggs and remove the yolks, mix with the asparagus purée, mayonnaise and seasoning. Pile back into the white cases and top with the tips of asparagus. Serve on a bed of lettuce.

178   DEVILLED EGGS

4 good sized hard-boiled
  eggs

little mayonnaise
1 oz. butter

little chutney
1 teaspoon curry powder
cucumber

seasoning
watercress

Halve the eggs, and remove the yolks. Mash and mix with the butter, chutney, curry powder, seasoning and a very little mayonnaise. Pile or pipe into white cases and serve on a bed of watercress with sliced cucumber.

179   SEA FOOD EGGS

4 hard-boiled eggs
4 oz. shrimps, prawns
  or flaked white fish

mayonnaise
lemon
lettuce

Halve the hard-boiled eggs, remove the yolks and mix with the chopped or flaked fish and mayonnaise. Pile back into the white cases and garnish with lemon. Serve on a bed of lettuce. If wished the white cases can just be filled with the fish and mayonnaise and the sieved egg yolk used as a colourful garnish.

180   ITALIAN EGGS

4 hard-boiled eggs
1 oz. Parmesan cheese
sliced green pepper

mayonnaise
few drops tomato purée
lettuce

Halve the eggs, remove the yolks and mix with the cheese and mayonnaise. Blend with a little tomato purée. Pile back into white cases and garnish with narrow strips of green pepper. Serve on lettuce.

181   FLEMISH FLAN

6 oz. self-raising flour
1 level teaspoon dry
  mustard
1 level teaspoon salt
4 oz. butter or margarine

2 eggs
1 teaspoon Worcestershire
  sauce
3 tablespoons cold water

Gas Mark 5) for 30—35 minutes. Turn out and cool on a wire tray.

Filling

2 large tomatoes
1 medium can tuna or
  salmon
4 tablespoons white sauce
  or salad cream

1 tablespoon tomato
  ketchup
1 tablespoon lemon juice
1 tablespoon finely chopped
  parsley seasoning to taste

Sift dry ingredients into a bowl. Rub in fat till mixture resembles fine breadcrumbs then mix to a soft dropping consistency with the beaten eggs, Worcestershire sauce and water. Beat thoroughly with a wooden spoon then turn mixture into an 8-inch well-greased sponge flan tin. Bake towards the top of a moderately hot oven (400°F. —

Cover base of flan with the sliced tomatoes. Mix filling ingredients well together and spread over the tomatoes Garnish with cucumber twists. Serve with salad.

182 LOBSTER MOUSSE

¼ pint white or Béchamel
    sauce (Recipes 242
    or 245)
2 tablespoons cream
1 — 2 tablespoons lemon
    juice or sherry
8 — 12 oz. minced or
    finely chopped lobster
    meat

2 eggs
seasoning
1 level dessertspoon
    powdered gelatine
¼ teacup water

Separate the egg whites from the yolks and cook the yolks
with the sauce for a few minutes, being careful the
mixture does not boil and therefore curdle. Dissolve the
gelatine in the very hot water, add to the sauce, together
with the cream, and when cooler the lemon juice or
sherry and fish. When the mixture is cool and just beginning to thicken slightly, FOLD in the stiffly beaten egg
whites. Pour into prepared mould or dish. When set
decorate with cucumber, lemon, lobster claws and salad.

184 CUCUMBER SALADS

Shrimp and Cucumber Boats

1 straight medium-sized
    cucumber
little vinegar or lemon
    juice
1 pint picked shrimps
    or 4—6 oz. frozen
    shrimps

2 hard-boiled eggs
lettuce
mayonnaise (Recipe 186)
seasoning

Cut the cucumber into four 2-inch lengths, then cut these
across the centre, scoop out and chop the centre pulp,
making a boat shape. If wished the peel can be entirely
removed or scored with a fork giving a 'stripey' effect.
Season the cucumber and sprinkle with lemon juice or
vinegar — this makes it more easily digested. Put the
cucumber pulp, hard-boiled egg whites and shrimps into
a basin. Mix with mayonnaise. Pile into the cucumber
boats and garnish with the chopped egg yolk. Serve on
a bed of lettuce.

Variations

Instead of shrimps use about 6 oz. canned pink or red
salmon or fresh salmon, or 4 oz. finely chopped ham, or
chicken.

183 STUFFED CUCUMBER SALAD

½ large cucumber
4 spring onions
1 teacup cooked peas
2 tomatoes

¼ teaspoon chopped mint
lettuce
lemon juice
mayonnaise (Recipe 186)

Peel the cucumber and cut into pieces about ½ inch in
depth. Take out centre and cut it finely. Put this into
a basin and mix with peas, mint, mayonnaise, seasoning
and chopped onion. Sprinkle the pieces of cucumber
with lemon juice, for that makes it more easily digested,
and let them stand for about 1 hour. Fill with vegetable
mixture, garnish with tomato rings and serve on lettuce.

185 CURRIED HADDOCK SALAD

1 lb. cooked fresh
    haddock
¼ teacup mayonnaise
    (Recipe 186)
1 dessertspoon curry
    powder
1 small onion

1 small sweet apple
1 oz. butter
lettuce
tomatoes
gherkins or cucumber
watercress

Mix curry in with fried onion and heat for a minute or
so. Fry finely chopped onion in butter until soft. Put
onion, curry and chopped apple into mayonnaise and
mix thoroughly. Flake fish. Arrange on lettuce leaves and
pour over curried mayonnaise sauce. Garnish with watercress, sliced tomatoes and cucumber.

Mayonnaise and Dressings

186 CLASSIC MAYONNAISE

1 egg yolk
good pinch salt, pepper
*   and mustard*
sugar if desired

½ — 1 gill olive oil
1 dessertspoon vinegar
1 dessertspoon warm
*   water*

Put the egg yolk and seasonings into a basin. Gradually beat in the oil, drop by drop, stirring all the time until the mixture is thick. When you find it creamy stop adding oil, for too much will make the mixture curdle. Beat in the vinegar gradually, then the warm water. Use when fresh. With an electric blender, put egg, seasoning and vinegar into goblet. Switch on for a few seconds, then pour oil in steadily.

Variations

187 Green Mayonnaise

Add finely chopped parsley, chives, sage and thyme to mayonnaise.

188 Curried Mayonnaise

Add little curry powder and curry paste to mayonnaise.

189 Tomato Mayonnaise

Add tomato purée or pulp and few drops tabasco or Worcestershire sauce to mayonnaise.

190 FRENCH DRESSING

1 tablespoon salad oil
1 dessertspoon vinegar
½ — 1 teaspoon English
*   or French mustard*

pinch sugar, salt and
*   pepper*
1 tablespoon finely
*   chopped parsley or*
*   chives*

Mix the dry ingredients for the dressing together in a basin, or on a saucer, then add the oil and vinegar, mixing very thoroughly into the dry ingredients.

191 VINAIGRETTE DRESSING

2 dessertspoons vinegar
*   (wine vinegar, cider*
*   vinegar or tarragon*
*   vinegar)*

5 dessertspoons olive oil
good fat pinch salt
pepper to taste

Mix all ingredients in bowl. Keep as cold as possible.

192 LEMON MILK DRESSING

small can full-cream,
*   unsweetened evaporated*
*   milk*

juice 1 lemon

Whisk the lemon juice into the evaporated milk, allow to stand for few minutes then stir together gently until thickened. Serve very cold. Seasoning can be added if wished.

193 YOGHOURT AND HONEY DRESSING

¼ pint yoghourt
1 level tablespoon thin
*   honey*
1 tablespoon lemon juice
*   or white wine vinegar*

good pinch salt
pepper
mustard
sugar

Put the salt, pepper, mustard and sugar into a basin, blend in first of all the honey, then gradually add the yoghourt. Lastly whisk in the lemon juice. Excellent with cheese salads.

194 CONDENSED MILK MAYONNAISE

1 gill sweetened
*   condensed milk*
2 tablespoons oil
2 tablespoons vinegar
*   or lemon juice*

¼ teaspoon salt
¼ teaspoon cayenne pepper
¼ teaspoon dry mustard

Gradually mix all the ingredients together. You may like to increase the amount of vinegar to give a more tart flavour.

Special Salad Dishes

MARGOT'S SALAD CAKE

8 oz. flour (with plain flour use 2 level teaspoons baking powder)	2 oz. fine semolina
	¼ level teaspoon salt
	4 oz. butter or margarine
good shake pepper	1 rounded tablespoon finely chopped parsley
2 rounded tablespoons finely grated onion	
2 eggs	1 rounded teaspoon vegetable extract
2 tablespoons hot water	8 oz. chive-flavoured cottage cheese or other fillings
1 tablespoon mayonnaise (Recipe 186)	
	cold water

Dissolve vegetable extract in hot water, then add enough cold water to give ¼ pint. Sift flour, semolina, salt and pepper into a bowl. Rub in fat until mixture resembles fine breadcrumbs then add onion and parsley. Mix to a soft dropping consistency with the eggs and water. Beat thoroughly with a wooden spoon. Transfer mixture to a well greased 2 lb. loaf tin. Bake in a moderately hot oven (400°F. — Gas Mark 5) for 45 minutes. Turn out on to a wire tray. When the loaf is completely cold, cut lengthwise into 3 layers. Sandwich together with 8 oz. cottage cheese well blended with 1—2 tablespoons mayonnaise or salad cream. Serve, cut in slices, with tomatoes, water cress and other salad vegetables.

196   AVOCADO PEAR SALAD

2 avocado pears	small piece cucumber
1 small grapefruit	endive or lettuce
2 tomatoes	French dressing (Recipe 190)

Peel the avocado pears, remove the skins and cut the fruit into thin slices. Put into a bowl with the sections of grapefruit, and toss in French dressing. Make a bed of the lettuce or endive, pile the pear mixture in the centre and arrange rings of cucumber and tomato around.

197   CRAB AND RICE SALAD

1 large dressed crab	2 teaspoons chopped gherkins
1 teacup cooked rice	
¼ teacup finely chopped celery	lettuce
	1 dessertspoon lemon juice or vinegar
1 teaspoon chopped parsley	1 tablespoon oil
	seasoning

Mix together all ingredients except the lettuce. Season well. Serve on individual dishes on a bed of lettuce. Garnish with small claws of the crab.

198 PEAR AND GINGER CHEESE SALAD

Fill halves of canned or dessert pears with grated Cheddar cheese, moistened with mayonnaise. Add a little chopped ginger and garnish with pieces of chopped stem ginger. If using fresh dessert pears moisten with lemon juice or French dressing to keep a good colour. Serve with lettuce and watercress.

199   AVOCADO PEAR

Avocado pears are an unusual but easily prepared hors d'oeuvre. Remove the stones and serve with oil, vinegar and seasoning. Allow to stand in a cool place before being served.

Fill the centre of the pears with shrimps or prawns in mayonnaise or French dressing. Serve on a bed of lettuce.

200   FRUIT JUICES

Grapefruit, pineapple, orange and a mixture of fruit juices all make a light hors d'oeuvre. Serve as cold as possible and add squeeze of fresh lemon juice to give a little 'bite'.

201   TOMATO JUICE COCKTAIL

Tomato juice has become a very popular hors d'oeuvre. Use canned or bottled tomato juice, or press the juice from fresh tomatoes when plentiful. To give a 'bite' serve as a cocktail with a pinch of celery salt, cayenne pepper, a few drops of Worcestershire sauce.

Always serve Worcestershire sauce with plain tomato juice, so that this may be added as desired.

In hot weather add a little crushed ice to tomato juice or actually freeze some of the tomato juice so that the flavour is not diluted. Garnish with sprigs of mint.

Tomato juice can also be heated and served as a tomato soup; this is a good choice when people are slimming.

202   MELON

Choose a firm but ripe melon, Charentais, which come
from Spain, Italy and France, or Dutch Cantaloupe
melons are considered by some people the best, but the
Honeydew types of melon, green or yellow, are excellent.
In season South Africa sends very excellent and economical Nett melons. Melon is at its best served slightly
iced, so keep for a time in the refrigerator. Cut into slices
and serve with castor sugar and powdered ginger — or
top with slices of preserved ginger. For easy serving cut
into slices, then into neat portions — but arrange these
on the slice so that they look attractive. Decorate with
glacé or Maraschino cherries.

203   MELON BASKET

For a more impressive hors d'oeuvre cut the top off the
melon carefully — this can be serrated — remove the fruit
pulp and dice. The melon in the colour picture No. 13 is
a water melon. Mix this with preserved ginger, top with
sprig of mint. Sweeten to taste and pile back into the
melon case. For special occasions pour over a little white
wine — a Graves is excellent for this — or sherry, some
time before serving.

204   MELON

with Angostura Bitters

If melon is sliced and just a few dashes of Angostura
Aromatic Bitters are put on the melon this will appeal
very much to people who do not like anything too sweet at
the beginning of a meal.

205   MELON AND SMOKED HAM

An unusual but delicious hors d'oeuvre is to serve a slice
of ripe melon with a slice of smoked Parma ham.

206   MELON COCKTAIL

ripe melon   *little sugar*
about 1 — 1¼ lb. mixed   *small amount of sherry*
    fresh fruit   *if desired*

Cut the top off the melon, and scoop out the centre pips,
then remove and ice the pulp. Mix with the rest of the
fruit, sweeten and moisten with a little sherry if wished —
or white wine. Pile back into melon. Serve on a bed of
strawberry leaves. Delicious for an hors d'oeuvre or
a sweet.

207   FRUIT COCKTAIL

Peel a pineapple carefully, trying to keep its shape intact. Replace leaves and arrange in a bowl. Put a mixture of diced fresh fruit all round and decorate with sprays of mint. As this is an hors d'oeuvre, put on very little sugar and add small quantity of dry sherry, if desired.

208   GRAPEFRUIT

Allow ½ grapefruit for each person. Cut away the pith and skin, loosen each section with a sharp fruit knife so it is easy to eat. Dust lightly with castor sugar and decorate with Maraschino cherries, glacé cherries or sprigs of mint. If using canned instead of fresh grapefruit serve in glasses topped with cherries. Grapefruit has a better flavour if served very cold, so if you have a refrigerator chill before serving.

209   GRAPEFRUIT BASKETS

Prepare the grapefruit in the usual way. Mix the sections with other fruit — fresh strawberries, canned Mandarin oranges, sliced preserved ginger are some of the most suitable. Make handles of angelica and decorate with sprigs of mint. If time permits serrate the edge of each grapefruit half.

210   HOT GRAPEFRUIT

Halve and prepare the grapefruit in the usual way. Spread just a small amount of butter over the top, add a sprinkling of brown sugar and mixed spice. Heat either in a moderate oven (375°F. or Gas Mark 4) or under the grill until the surface of the fruit is golden-brown and the juice begins to flow. For special occasions add a little dry sherry to the fruit as well as butter, spice and sugar.

211   ICED FRUIT COOLER

1 can orange juice
1 can pineapple juice
2 tablespoons fresh lemon juice
ice balls or ice cubes

Maraschino cherries
1 or 2 sprigs of fresh mint
1 or 2 slices of orange and or lemon

Blend juices, add lemon juice and chill with ice balls or cubes. Bruise 1 or 2 sprigs of mint (reserving the tender end-tips for garnish) and stir in the fruit juices. Remove mint before serving, and garnish with cherries.

212 PINEAPPLE AND MELON COCKTAIL

ripe melon
diced fresh or canned
    pineapple
little sherry if wished

mint leaves
squeeze lemon juice
sugar

Mix the pineapple and melon together in a bowl, cutting both into small easy to serve dice — or if you have a vegetable scoop the melon can be cut into balls. Mix with a little lemon juice, sherry and sugar and leave in a really cold place. Pile into glasses and top with mint when ready to serve.

213 PINEAPPLE AND CREAM CHEESE SALADS

fresh pineapple or canned
    pineapple rings
chopped walnuts

cream cheese
lettuce
cucumber

Cut the fresh pineapple into rings, or drain canned pineapple. Arrange on crisp lettuce. Fill the centre of each pineapple ring with cream cheese and top with chopped walnuts. Serve with sliced cucumber.

214
PINEAPPLE AND GRAPEFRUIT BASKETS

2 good sized grapefruit
approximately 1 teacup
    diced fresh or canned
    pineapple

little sugar
cherries
mint

Cut the grapefruit into halves through the centre, remove the pulp and mix with the pineapple, any juice from fresh pineapple and a little canned pineapple syrup. Sweeten to taste, pile back into grapefruit cases and decorate with cherries and mint sprigs. Put a handle of pineapple skin or grapefruit skin over the top if wished.

In cold weather the mixture of pineapple and grapefruit can be heated. Top with a little sugar, butter and spice and heat as directed under Recipe 210.

215 STUFFED TOMATO HORS D'OEUVRE

Fresh tomatoes can be stuffed in an almost endless variety of ways, and many of these are suitable as an hors d'oeuvre. Cut the tops off tomatoes. Scoop out centre pulp, and turn the cases upside down for a few minutes to 'drain'. Season the cases lightly. Mix the pulp with fillings as suggested then pile back into the tomato cases. Serve on crisp lettuce.

Eggs. Mix the tomato pulp with lightly scrambled egg, chopped hard-boiled egg, a little mayonnaise and seasoning.

Cheese. Mix the pulp with diced cheese, grated Parmesan cheese (moistened with little cream), grated cheese, cream or cottage cheese. Add chopped cucumber, gherkins, capers, parsley and mayonnaise.

Fish. Mix the pulp with chopped prawns, shrimps or any other shell or flaked white fish. Moisten with mayonnaise. chopped cucumber, gherkins etc. can be added.

Meat. Mix the pulp with diced ham, tongue, cooked salami, sausages, moisten with French dressing or mayonnaise. Add chopped cucumber.

Vegetables. Mix the pulp with freshly cooked drained vegetables, season well and moisten with mayonnaise if wished. Or mix with chopped cucumber, grated carrot and chopped watercress.

13   MELON (Recipe 202)

Hot Hors d'oeuvre

Choose dishes that can be prepared beforehand if possible and just heated with little attention at the last minute. Take care that fish dishes, and in particular shell fish dishes are not overcooked, since this spoils both flavour and texture.

216   LOBSTER THERMIDOR

2 medium sized lobsters	1¼ teacups milk
4 oz. mushrooms	1 — 2 oz. grated cheese
8 oz. tomatoes	seasoning
2 oz. butter or margarine	¼ teacup sherry or white
1 oz. flour	wine

Fry the chopped, skinned and sliced tomatoes until very soft. Stir in the flour and cook for 3 minutes, then gradually add the milk. Bring to the boil and cook until thickened. Season well, then stir in the flaked lobster meat and the wine. Pile into the halved lobster shells, sprinkle cheese on top and brown under a hot grill.

217   LOBSTER NEWBURG

1 lobster	little brandy
¼ pint cream or white	2 eggs
sauce and cream mixed	tablespoon sherry
2 oz. butter	little milk
	pepper

Remove the lobster meat from the body and claws, dice and toss in the hot butter, add the white sauce or cream, brandy. Blend the eggs with 2 or 3 tablespoons milk, add to the mixture and thicken WITHOUT BOILING for a few minutes. Add pepper and sherry and pile back into the lobster shells. Serve very hot.

218   LOBSTER AMÉRICAINE

1 lobster	2 oz. butter
1 small onion	3 skinned tomatoes
little white wine	1 tablespoon brandy
seasoning	(could be omitted)

Fry the finely chopped onion and tomatoes in the hot butter, add the diced lobster meat, enough white wine to moisten, add brandy and seasoning and pile back into lobster shells.

Note. Mention has been made in Recipes 216, 217, 218 of putting the mixture back into the lobster shells. If a lighter hors d'oeuvre is required it should be put into 4 small scallop shells and garnished with small lobster claws. In this way 1 lobster will serve 4 people. If wine etc. is omitted in these recipes use lemon juice or white wine vinegar to flavour. DO NOT OVER-COOK THE LOBSTER MEAT.

219   SOLE AND LOBSTER MORNAY DE LUXE

4 fillets sole	2 oz. grated cheese
¼ pint white wine	1 oz. flour
1 very small lobster or	3 oz. butter
part of lobster	¼ pint milk
1 hard-boiled egg	¼ gill cream
lemon	seasoning
	2 slices bread

Put the sole into a dish with a little seasoning, squeeze of lemon juice, 1 oz. butter and white wine. Bake for about 10 minutes with the top covered carefully with paper in a moderate oven (375°F. — Gas Mark 4). Meanwhile dice the sliced bread and fry in 1 oz. butter until crisp and dark golden-brown. Heat the rest of the butter in a pan, stir in the flour, cook for a few minutes and then add the milk, the cream and the diced lobster meat. Lift the fillets of sole into a hot dish, add all the liquid to the sauce. Pour this over the sole and garnish with the cheese, bread and hard-boiled egg. *Illustrated in colour picture opposite.*

220   CURRIED PRAWNS

8 oz. frozen or freshly shelled	curry sauce (Recipe 236)
prawns	

Make the curry sauce, and simmer well for approximately 1 hour. Add the prawns and cook gently until hot. Do NOT over-cook or you will toughen shell fish. Serve with Patna rice. To get grains of boiled rice really separate wash the uncooked rice in two changes of water, then drain. Cook in a large saucepan, covering with plenty of water. Bring to the boil quickly, season, and simmer for 20 minutes or more until each grain is soft but not mushy. Drain through a colander, rinse in running cold water, then stand colander over a pan of simmering water or put rice in a shallow dish in a very low oven until it has warmed through.

221 FRIED SCAMPI

The large prawns known as scampi have become very popular. You can buy either frozen uncooked scampi, or the large cooked Dublin Bay prawns — which can be served instead of lobster. For this and the other scampi recipes the uncooked type are better. Allow to defrost and use AT ONCE — do not try and keep without a deep freeze.

Coat the fish in egg and breadcrumbs or a thin batter.

Fry in hot deep fat until crisp and golden brown — do not over-cook; about 3—4 minutes is plenty. Drain on crumpled tissue paper or kitchen roll, and serve with wedges of lemon and tartare sauce (Recipe 250).

222 SCAMPI PROVENÇALE

about 18 large prawns cooked or raw	little chopped parsley, to garnish
small onion	2 or 3 tomatoes
clove garlic	little white wine
chopped parsley	seasoning
	2 tablespoons olive oil

Fry the chopped onion, garlic and tomatoes in the hot oil. If using raw scampi add these together with chopped parsley and white wine to moisten. Cook steadily for about 5—6 minutes. If using cooked prawns add white wine, parsley and seasoning to the onion mixture; get this very hot before heating the prawns for 2 or 3 minutes. Serve garnished with chopped parsley.

223 SCAMPI MEUNIÈRE

about 18 large prawns, cooked or raw	little lemon juice
3 oz. butter	1 dessertspoon chopped parsley
seasoning	lemon

Heat the butter and add the prawns. If using ready cooked prawns they need just be heated, but if using raw prawns, cook steadily for about 4 minutes. Lift on to a hot dish, and continue cooking the butter until it becomes dark brown, add seasoning, lemon juice, chopped parsley and capers, and pour over the Scampi. Garnish with lemon.

224 WHITEBAIT

These tiny fish are delicious when cooked in deep fat. Wash and dry the fish; do not remove the heads. Toss in well seasoned flour, and shake off any surplus flour. Put into a frying basket, and lower into a pan of hot deep fat. Fry until just golden coloured. Lift out of the fat; re-heat this for a minute or two then put in the fish for the second time. Allow about 1 minute cooking, take out, drain on crumpled tissue or kitchen paper. Serve with lemon, parsley and cayenne or paprika pepper, and accompanied by brown bread and butter. Whitebait are not always easy to obtain, and small sprats could be served instead. Remove the heads and cook as above.

225 SCALLOPED PRAWNS

1 lb. potatoes	¼ pint white sauce (Recipe 241)
1 small egg	
½ oz. butter	¼ pint prawns
little top of the milk	1 small teaspoon anchovy essence
pepper	1 dessertspoon lemon juice
salt	¼ teaspoon grated lemon rind
	paprika
	3—4 scallop shells

Cook potatoes, mash and cream thoroughly, adding beaten egg, small piece of butter, cream and seasonings. Butter 3—4 scallop shells and line with potato mixture, making an edging of potato rosettes round shells. Blend remainder of potato cream with white sauce, adding most of the prawns (chopped) but saving a few for garnish later. Flavour with anchovy essence and lemon, adjusting seasoning to taste. Bake the lined shells in a hot oven (425—450°F. — Gas Mark 6—7) about 15—20 minutes, until lightly browned. Fill with prawn cream. Sprinkle a little paprika on each and garnish with whole prawns before serving.

226   POTATO AND SARDINE SCALLOPS

6 — 7 scallop shells*
1 lb. cooked potatoes
1 egg
1 tin sardines
little butter

small sprigs watercress
2 hard-boiled eggs (these
  should be shelled and
  sliced while still hot and
  used hot)

* These may be bought from the fishmonger

Grease the scallop shells with butter and mash the sardines, removing the centre backbone if wished, cream potatoes, mix with egg, sardines and butter. Divide the mixture between the scallop shells, roughing them up into peaks with the back of a fork. Top each scallop with one or two shavings of butter and bake in a hot oven (450°F. — Gas Mark 7) for 10 — 15 minutes. Prepare the hard-boiled eggs. Place a sprig of watercress in the centre of each scallop mixture and surround with slices of hard-boiled egg, so that they overlap each other. Serve with brown bread and butter.

227   LOBSTER A LA CATALANE

3 sherry glasses tomato
  ketchup
2 oz. oil or butter
1 small onion (grated
  or finely chopped)
1 clove garlic (crushed)
1 dessertspoon chopped
  parsley
Duchesse potato rosettes
  (Recipe 36)

1 large or 2 small
  lobsters (split and meat
  removed from shell as
  whole as possible)
1 sherry glass white wine
pepper
salt

Fry the halves of lobsters in heated oil or butter until lightly browned. Do not over-cook as this toughens flesh. Dish up on a hot serving dish. Put tomato ketchup into a pan, add onion and garlic, pepper and salt and white wine. Stir over heat until onion is slightly softened, then pour — or strain, if clear sauce is required — over lobsters before serving. Garnish with Duchesse potato rosettes, lightly browned in a hot oven. Serve wedges of lemon separately.

228   SCALLOPS OR COQUILLE ST. JACQUES

5 medium sized scallops
2 oz. butter
1 tablespoon white wine
  or sherry
seasoning

½ pint milk
1 oz. flour
little mashed potato
few crisp breadcrumbs
1 oz. grated cheese

Simmer the scallops in the milk for approximately 10 minutes, until quite soft. It is important that this is done slowly, for too quick cooking makes them tough. When cooked, put the scallops on to their shells. Pipe round a border of mashed potato. Melt the butter in the pan, stir in the flour and cook gently for 3 minutes. Gradually add the milk. This should be made up again to ½ pint — some will have evaporated when cooking the scallops. Cook the sauce until thick, adding seasoning and the wine. Carefully mask the tops of the scallops with this. Sprinkle with the crumbs and cheese and either put into a hot oven or under the grill until heated through and crisp and brown on top.

229 MUSSELS MARINIÈRE

2 pints mussels	liquid to cover
1 small onion	1 bunch parsley
1 tablespoon tarragon vinegar	seasoning
	2 or 3 pieces celery when available

Scrub the mussels well, discarding any that are open and will not close when sharply tapped. Put into a large saucepan together with water, onion, celery, a good pinch of salt and pepper and the bunch of parsley. Heat slowly until the mussels open. Remove the beards from the mussels. Sometimes you will find a small growth, looking like a weed, in the mussels. This must be taken out. Leave the mussels on half the shell. Re-boil the liquid and strain over them. Garnish with chopped parsley. A little wine can be added if wished.

230 CHINESE PRAWNS WITH BACON

4 oz. shelled prawns (frozen, canned or fresh)	1 teaspoon cornflour
	1 egg
6 lean rashers bacon	oil for frying — about 2 tablespoons

Sauce

1 small onion	1 level teaspoon cornflour
1 oz. bamboo shoots	
2 oz. mushrooms	1 teaspoon soy sauce
	¼ pint stock

Chop the prawns finely and spread on to the bacon rashers. Roll up tightly, coat with cornflour and dip in egg, then fry until brown in the hot oil turning as necessary. Remove to a hot serving dish and keep warm. To make the sauce, slice the onions, bamboo shoots and mushrooms in small pieces and brown in the oil in the frying pan. Mix the cornflour smoothly with the soy sauce and stock then pour into the pan. Simmer gently for 3 minutes and pour over the bacon rolls. Serve hot, on a bed of rice.

231 CREAMY HADDOCK CASSEROLE

1 lb. haddock or cod	squeeze lemon juice
8 oz. cottage cheese	pepper and salt
¼ pint white sauce (Recipe 242)	8 oz. cooked peas
	1 lb. freshly cooked potatoes
1 egg	
1 level teaspoon mild mustard	butter
	milk

Poach fish gently in lightly salted water until tender and white, about 15 minutes. Drain fish (some of the stock could be used in the white sauce), remove skin and bones and flake the flesh with a fork. Rub cheese through a sieve and whip it into the sauce; add beaten egg and season to taste with the mild mustard, lemon juice, pepper and salt. Combine fish, sauce, peas and half the creamed potato. Turn this into a well greased heat proof dish and top with remaining potato in piped lines, or pile a border of potato round the edge of the dish and rough it up with a fork. Brush top with beaten egg or milk and reheat, browning lightly, in a moderately hot oven (400°F. — Gas Mark 5) for about 15 minutes. Serve with buttered carrots or baked tomatoes. As a variation add 4 oz. chopped grilled mushrooms and few chopped chives.

232   TUNA FLORENTINE

1 lb. spinach	*2 hard-boiled eggs*
1 level teaspoon salt	*¼ pint white sauce*
dash pepper	*2 oz. grated cheese*
½ oz. butter	*1 tablespoon soft*
*2 cans tuna fillets **	*breadcrumbs*
	extra ¼ oz. butter

* Canned salmon or cooked white fish can be used instead

Wash spinach thoroughly, removing tough stems and wilted leaves. Place in large pan. Cover tightly and cook, shaking the pan several times, about 8 minutes or until tender. Drain if necessary, chop finely; add pepper and salt and butter. Place in casserole or deep heatproof dish. Top spinach with sliced eggs and then with tuna fillets. Add cheese to the sauce and pour over the tuna. Sprinkle with breadcrumbs and dot with butter. Bake in moderately hot oven (400°F. — Gas Mark 5) about 20 minutes. This dish may be garnished with a dusting of parsley or paprika.

233   PACIFIC PIE

7 oz. can tuna
2 tablespoons milk
1 egg
seasoning
1 lb. cooked potatoes —
*   mash while hot*
3 oz. grated Cheddar
*   cheese*
1 rounded teaspoon made
*   mustard*
1 or 2 tomatoes

Remove tuna from tin, flake, and combine with the potatoes, milk, 2 oz. cheese, egg and mustard. Mix thoroughly and season well to taste. Put into well greased fireproof dish and bake near the top of a very hot oven (475°F. — Gas Mark 8) for about 10 minutes. Garnish with tomato slices and the rest of the cheese.

234   TUNA SQUARES

4 oz. flaky or short crust	*1 tablespoon lemon juice*
pastry (Recipes 484,	*pepper and salt*
*485) **	*3 oz. grated cheese*
4 medium tomatoes	*4 gherkins or stuffed*
1 can (4½ oz.) tuna	*olives (optional)*
fillets	*parsley*

* or hot buttered toast can be used

Roll pastry to about ¼ inch thickness and cut into squares of about 4 inches. Bake in hot oven (450°F. — Gas Mark 7) until crisp and lightly browned, for about 7 minutes. Meanwhile slice tomatoes and lightly sprinkle fillets with lemon juice and pepper and salt. Slip these into the oven or under grill for 3 minutes to warm through. Then top pastry squares (or buttered toast) with tomato and fillets and sprinkle liberally with grated cheese. Slip back into oven or under hot grill to heat and to melt and to brown the cheese lightly. Garnish each square with a fan of sliced gherkin or sliced olive or parsley.

235 CURRIED BANANAS

4—8 bananas
curry sauce (Recipe 236)
cooked rice

Cut the bananas lengthwise, brush with a little oil or melted butter and fry until golden brown. Place in a dish on a bed of cooked rice and coat with the curry sauce. Serve with chutney, pickles, etc.

236 CURRY SAUCE

1 medium sized onion
1 cooking apple
1 oz. butter
1 level tablespoon curry powder
1 level tablespoon cornflour
1 teaspoon curry paste
*1—2 tablespoons milk or cream**
½ pint stock or water
salt
1 dessertspoon chutney
1 tablespoon desiccated coconut
1 dessertspoon sultanas
1 teaspoon lemon juice

* *This can be omitted with meat curries*

Chop the onion and cooking apple and sauté in the butter. Then add curry powder, paste and cornflour. Stir until blended, cook a few minutes and then stir in stock. Bring to the boil, stirring all the time. Add chutney, coconut and sultanas. Cover and simmer for at least an hour. Stir in the lemon juice, add seasoning and the milk or cream.

237 SPANISH RICE

1½ pints water
4 oz. rice
2 green peppers
1 teaspoon salt
2 tablespoons oil
8 oz. sliced tomatoes
2 large sliced onions
cayenne pepper
½ teaspoon chili powder or ½ chopped chili
cheese

Heat the oil in a large saucepan, fry the onions and tomatoes until soft: add the water, bring to the boil, then put in the salt and rice. Slice the peppers, add to the rice together with chili powder. Cook gently for 25 minutes, stirring from time to time. Serve very hot with plenty of grated cheese if desired.

238 CURRIED RICE

8 oz. Patna rice
2 really large onions
1½ oz. margarine
1 apple
¾ teacup stock
½—1 level tablespoon curry powder

Heat margarine in saucepan and fry in it the sliced apple and onions. Add the rice (cooked in boiling salted water sufficiently to make just tender, but not over-soft) and the stock blended with the curry powder. Simmer together until the onions and apples are quite tender. Chutney and a few sultanas may be added if wished.

For variation a few pieces of cooked meat can be added.

239 PRAWN AND RICE MORNAY

4—5 oz. rice
½ pint cheese sauce (Recipe 242)
½—1 pint shrimps or prawns
2 chopped gherkins
1 chopped red pepper (can be omitted)
little butter
2 oz. sliced mushrooms

Boil rice in salted water. While rice is cooking, heat prawns gently in sauce, add gherkins and chopped pepper. Fry mushrooms in the butter. Strain rice and mix with the cheese mixture. Garnish with mushrooms.

240 HAM BASKETS

2—4 oz. luxury margarine
2 lb. mashed potatoes
1 egg
approximately 1 tablespoon milk to mix
salt and pepper to taste
milk for glazing

Filling

1 tablespoon finely chopped onion
2 oz. luxury margarine
1½ oz. plain flour
½ pint milk
3 oz. finely grated Cheddar cheese
salt, pepper and mustard
8 oz. lean ham, cut into ½-inch cubes

Add margarine to mashed potatoes and mix thoroughly. Add beaten egg and milk and whisk lightly with a fork. Season to taste, then pile in eight heaps on a well-greased baking sheet and hollow out centres to form oval nest shapes. Alternatively, pipe mixture, using a forcing bag and large star tube, into oval nests. Brush with milk and bake in a hot oven (450°F. — Gas Mark 7) for 15 minutes. Fill with ham mixture, garnish with watercress or parsley and serve with salad or hot vegetables.

Fry onion in margarine till tender and golden, about 5 minutes. Stir in flour and cook for 1 minute, remove from heat, and very gradually add the milk. Bring slowly to the boil, stirring all the time with a wooden spoon, then cook for 3 minutes. Add cheese and seasoning to taste, reheat, then finally stir in ham and put into hot potato cases.

241 EGGS BENEDICT

Arrange slices of tongue or luncheon meat on fried bread. Top with poached eggs and Hollandaise sauce (Recipe 259). Serve with canned vegetables.

Sauces

WHITE SAUCE

242

1 oz. butter or margarine
salt
1 oz. flour
pepper

½ pint milk for coating
consistency, i. e. sauce
1 pint milk for thin white
sauce for soups
¼ pint milk for panada
binding consistency

Heat the butter gently, remove from the heat and stir in the flour. Return to the heat and cook gently for a few minutes so that the *roux*, as the butter and flour mixture is called, does not brown. Bring to the boil and cook, stirring with a wooden spoon, until smooth. Season well. If any small lumps have formed whisk sharply.

Variations on White Sauce

243
Cheese sauce

Stir in 3—6 oz. grated cheese when sauce has thickened, add mustard

Serve with vegetable, meat, fish and savoury dishes

244
Parsley sauce

Add 1—2 teaspoons chopped parsley

Serve with fish, etc.

More elaborate variations on white sauce
Method   *Use*

245
Béchamel sauce

Infuse a piece each of very finely chopped onion, carrot celery in milk. Strain and make as white sauce

In place of white sauce

246
Economical Hollandaise sauce

Make white sauce, remove from heat and whisk in 1 egg, 1 desertspoon lemon juice or vinegar. Cook gently without boiling for a few minutes

Vegetable dishes etc.

247
Maître d'Hôtel sauce

As white sauce, but use half fish stock. Add 2 teaspoons chopped parsley and 3 tablespoons thick cream just before serving

Fish dishes

248
Oyster sauce

Make Béchamel sauce, add about 12 oysters and little cream just before serving

Fish dishes

249
Prawn sauce or Shrimp sauce

Make white sauce, add about ½—1 teacup chopped prawns and a little anchovy essence just before serving. If using fresh prawns simmer shells and use ¼ pint stock instead of the same amount milk

Fish dishes

250
Tartare sauce (Hot)

Make Béchamel sauce, then whisk in 2 egg yolks, 1 tablespoon cream, 1 teaspoon capers, 1 teaspoon chopped gherkin, 1 teaspoon chopped parsley and a squeeze of lemon juice. Cook gently for a few minutes without boiling

Fish, vegetable and some meat dishes; excellent with **veal**

Vegetables with white sauce

	Method	Use
251 Creamed tomato sauce	Whisk a thick tomato purée (which should be hot but not boiling) into hot white sauce. Do not boil together	Fish, meat and savoury dishes
252 Cucumber sauce	Whisk about ¼ pint thick cucumber purée into white sauce, add little lemon juice, green colouring and cream	Fish and vegetable dishes
253 Horseradish sauce (Hot)	Whisk about a dessertspoon vinegar and 2 tablespoons grated horseradish into sauce. Add small amount of cream and pinch sugar	Beef, hot trout
254 Mushroom sauce	Simmer 2—4 oz. chopped mushrooms in the milk until tender. Use this in the white sauce	All types of savoury dishes

255 CHEESE SAUCE MADE WITH EVAPORATED MILK

1 small can evaporated milk
4—6 oz. grated processed cheese
salt and pepper
little made mustard

Put all the ingredients into a saucepan, top of a double saucepan or basin over hot water. Beat gently, stirring, until cheese dissolves, then cook until thick. Serve at once. Delicious with vegetable dishes.

256 TOMATO SAUCE

5 large fresh or canned tomatoes
¼ pint stock or liquid from can
1 rasher bacon
good pinch sugar
1 small onion
bay leaf
1 oz. butter
¼ oz. flour
salt and pepper

Dice onion, carrot and bacon. Heat butter and toss them in this — do not brown. Add tomatoes and simmer for a few minutes with canned tomatoes, rather longer with fresh ones. Take time doing this, since it improves the flavour of the sauce. Blend flour with stock, add to ingredients and simmer gently for about 30 minutes. Stir from time to time. Rub through a sieve or beat with a wooden spoon, add seasoning and sugar. The bay leaf can be put in at the same time as the tomatoes, but for a milder flavour add with stock. For a vegetarian sauce omit bacon. Garlic or garlic salt can be added.

257 TEN-MINUTE TOMATO SAUCE

1 small tube or can tomato purée
1 oz. butter or margarine
2 level teaspoons cornflour
1 small apple
1 small onion
½ pint water
good pinch sugar
salt and pepper

Peel and grate both onion and apple. Heat butter and fry onion for a few minutes, then apple. Add purée, cornflour blended with water, and seasoning. Bring to the boil, and stir until smooth. Simmer gently for about 10 minutes, taste and re-season. Add sugar if wished.

258 HOLLANDAISE SAUCE

2 egg yolks
2—4 oz. butter
pinch cayenne pepper
1—2 tablespoons lemon juice or white wine vinegar
salt and pepper

Try to use a double saucepan for Hollandaise and similar sauces. Put the egg yolks, seasonings and vinegar into the top of the pan. Whisk over hot water until sauce begins to thicken. Add the butter in very small pieces, whisking in each pat and allowing it to melt before adding the next. DO NOT ALLOW TO BOIL as it will curdle. If too thick, add a little cream.

Variations on Hollandaise Sauce

	Method	Use
259 Béarnaise sauce	Add finely chopped shallot and extra pepper to ingredients for Hollandaise sauce. Add a little chopped parsley and Tarragon vinegar. A more economical sauce is made by adding vinegar, shallot and pepper to rich white sauce	Steak
260. Mousseline sauce	Use only 1 oz. butter to the 2 egg yolks and add a little cream and grated nutmeg	Asparagus, broccoli and other vegetables

COLD SAUCES

Mayonnaises, salad dressing and French dressings are to be found under Recipes 186—192.

261 TARTARE SAUCE (Cold)

Make any of the mayonnaises and add little chopped parsley, gherkins, capers. If available also add a very little chopped fresh tarragon, or add a few drops tarragon vinegar.

262 HORSERADISH SAUCE (Cold)

¼ pint cream
2 good tablespoons grated horseradish
mustard
1 tablespoon white vinegar
salt and pepper
good pinch sugar

Mix all seasonings with the cream and whip slightly. Add the horseradish and the vinegar.

16 SPAGHETTI WITH TOMATO SAUCE AND GRUYERE CHEESE (Recipe 264)

19   CREAMED SALT COD PROVENCALE (Recipe 173)

20   VEAL AND HAM PIE WITH SALAD (Recipe 492)

Substantial Savoury Dishes

In this chapter are a variety of savoury dishes, which could be served either for a supper dish, or as an hors d'oeuvre.

Pasta Dishes

263 There are a great variety of different kinds of pasta, and they provide not only nutritious, but easily prepared savoury dishes. Many of the modern pastas cook within minutes.

Do not overcook pasta; to be perfect it should be slightly firm in texture. Serve with a variety of sauces.

Always have plenty of boiling salted water for cooking pasta, so that it cannot stick in the pan.

264 SPAGHETTI WITH TOMATO SAUCE AND GRUYÈRE CHEESE

approximately 6 oz spaghetti

For the sauce:

3 tablespoons tomato purée
1 oz. flour
¾ — 1 pint stock or water with a bouillon cube
seasoning
1 oz. butter
1 medium sized onion
clove garlic
3 — 4 triangles Swiss Gruyère cheese

Melt the butter and cook the chopped onion and garlic until soft. Stir in the flour, and gradually add the stock. Bring to the boil, and when thickened add the purée, seasoning and if desired a little chopped parsley, thyme and marjoram. Bring to the boil again and simmer for about 20 minutes. Meanwhile cook the spaghetti in plenty of boiling salted water, and strain. Add chopped cheese to the hot sauce, heat for 2 minutes until beginning to melt, then pour over the spaghetti. *Illustrated in colour picture No. 16.*

265 MACARONI WITH TOMATO SAUCE

This is an easy and economical savoury. If you use quick cooking macaroni with the Ten Minute tomato sauce (Recipe 257) the whole dish can be ready within a quarter of an hour. Serve with plenty of grated cheese.

266 PRAWN AND MACARONI RING

4 oz. mushrooms
1 pint prawns (or shrimps)
1 or 2 diced tomatoes
2 oz. elbow macaroni
1 or 2 hard-boiled eggs
¼ pint tomato sauce (Recipe 256 or 257)
little sherry
lemon
1 oz. butter

Make the sauce and add diced mushrooms, sherry, tomatoes and most of the prawns. Meanwhile cook the macaroni and form into a ring, tossing the pasta in a little butter to keep it moist. Fill the ring with the prawn mixture, flavouring with a little lemon juice. Garnish with prawns and sections of egg. If desired cook a few small mushrooms and arrange round the dish.

267 SPAGHETTI SOUFFLÉ

3 oz. spaghetti
¼ pint cheese sauce (Recipe 243)
2 eggs
chopped chives or spring onions

Cook the spaghetti, drain and mix with the cheese, add egg yolks, seasoning and chives. Finely fold in stiffly beaten egg whites. Bake for approximately 25 minutes in centre of moderately hot oven (400°F. — Gas Mark 5). Serve hot.

268   SPAGHETTI BOLOGNESE

6 — 8 oz. spaghetti   *Parmesan cheese*

Bolognese Sauce

1 can tomatoes,	*seasoning*
preferably Italian	*¼ pint good brown stock*
plum tomatoes or	*if using tinned*
1 tube or small can	*tomatoes or*
tomato purée or 4 fresh	*2¼ gills with fresh*
tomatoes	*tomatoes or*
approx. 6 oz. minced	*2¼ gills with tomato*
raw beef	*purée*
1 carrot, shredded	*1 wineglass red wine*
1 — 1½ oz. butter } *or 2 oz.*	*2 oz. mushrooms finely*
1 tablespoon } *butter*	*chopped*
olive oil }	*½ — 1 clove garlic (could*
1 onion finely chopped	*be omitted)*

Heat the butter and oil in a pan, then gently fry the crushed garlic, onion, mushrooms and carrot for several minutes. Add the meat and the rest of the ingredients and simmer until the sauce has thickened. Although not correct, you can include a sliced red or green pepper in this sauce. A little chopped parsley can be added to the sauce just before serving. Cook the spaghetti in boiling salted water — the quick cooking variety takes only 7 minutes. Strain. Pour the sauce on top and serve with grated Parmesan cheese.

269   LASAGNA

This wide ribbon type of pasta forms the basis for many delicious dishes. You can obtain the green spinach-flavoured lasagna as well as the plain pasta. Always use plenty of boiling salted water and a very large pan. Either break into convenient pieces or lower one end of the long sticks into the boiling salted water, and wait for this to soften before allowing the rest of the pasta to go into the saucepan.

6 oz. lasagna	*2 oz. grated Parmesan*
4 — 6 oz. Gruyère	*cheese*
cheese	*4 oz. cream cheese*
sliced thinly	*Bolognese sauce*
	(Recipe 268)

Cook the lasagna in boiling salted water for about 20 — 25 minutes until tender. Strain and if using long pieces put these over the top of a saucepan to dry out. Cut into convenient lengths. Make the sauce. Put a layer of the lasagna into a buttered dish, then a layer of sauce, then a little cream cheese, Parmesan cheese and Gruyère cheese. Fill the dish like this, ending with the Parmesan and Gruyère cheese. Bake for approximately 30 minutes in the centre of a moderately hot oven (400°F. — Gas Mark 5).

270   SPAGHETTI WITH TOMATO AND RED PEPPER SAUCE

8 oz. spaghetti	*2 tablespoons chopped*
1 onion	*parsley*
8 oz. tomatoes	*oil for frying*
1 red pepper (small)	*salt and pepper*
¼ — 1 clove garlic	*2 — 3 tablespoons*
4 oz. cooked minced	*Parmesan or Pecorino*
pork	*cheese*

Start cooking the sauce first as it takes longer than the spaghetti. Heat the oil in a pan, brown the garlic, onion and pork. Take out the garlic, add the chopped tomatoes, sliced red pepper and parsley, cook for 5 minutes before adding sufficient hot water or stock to make a sauce. Add the salt and pepper last. Simmer until the tomatoes are reduced to a pulp, stirring occasionally. The longer you cook the better the flavour, but make sure the sauce does not become too dry.

Cook the spaghetti in the usual way, drain it and mix it well with grated cheese. Pour the sauce over it. Serve extra grated cheese.

271   SPAGHETTI AND MUSHROOM LOAF

1 small can cooked	*few breadcrumbs*
spaghetti	*1 or 2 eggs*
1 oz. margarine	*seasoning*
2 oz. mushrooms	*1 tablespoon grated*
1 tomato	*cheese*

Chop the spaghetti into small pieces. Heat the margarine and fry the chopped mushrooms and tomato until soft. Stir these into the spaghetti, adding other ingredients. Press into greased tin and bake for good 30 minutes in centre of a hot oven (450°F. — Gas Mark 7). Serve with tomatoes.

272   MACARONI CREOLE

6 — 8 oz. quick cooking	*8 oz. cooked ham or*
elbow length macaroni	*cooked meat*
1 green or red pepper	*3 or 4 tomatoes*
2 oz. butter or margarine	*few cooked beans if*
1 teacup stock	*available*
seasoning	*few cooked carrots*
	2 onions

Fry the sliced onions and pepper in the butter. Add stock and the diced meat etc. Heat thoroughly. Cook macaroni for 7 minutes in boiling salted water. Strain and mix with the meat and vegetable mixture. Serve at once. *Illustrated in colour picture No. 15.*

273   SPAGHETTI MARINARA

8 oz. spaghetti	*2 bay leaves*
1 large tin anchovies	*4 oz. mushrooms*
4 rashers bacon	*2 oz. grated cheese*
1 sliced onion	*(preferably Parmesan)*
1 lb. tomatoes	*1 tablespoon oil*
seasoning	

Half fill a large saucepan with water, bring to the boil, adding a good teaspoon salt. Drop in the spaghetti and cook steadily for 10 minutes — no longer. Drain thoroughly and keep warm. While the spaghetti is cooking prepare the rest of the mixture. Drain off the oil from the anchovies and put this, together with the other tablespoon of oil, into another saucepan. When this is hot, fry the sliced onion, sliced tomatoes and mushrooms until they form a soft sauce. Put the spaghetti into this, add seasoning to taste — remembering that the anchovies will make it very salty — and the bay leaves. Simmer gently for 10 — 15 minutes, adding most of the anchovies during the last 5 minutes. Cut the bacon into small dice and fry until crisp and brown. Take out the bay leaves. Pile the spaghetti mixture into a hot dish, garnish with the remaining anchovies, pieces of bacon and grated cheese.

274 SPAGHETTI WITH BARBECUE SAUCE

8 — 12 oz spaghetti

For the sauce

2 tablespoons corn oil
1 small onion chopped
¼ oz. cornflour
1 lb. tomatoes — peeled and sliced
1 pint water
2 oz. chopped lean ham
2 oz. soft brown sugar

grated cheese

¼ level teaspoon paprika
salt
1 tablespoon Worcestershire sauce
1 dessertspoon vinegar
dash of Tabasco sauce
stuffed olives

Cook spaghetti in boiling salted water. Meanwhile make sauce. Heat the oil in a saucepan, add the onion and cook for a few minutes without browning. Stir in the cornflour and mix well. Add tomatoes, water and ham and simmer gently for 10 — 15 minutes. Add all remaining ingredients except olives and cook a further few minutes. Correct the seasoning. Lastly, stir in the sliced stuffed olives.

Put the spaghetti into a serving dish. Pour over the sauce. Sprinkle some grated cheese over and top with a nut of butter.

Vegetable Dishes

275 HARD-BOILED EGGS FLORENTINE

4—6 hard-boiled eggs
1 lb. cooked spinach*
little butter

evaporated milk cheese
sauce (Recipe 255)
seasoning

Frozen chopped spinach is ideal for this dish

Cook the spinach, drain well and chop finely, then add butter and plenty of seasoning. Arrange at the bottom of a buttered dish and arrange the eggs on top. These can be halved, in which case put the cut side downwards. Cover with the sauce and serve. If desired the mixture can be put into 4 individual scallop shells, the top covered with breadcrumbs and grated cheese and browned under the grill.

276 SWISS SPINACH FLAN

6 oz. short crust pastry
   (Recipe 485)
1 lb. spinach
salt and pepper
nutmeg
3 triangles Swiss
   Gruyère cheese

2 tablespoons butter
2 eggs
6 tablespoons cream or
   top of the milk or
   evaporated milk
few anchovies

Cook the spinach and chop finely, adding the butter, seasoning. Line a very deep flan ring or tin with the pastry, or use the inside of an oven-proof dish. Put the spinach at the bottom of this. Beat together eggs and cream, season lightly, pour over the spinach. Arrange the Gruyère cheese sections and anchovy fillets on top. Bake for approximately 25 minutes in a moderately hot oven (400°F. — Gas Mark 5), just above centre of oven. *Illustrated in colour picture No. 8.*

Note. The pastry must be rolled out very thinly in this recipe.

277 SPINACH RAMEKINS

1 teacup cooked creamed
   spinach
2 oz. finely grated
   cheese (including a
   little Parmesan if
   possible)

2 eggs
seasoning — including
   paprika pepper

Divide the spinach between 4 small ramekin dishes. Beat the eggs well, adding seasoning and most of the cheese. Pour over the spinach, dusting the top of each ramekin with the last of the cheese. Put near the top of a hot oven (425—450°F. — Gas Mark 6—7) for 10 minutes until the egg mixture is just set. Dust with cayenne pepper and serve at once.

278 RATATOUILLE

2 onions
1 lb. tomatoes
1 medium marrow
4 small aubergines or
   eggplant

1 red or green pepper
little bacon fat or rind
   from gammon
1 or 2 cloves garlic
seasoning
little chopped parsley

Chop the onions and skin the tomatoes, cut the latter in half, sprinkle with salt and leave upturned to drain. Peel the marrow, cut in large chunks, remove the stalks of the aubergines, cut in half, scoop out slightly and cut into chunks. Seed and slice the pepper. Heat the fat or rind in a strong pan and gently fry the onions and the crushed garlic. Add the aubergines, marrow, tomatoes and pepper. Season well and simmer slowly, with well-fitting lid on the pan, until the vegetables are tender. Serve sprinkled with parsley, if wished.

279 GNOCCHI

4 oz. semolina
1 pint milk
pepper and salt

3 oz grated cheese
2 oz. butter
1 beaten egg

Heat milk with a sprinkling of pepper and salt. Stir in the semolina and bring to the boil, stirring. Cook gently for 3 minutes until thickened. Remove from heat and add 1½ oz. grated cheese and 1 oz. butter. Beat in the egg. Stir over low heat, without boiling, for a minute or two. Turn out on to an oiled or wetted shallow oblong tin, spreading ¼ inch thick. Cool. Cut into rounds about size of a penny with a wetted cutter. Arrange in overlapping rows on buttered dish. Sprinkle with remaining cheese and dot with butter. Heat under grill, slowly at first, then more quickly to brown. Garnish with parsley. Serve with tossed green salad or cheese sauce or with hot lamb or veal. *Illustrated in colour picture No. 38.*

280 SCALLOPED MOUSSE FLAN

6 oz. plain flour	*3 oz. butter or margarine*
¼ level teaspoon salt	*2 oz. Cheddar or*
¼ level teaspoon dry	*Parmesan cheese*
mustard	*2 tablespoons cold water to*
pinch cayenne pepper	*mix (approximately)*

Sift dry ingredients together. Rub in fat till mixture resembles fine breadcrumbs, add finely grated cheese then mix to a stiff paste with cold water. Turn out on to a lightly floured board, knead quickly till smooth then divide pastry in two. Roll one half into a circle and with it line the bottom of a well greased 9-inch pie plate. Add trimmings to rest of pastry, roll out thinly, then cut into approximately 28—30 rounds with a 1¾-inch plain cutter. Overlap these round side of pie plate (see first picture), moistening each with a little cold water to seal and hold them together. Prick base well, then bake just above centre of a hot oven (425—450°F. — Gas Mark 6—7) for 15 minutes, then at 375°F. — Gas Mark 4 for 10—15 minutes. When cool, transfer flan case to a serving dish.

Filling

¼ gill boiling water	*2 tablespoons chopped*
1 rounded teaspoon sugar	*stuffed olives*
¼ oz. gelatine	*4 tablespoons cooked peas*
3 chopped hard-boiled	*1 gill evaporated milk*
eggs	*seasoning to taste*
3 tablespoons lemon juice	

Dissolve gelatine and sugar in the boiling water then add eggs, olives and peas. When mixture is cold and starting to thicken fold in evaporated milk, whisked till thick and frothy, and the lemon juice. Season to taste and pour filling into flan case (see second picture). Decorate top with slices of stuffed olives. Chill before serving.

281 STUFFED AUBERGINES OR EGGPLANT

2 medium sized	*1 skinned chopped*
aubergines	*tomato*
¼ teaspoon salt	*2 oz. fresh breadcrumb*
2 teaspoons olive oil or	*salt and pepper*
butter	*4 oz. grated Cheddar*
2 oz. diced cooked	*cheese*
bacon	*1 oz. extra grated*
1 tablespoon chopped	*Cheddar cheese*
eggs	*¼ pint tomato sauce*
1 tablespoon finely	*(Recipe 251) or*
chopped cooked onion	*¼ pint cheese sauce*
	(Recipe 243)

Wash the aubergines and remove the stalk, then cut in half lengthwise. Cut round each half aubergine ¼ inch

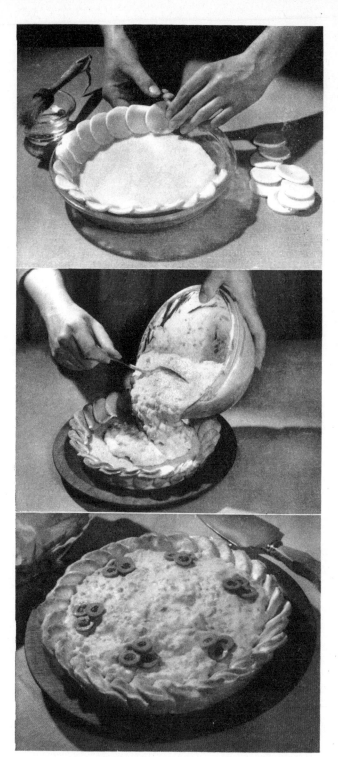

from the skin and then criss-cross cut the surface lightly to ensure even cooking. Sprinkle with salt and olive oil or melted butter. Put on a greased baking tin in a moderately hot oven (400°F. — Gas Mark 5) until the centre is nearly cooked (15—20 minutes). Make the stuffing by mixing all the ingredients together. Scoop out about half the flesh from the centre of the cooked aubergines, chop up and add to the stuffing. Fill the aubergine cases with the stuffing, sprinkle with grated cheese and return to the oven for a further 15 minutes. Serve hot with tomato or cheese sauce.

Quiches

282 QUICHE LORRAINE OR CHEESE FLAN

6 oz. flaky pastry
(Recipe 484)
6 oz. grated cheese
¼ pint milk

¼ pint cream
seasoning
2 or 3 rashers of bacon
2 eggs

Chop bacon finely and fry very lightly. Line a really deep flan ring with pastry, beat eggs, add cream, milk, grated cheese, bacon and seasoning. Pour in carefully and bake in the centre of a moderately hot oven (400°F. — Gas Mark 5) until the pastry is well risen and brown and the filling firm. *Illustrated in colour picture No. 42.*

For a more economical flan, use more milk and just the egg yolks.

283 PRAWN QUICHE

6 oz. short crust pastry
or flaky pastry
(Recipes 485 or 484)
4—6 oz. chopped prawns
or shrimps
little grated cheese if
desired

2 eggs
¼ pint milk or ⅛ pint milk
and ⅛ pint cream
seasoning

Line a really deep flan ring with the pastry. Beat the eggs, add milk or milk and cream, seasoning, prawns or shrimps and the cheese. Pour mixture carefully into pastry cases, and bake in the centre of a moderately hot oven (400°F. — Gas Mark 5) for approximately 30 minutes until the pastry is cooked and the filling set.

284 MUSHROOM AND ONION QUICHE

6 oz. short crust pastry
(Recipe 485)
2 onions
small can evaporated milk
2 oz. butter
1 teaspoon lemon juice

12 small mushrooms
2 eggs
pinch dried mustard
3 oz. grated cheese (could
be omitted)

Roll out pastry and line 8-inch sandwich tin or flan ring. Prepare and slice the onions and peel about half the mushrooms, leaving the stalks on. Fry these mushrooms and the onions in butter, and place on the bottom of the flan case. Put 3 oz. grated cheese in a bowl, season with salt and pepper and pinch of dried mustard. Add 2 eggs and the contents of a small can of evaporated milk. Stir well, and then pour the mixture into the flan case. Cook in centre of moderately hot oven (400°F. — Gas Mark 5) for 30—40 minutes.

Simmer the rest of the mushrooms in a little boiling salted water (to which 1 teaspoon lemon juice has been added) until tender. Cut into slices, and use for decorating the quiche. Serve hot.

285 BACON QUICHE

Ingredients and method of cooking as Quiche Lorraine, but halfway through cooking put a lattice of thin bacon strips on top and allow these to cook with the quiche. Or if preferred cook the quiche, and when ready garnish with crisp strips of bacon and stuffed olives.

286   BANANAS SINGAPORE

1 lb. bananas*	*1 pint curry sauce made*
1¼ oz. melted butter or	*from:*
margarine	*3 oz. butter*
¾ pint shrimps or	*2 oz. flour*
prawns, cooked and	*2 level teaspoons curry*
picked	*powder*
4 oz. hot coodek rice	*1 level teaspoon ground*
	black pepper
* Use slightly under-ripe	*just under 1 pint hot*
bananas — green tipped or	*chicken stock,*
all yellow peel	*consommé or water*
	with bouillon cube

To make the curry sauce, melt butter, blend in flour, curry powder, salt and pepper. Add hot chicken stock. Cook until thick, stirring constantly. Peel bananas. Keep whole or cut into halves lengthwise or crosswise. Place in greased baking pans. Brush or coat bananas with butter or margarine. Pour half the curry sauce over bananas. Bake in a moderate oven (375°F. — Gas Mark 4) 15—18 minutes. Heat shrimps in remaining curry sauce. Serve hot with bananas on a bed of hot rice.

287   PAELLA

4 pieces cooked or raw	*8 oz. frozen peas*
chicken*	*2 pints water*
4 Dublin Bay prawns	*1 chicken bouillon cube*
or 8 — 10 large prawns	*¼ can pimento or red*
1 small cooked lobster	*pepper*
or can lobster	*2 medium size tomatoes*
2 tablespoons olive oil	*little saffron if possible*
4 oz. rice	*1 onion*
1 clove garlic	*6 — 8 mussels*

* If using raw chicken it should be jointed young frying chicken

Cut up chicken, onion and garlic and fry in the oil until golden. Add half the water and simmer for 15 minutes. Add the tomatoes skinned and cut up, add the rice and the remaining water and bouillon cube. Simmer 5 minutes, stir in saffron. Arrange the lobster pieces, prawns, mussels and peas attractively with the pimentos. Continue cooking until rice is cooked and has absorbed most of the liquid, 15—20 minutes.

The above is a true paella with its wonderful mixture of ingredients. Many of these can be omitted but to keep the interest of the dish you MUST mix some shell fish with the chicken.

288   SPANISH SAVOURY RICE

A recipe for the real Spanish rice will be found in Recipe 237 but this quick version makes a pleasant savoury snack

10 oz. can condensed	*2 oz. chopped green*
tomato soup	*pepper*
4 oz. Patna rice	*4 tablespoons water*
4 rashers of bacon	*pepper*
2 oz. chopped onion	*olives*

Cook the rice in salted water till tender. Drain and rinse. Cut up the bacon and fry until crisp. Remove from pan and sauté the onion and pepper until tender, add bacon, rice and remaining ingredients. Heat through and serve on small cheese biscuits, topped with sliced olives.

Fish Dishes

289 CRISPY TUNA PUFFS

with Sweet-Sour Sauce

7-oz. can middle-cut tuna
2 egg yolks
1 oz. plain flour
½ level teaspoon salt
good sprinkle of pepper
2 egg whites

Remove tuna from can and finely flake with a fork. Beat egg yolks until creamy, stir in the flour and seasoning. Blend in the tuna. Whisk the egg whites to a stiff froth and lightly but thoroughly fold into the tuna mixture. Drop neat spoonfuls into deep hot fat and fry until crisp and golden. Drain on crumpled kitchen paper. Serve in a hot dish, with hot greens or a crisp salad and sweet-sour sauce.

290 Sweet-Sour Sauce

Melt 3 tablespoons redcurrant jelly. Blend in 1 tablespoon made mustard. Simmer for a minute or two. Add 1 tablespoon sliced pickled gherkin or stuffed olives.

291 SEA FISH PIE

12 oz. short crust pastry (Recipe 485)
8 oz. cooked fish (or canned salmon or tuna)
½ oz. butter
1 oz. cornflour
½ pint milk
salt and pepper
1 egg
½ teaspoon anchovy essence
1 teaspoon lemon juice
½ small onion finely chopped
1 teaspoon chopped parsley

To garnish: *radishes, cucumber, tomato*

Line an 8-inch pie plate with half the short crust pastry. Flake the fish finely. Melt the butter in a pan, add the cornflour and cook for a few minutes. Remove from the heat, add the milk stirring all the time. Return to the heat, stir until boiling and boil for 1 minute. Remove from the heat and stir in the slightly beaten egg. Add all the seasonings and the fish. Turn most of the mixture into the prepared pie plate and cover with the rest of the pastry. If desired a small circle can be cut from top round as shown in the picture. Brush with a little beaten egg or milk. Bake for about 1 hour in centre of a moderately hot oven (400°F. – Gas Mark 5). When cooked top centre circle with the small amount of filling left and garnish with radish 'roses' and sliced cucumber and tomato. *Illustrated in colour picture opposite.*

292 SALMON SUPPER RING

Scone Mixture

7 oz. plain flour
1 oz. cornflour
pinch salt
2 level teaspoons baking powder
1 oz. butter or fat
milk to mix

Filling

½ oz. butter
1 level tablespoon cornflour
½ pint milk
salt and pepper
1 teaspoon lemon juice
8-oz. can salmon or 1 lb. cooked white fish
few chopped capers
½ teaspoon anchovy essence (omit if using salmon)

Sieve the dry ingredients for the scone mixture together. Rub in the fat. Mix with sufficient milk to form a soft dough. Roll out thinly into an oblong shape.

Melt the butter in a pan, add cornflour and cook for a few minutes. Remove from the heat, add the milk stirring all the time. Return to the heat, stir until boiling and boil for 1 minute stirring constantly. Season well. Add the flaked fish, chopped capers, anchovy essence and lemon juice. Spread this savoury mixture on the dough – moisten the edges and roll up like a Swiss roll. Put carefully on to a greased baking sheet, then shape into a horseshoe. Using a pair of kitchen scissors or a sharp knife make some cuts two-thirds of the way into the roll. Turn each section out a little on to its side. Brush with a little beaten egg or milk. Bake for about 15 minutes in centre of a hot oven (450°F. – Gas Mark 7). Serve hot or cold. *Illustrated in colour picture opposite.*

21   SEA FISH PIE (Recipe 291)

22   SALMON SUPPER RING (Recipe 292)

23   **CHEESE AND TOMATO BAKES** (Recipe 329)
        SCOTCH WOODCOCK (Recipe 326)
        SOUFFLÉ TARTS (Recipe 324)

24   **BACON ROLLS** (Recipe 339)

After-dinner Savouries, Soufflés and Cocktail Savouries

Many people prefer a savoury to a sweet at the end of the meal;
for a formal dinner serve the savoury after the sweet.

FOODS TO SERVE AS AFTER-DINNER SAVOURIES

293   The savoury at the end of a meal should be small and quite strongly flavoured to 'round off' a good meal.
Most cheese dishes make a good savoury; bacon with other ingredients is a good choice or such fish dishes as sardines, anchovies with egg etc. will all be popular.

Cheese Savouries

294   WELSH RAREBIT

4 — 6 large slices of toast	salt
8 oz. cheese*	pepper
1 teaspoon made mustard	1 oz. butter
1 tablespoon beer or ale	1 oz. flour
or Worcestershire sauce	¼ pint milk
butter for toast	

* A Dutch Gouda or Edam makes a soft creamy Welsh Rarebit,
or use Cheddar or Cheshire for a creamy mild flavour, or mix
a very little Parmesan cheese in to give real 'bite'

Heat the butter in a saucepan, stir in the flour and cook steadily for several minutes, then gradually add the cold milk. Bring to the boil and cook until smooth and thick. Add the mustard, salt, pepper, most of the cheese and the beer. Heat steadily, without boiling too quickly, until the cheese has melted. Spread over the hot buttered toast, sprinkle with the remainder of the cheese and brown under a hot grill. Serve at once. *Illustrated in colour frontispiece.*

This Welsh Rarebit mixture can be stored in covered jars for some days in a refrigerator.

294 (cont.)   Variations on Welsh Rarebit:

Tomato Rarebit. Blend the mixture with tomato juice or soup instead of milk. If using soup use a little less flour.
Celery Rarebit. Arrange neat pieces of well drained cooked celery on the toast and coat with the Welsh Rarebit mixture. The celery stock can be used instead of milk.
Buck Rarebit. Top the mixture with a poached egg.
Creole Rarebit. Mix the rarebit mixture with fried onion and tomatoes and little corn on the cob.
Vegetable Rarebit. Mix the rarebit mixture with few cooked well drained vegetables.

295   YORK RAREBIT

Ingredients and method as Welsh Rarebit, but put a thick sliced of cooked ham on each piece of toast and cover with the cheese mixture.

296 WELSH RAREBIT SAUCE WITH EGG AND TOMATO

4 slices toast
4 hard-boiled eggs
8 thick slices of tomato

Welsh Rarebit Sauce

1 oz. butter
8 oz. grated Cheddar cheese
2 tablespoons milk
salt and pepper to taste

Prepare the Welsh Rarebit sauce: melt the butter. Add the grated cheese and the milk. Stir over low heat until the cheese melts. Season and adjust consistency with a little extra milk if necessary.

Lay the required number of trimmed toast slices in a shallow fireproof dish and put 2 tomato slices on each piece. Heat through in a moderate oven (375°F. — Gas Mark 4) or under the grill for a few minutes. Cut the shelled hard-boiled eggs across in half (while still hot) and lay one half on each tomato slice. Pour over the Welsh Rarebit sauce. Garnish with piles of freshly cooked green peas and serve at once.

297 CHEESE ON TOAST

If you do not want the bother of making Welsh Rarebit just put slices of cheese on top of hot buttered toast, and put under a hot grill. Do not overcook or the cheese becomes tough.

298 ICED CAMEMBERT CHEESE

Iced Camembert cheese is a delicious savoury at the end of a meal, particularly in hot weather. Remove rinds from the cheese if wished, mix with a little cream and put into the freezing tray and leave until lightly frozen. Serve with biscuits, radishes and lettuce.

299 CHEESE PUDDING

4 — 5 oz. grated cheese
4 oz. white bread
2 oz. butter
seasoning
¾ pint milk
2 eggs

Cut the bread into neat dice or make into bread crumbs, and put into a basin. Heat the butter with the milk, pour over the bread. Allow to cool slightly, then add the beaten eggs and most of the grated cheese. Season well. Pour into a pie or entrée dish and cover the top with the remainder of the cheese. Bake for approximately 30 — 40 minutes in the centre of moderate oven (375°F. — Gas Mark 4) until firm.

300 CAMEMBERT MOUSSE

1 oz. butter
1 oz. flour
½ pint milk
2 oz. Camembert cheese (weighed without the rind)
1 oz. grated Parmesan cheese
1 heaped teaspoon tomato purée
1 heaped teaspoon French mustard
pinch salt and cayenne pepper
1 heaped teaspoon powdered gelatine
2 eggs

Prepare a 5-inch soufflé case by tying a wide band of double greaseproof paper round the outside so that it extends above the rim. Melt the butter in a pan, stir in the flour and cook for a minute. Add the milk gradually, bring to the boil and boil for 1 minute, stirring. Add the creamed Camembert and grated Parmesan cheese and seasonings and stir until smooth. Soften the gelatine in 1 tablespoon of cold water and dissolve in 2 tablespoons of boiling water. Add the egg yolks and dissolved gelatine to the cheese sauce, stirring over gentle heat until it thickens. Cool, stirring occasionally, and when almost set fold in the stiffly beaten egg whites. Pour into the soufflé case and put in a cool place to set. Remove the paper carefully, garnish and serve with a lettuce salad.

301 ANGELS ON HORSEBACK

Allow 1 or 2 oysters per person and proceed just as for Devils on Horseback (Recipe 302) but season the oyster and add a squeeze of lemon before rolling bacon round it. Do not over-cook as this toughens the oysters.

302 DEVILS ON HORSEBACK

8 large juicy cooked prunes	8 fingers buttered toast
4 long rashers bacon	paprika (red) pepper

Stone the prunes, cut each rasher of bacon into halves and wrap round the prune, securing with a cocktail stick. Cook under the grill until the bacon is crisp and brown. Serve on toast dusted with red pepper. If wished, a little liver pâté can be inserted into the centre of the prune.

303 BENGAL CANAPÉS

1 oz. margarine) for	dash of cream
¼ oz. cornflour } white	4 oz. diced ham (cooked)
¼ pint milk) sauce	seasoning
4 slices bread	parsley
2 tablespoons grated cheese	chutney

Make the white sauce. Add cream, ham and seasoning. Toast or fry the bread and spread with chutney, then the ham mixture. Cover with the grated cheese and brown under the grill or in the oven. Garnish with parsley and more chutney.

304 BRETON FINGERS

1 small tin sardines in oil	little margarine or butter, if necessary
seasoning	¼ teaspoon made mustard
1 teaspoon Worcestershire sauce	4 slices buttered toast
¼ teacup breadcrumbs	1 tomato
2 oz. grated Cheddar cheese	

Mash the sardines very well and season. Mix the oil from the tin of sardines with the breadcrumbs, seasoning, Worcestershire sauce and cheese. If there is not sufficient oil to give a soft mixture then add a little margarine or butter and cream well. Spread the mashed sardines on the slices of toast, and cover with the crumb mixture. Put under a hot grill for a few minutes until crisp and golden brown. Garnish with a small piece of tomato, and serve hot or cold. If serving hot the fingers can be prepared earlier and just heated in oven.

305 KIDNEYS ON TOAST

Skin and halve the kidneys, season well and fry in hot butter until tender, OR

Quarter kidneys, coat in well seasoned flour. Fry chopped bacon in a pan, add a little butter then the kidneys and cook steadily, adding little water or port wine to moisten. Excellent topped with a poached egg. Serve on buttered toast.

306 KIDNEYS AND BACON ON TOAST

Put a small roll of bacon, a tiny mushroom and ½ kidney on skewers. Brush with melted butter and season, then cook under the grill. When cooked serve on strips of crisp buttered toast.

Fish Savouries

307 SARDINES ON TOAST

Arrange well drained sardines on hot buttered toast, season lightly, and heat for 1 minute under the grill.

Sardines on toast are delicious if you make savoury butter by adding a squeeze of lemon juice, a pinch of celery salt and a pinch of cayenne pepper to the butter.

208 Variations

Mash sardines, season well, spread on toast. Cover with grated cheese and brown under the grill.

309

Mash sardines, season well, spread on toast. Cover with thickly sliced skinned tomatoes, brush with little butter and cook under medium grill.

310   CREAMED HADDOCK

Heat a good knob of butter in a pan, add little milk and flaked cooked smoked haddock. Heat together until a thick mixture. If wished a beaten egg can be stirred into the mixture. Garnish with paprika pepper.

311   COD'S ROE

As well as being served as an hors d'oeuvre, cod's roe makes an excellent after-dinner savoury. If uncooked steam the roe until just tender, cut into slices and fry. If purchased already cooked, just slice. Cook gently in hot fat or bacon fat until pale golden brown. Serve with rolls or small strips of bacon on strips of toast.

312   ROES ON TOAST

Either fry the soft roes in hot butter or cook in milk and butter in a pan or on a dish over hot water. Drain well and garnish with paprika pepper.

313   CHEESE CHARLOTTE

few slices thinly cut brown and white bread and butter
3 eggs
2 level teaspoons gelatine
3 tablespoons water
2 oz. cream cheese
2 oz. Cheddar cheese
¼ teaspoon French mustard
pinch salt and cayenne pepper
¼ pint single cream or top milk
almonds to decorate

Grate Cheddar cheese. Line a buttered Charlotte mould or 5-inch cake tin with the bread, using alternate fingers of white and brown. Whisk the egg yolks until thick, and add the gelatine dissolved in the very hot water. Stir in the cream, cheeses and seasonings, then fold in the stiffly whipped whites. Turn the mixture into the Charlotte mould and chill. Turn out and serve garnished with watercress and decorated with almonds.

314   DANISH BLUE CHEESE GRATIN

6 oz. Danish pork luncheon meat
6 oz. Danish Blue cheese
2½ oz. butter
1½ oz. flour
1 large onion
2 tomatoes
¼ small clove of garlic
2 eggs
¼ pint milk

Melt 1½ oz. butter in a saucepan, add the flour and cook over a low heat for 2 minutes. Add the milk gradually, stirring all the time until the sauce thickens. Remove from the heat and stir in the beaten egg yolks.

Slice thinly the onion, tomatoes and garlic and fry in 1 oz. butter. Add this to the sauce, also the chopped pork luncheon meat and the mashed Danish Blue cheese. Whisk the egg whites till stiff and fold into the mixture.

Put the mixture into a greased oven-proof dish. Bake in a very hot oven for 10 minutes, then turn down to moderate for 20 minutes.

315   CHEESE CAKE

Rich Short Crust Pastry

5 oz. plain flour
pinch salt
2¼ oz. butter

2 teaspoons castor sugar
1 egg yolk and a little
   cold water to bind

Filling

8 oz. cream cheese
2 oz. castor sugar
2 oz. raisins

few drops vanilla essence
1 tablespoon milk or cream
2 egg whites and 1 yolk

Prepare the shortcrust pastry, sieve the flour and salt, rub in the butter. Add the sugar and bind with the egg yolk and a little water. Roll out and line a 7-inch flan ring. Re-roll the pastry scraps and cut into a circle 3—4 inches in diameter. Cut across to form six triangular pieces and keep for the decoration. Bake the pastry case 'blind' in a moderately hot oven (400°F. — Gas Mark 5) for 15 minutes. Meanwhile mix the cream cheese, castor sugar, cleaned raisins, egg yolk, vanilla essence and milk or cream, and fold in the stiffly beaten egg whites. Fill the half-cooked flan case with the cream cheese mixture. Place the pastry decoration on top and return to the oven. Bake for 15 minutes until the top is golden brown.

316   CREAMY CHEESE CAKE

with strawberries

1 lb. cottage cheese
2 oz. butter
4 oz. castor sugar
4 eggs
2 tablespoons stiffly
   whipped cream

1 tablespoon cornflour
1½ tablespoons lemon juice
1 teaspoon finely grated
   lemon rind
2 oz. semi-sweet biscuit
   crumbs

Rub the cheese through sieve. Cream the butter with the sugar, then beat in the egg yolks. Add the cream, cornflour, lemon juice and rind and cottage cheese. Mix thoroughly to blend ingredients. Fold in the egg whites, whisked to a stiff snow. Butter a cake tin, preferably a loose bottomed one about 7½ inches by 3 inches deep, and dust it with fine biscuit crumbs. Turn the creamy mixture into this. Bake in the centre of a very moderate oven (325—350°F. — Gas Mark 2—3) for 1¼ hours. Leave to cool in oven. Turn out to serve. This is delicious served plain. It is extra special when topped with cream and served with sugared strawberries or raspberries.

317 SECRETS OF A GOOD SOUFFLÉ

Soufflés are not difficult to make; they simply consist of eggs, either a sauce or purée base, and some form of flavouring. The way the eggs are added to the mixture makes an enormous difference however — the egg yolks and whites are separated, the yolks being beaten in and the stiffly beaten whites folded in afterwards. To separate the yolks and the whites of eggs, either crack the egg shell gently, allow the white to drop in a basin; tilt the halved shells gently, so all the white goes into the basin and then put the yolk in a separate container, *or* break the egg, put it on to a flat plate or saucer, invert an egg cup over the yolk, and pour away the white into a basin.

To whisk the egg whites you need a clean basin, free from any grease, eggs that are not less then 24 hours old and a good egg whisk. If stored in a refrigerator the eggs whisk more quickly if kept in room temperature for an hour. If you have no whisk, whip with a palette knife on a flat plate.

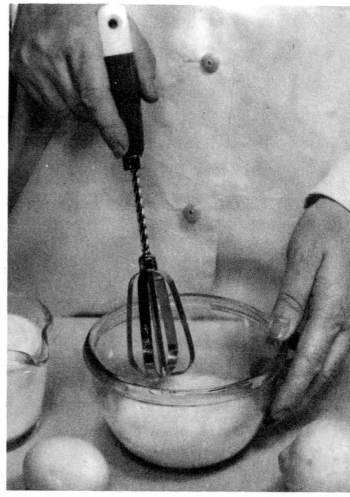

318 CHEESE SOUFFLÉ

Ingredients as Cheese and Spinach soufflè (Recipe 319) except that the spinach is omitted. If you like a very liquid soft soufflè use about 1½ gills milk, instead of the 1 gill (¼ pint).

For a very strong flavour use 2—3 oz. grated Cheddar cheese and 1 oz. grated Parmesan cheese.

319 CHEESE AND SPINACH SOUFFLÉ

1 lb. cooked spinach	pinch salt
3 egg yolks	cayenne pepper
3 oz. grated Cheddar cheese	4 egg whites

For the Sauce

1 oz. butter	¼ pint milk
½ oz. flour	

Prepare a 6-inch soufflé case by tying a greased double band of paper round the outside of the case, to come 3 inches above the rim. Put the cooked and well drained spinach in the base of the soufflé case. Make the thick white sauce (or panada) in the usual way. Reduce the heat and stir in the grated Cheddar cheese. Cool, and add the egg yolks one at a time. Add the seasoning. Whip up the egg whites until stiff — take about a quarter and whisk into the cool cheese sauce to soften it. Fold in the remainder very carefully and lightly, using a metal spoon. Pour into the prepared soufflé case. Bake in the middle of a moderate oven (375°F. — Gas Mark 4) approximately 40 minutes, until well risen, golden brown and just firm. Remove the paper and serve immediately.

320 HAM AND CHEESE SOUFFLÉ

1 pint milk	2 oz. grated cheese
¼ level teaspoon salt	2 oz. chopped ham
2 rounded tablespoons	3 eggs
fine semolina	

Warm the milk and sprinkle in the salt and semolina. Bring to the boil, stirring. Remove from the heat and stir in the cheese and ham. Separate yolks from whites of eggs. Beat in the egg yolks, Fold in the egg whites, beaten to a stiff froth. Turn into a greased soufflé dish, casserole or pie-dish. Do not fill the dish more than two-thirds. Bake in centre of a moderately hot oven (400°F. — Gas Mark 5) until well risen and golden, about 35 minutes. Serve at once with French mustard.

321 CELERY AND CHEESE SOUFFLÉ

1 oz. butter	¼ pint milk
1 oz. flour	3 eggs
4 tablespoons condensed	seasoning
cream of celery soup*	2 oz. cheese

Or simmer about 1 teacup chopped celery in same amount of milk until tender, then rub through sieve. Season well

Melt butter in medium saucepan, add flour and, stirring, cook for 1 minute. Add soup and milk and, still stirring, cook gently for a further 2 minutes. Allow to cool slightly. Beat in egg yolks, seasoning and cheese. Whisk egg whites until thick and fold into mixture. Pour into greased soufflé dish and bake in centre of moderately hot oven (400°F. — Gas Mark 5) for 25 — 30 minutes. Serve at once.

322 SMOKED HADDOCK SOUFFLÉ

1 oz. butter	1 oz. Parmesan cheese
½ oz. flour	(grated)
¾ gill milk	1 or 2 tablespoons cream
4 — 5 oz. smoked haddock	seasoning
4 egg whites	3 egg yolks

The haddock may be used cooked or raw as preferred. If using raw fish, remove skin and pound the fish until smooth. If using cooked smoked haddock flake finely. Make a thick sauce of the butter, flour and milk, add the haddock and seasoning. Do not add too much salt to the mixture, since the smoked haddock gives a salt taste. Add the cheese, the cream, and the egg yolks and mix well. Fold in the stiffly beaten egg whites then pour into prepared soufflé dish and bake in the centre of a moderately hot oven (400°F. — Gas Mark 5) for approximately 25 minutes until golden brown and well risen. Serve at once.

323 PARMESAN AND ASPARAGUS SOUFFLÉ

8 — 12 oz. asparagus*	little milk or cream
1 oz butter	seasoning
½ oz. flour	1 — 2 oz. grated
3 or 4 eggs	Parmesan cheese

The extreme tips could be used for garnishing another dish, and the stems used for the pureé

Simmer the asparagus in boiling salted water until tender, then rub through a sieve giving a smooth purée. Blend the flour with about 2 or 3 tablespoons milk or cream, add this to the purée, together with the butter, and cook until smooth. Add grated cheese, egg yolks and seasoning. Fold in the stiffly beaten egg whites and pour into soufflé dish. Bake for approximately 25 — 30 minutes in the centre of a moderately hot oven (400°F. or Gas Mark 5). Serve at once.

324 CHEESE SOUFFLÉ TARTS

4 oz. short crust pastry	good pinch salt
(Recipe 485)	pinch pepper
2 eggs	¼ teaspoon chopped
2 oz. finely grated	parsley
cheese	watercress
pinch cayenne pepper	

Roll out the pastry very thinly and line 9 or 12 patty tins with this. Beat the egg yolks with the cheese and seasonings, add the parsley and lastly the stiffly beaten egg whites. Put into the pastry cases and bake for approximately 12 — 15 minutes in centre of a hot oven (425°F. — Gas Mark 7). Serve hot or cold garnished with watercress. *Illustrated in colour picture No. 23.*

325 MUSHROOM SOUFFLÉ TARTS

Recipe as above, but use 2 oz. chopped cooked mushrooms and a little chopped onion instead of grated cheese.

More Small Savouries

326 SCOTCH WOODCOCK

4—6 eggs
1½ oz. butter
seasoning
few capers

little milk
8 anchovy fillets
4 slices buttered toast

Heat the butter in a pan, beat the eggs with seasoning and a little milk. Scramble slowly and when set pile on to buttered toast and garnish with the anchovy fillets. A few capers can also be put on top. The toast should be cut into 8 fingers to form an after-dinner savoury. *Illustrated in colour picture No. 23.*

324 KIDNEYS AND SCRAMBLED EGG

2 lambs kidneys
4 eggs
2 oz. butter

seasoning
squeeze lemon juice
4 slices fried bread or
    buttered toast

Cut the kidneys into small pieces, season well. Heat butter and cook kidneys in this for about 7—8 minutes: if necessary add 1 tablespoon water to prevent sticking. Add lemon juice. Beat and season eggs lightly — add to kidney and continue cooking until firm. Serve on toast or fried bread.

328 DEVILLED MUSHROOMS AND EGGS

4 rounds toast
2 oz. mushrooms
3 hard-boiled eggs
2 oz. butter
good pinch curry powder

½ — 1 teaspoon made
    mustard
1 teaspoon Worcester-
    shire sauce
1 teaspoon mustard
    ketchup

Heat butter, fry chopped mushrooms in it, add flavourings. When mushrooms are cooked add quartered hard-boiled eggs. Heat and serve at once.

329 CHEESE AND TOMATO BAKES

8 good sized tomatoes
4—6 oz. diced Cheddar
    cheese
seasoning

toast or crisp bread
little butter

Cut the tops off the tomatoes and scoop out the centre pulp. Mix this with the diced cheese and pack back tightly into the seasoned tomato cases, put a little butter on top and cover with the lid. Bake for about 10 minutes in a moderately hot oven (400°F. — Gas Mark 5) and serve at once, with crisp toast or bread. *Illustrated in colour picture No. 23.*

330 ENGLISH MONKEY

4 slices toast
1 oz. butter
¼ pint milk
2 oz. soft breadcrumbs

4 oz. grated cheese
1 beaten egg
mustard
Worcestershire sauce
1 tomato

Heat butter in a pan, add milk and breadcrumbs. When very hot add the grated cheese and beaten egg. Season well, adding a little made mustard and few drops Worcestershire sauce.

Stir together until thick and creamy. Pour on to toast, garnish with sliced tomato.

331 TOMATOES ON TOAST

Halve or slice the tomatoes and fry steadily in butter or margarine, season and add pinch sugar to taste.

Garnish with chopped parsley, or serve with crisp bacon or poached or fried eggs on top.

332   TOMATO CHEESE TOASTS

¾ oz. butter
¾ oz. flour
¼ pint milk
½ teaspoon prepared
   mustard
dash of cayenne pepper

8 oz. grated Cheddar
   cheese
4 slices buttered toast
4 tomatoes, skinned and
   sliced
2 rashers bacon cut
   across in half

Melt the butter in a small pan. Add the flour and cook
for a minute. Add the milk gradually, bring to the boil and
boil for a minute stirring. Add the seasonings and grated
Cheddar cheese and stir over gentle heat until the cheese
has melted. Prepare the toast and grill the bacon. Arrange
the tomato slices on the toast and put under the grill to
heat through. Pour the hot cheese sauce over and garnish
with crisp pieces of bacon.

333   PEPPERS AU GRATIN

slices of toast
grated cheese

slices of ham (if desired)
slices of red pepper
butter

Toss the sliced red pepper in a little hot butter. Toast
the bread, cut into neat squares and butter lavishly. Cover
with slices of ham and the thick slices of red pepper.
Cover with grated cheese and brown under grill.

334   DEVILLED BEANS

Open a can of beans, put into a saucepan with a sprinkling
of curry powder, a spoonful of chutney and a few drops
of Worcestershire sauce. Heat well and serve on buttered
toast.

335   MUSHROOMS ON TOAST

Fry the mushrooms in hot dripping or fat and serve on
toast.

336   DANISH BLUE CHEESE MOUSSE

1 packet lemon jelly
4 oz. Danish Blue
   cheese
2 heaped tablespoons
   mayonnaise
1 small red pepper

2 stalks celery
2 eating apples
¼ pint evaporated milk
   or cream
1 tablespoon lemon juice
1 tablespoon Worcesteshire
   sauce

Make up the jelly with half a pint of water and leave until
nearly setting. Crumble the cheese and mash down with
a fork, add the mayonnaise, diced pepper, celery and
apple. Whip the evaporated milk with 1 tablespoon lemon
juice and fold into the cheese mixture, then fold in the
jelly and Worcestershire sauce. Mix well and pour into
a mould and leave to set. When firm, turn out and serve.

Cocktail Savouries

A cocktail party is one of the easiest ways of entertaining a comparatively large number of people, without either taking up a lot of time to prepare, or, in these days of smaller houses, without needing as much space as more formal entertaining. When preparing food for cocktail parties remember that people have to hold the food in their fingers and it is much easier to eat if very small portions are served.

Hot Savouries

337 NEW POTATOES FOR THE COCKTAIL PARTY

An easy idea for a cocktail party is to scrub small new potatoes and to boil them in their skins until tender but not flaky. Glaze with butter and arrange in a large bowl garnished with parsley and with plenty of cocktail sticks so that the potatoes can be dunked in a variety of sauces and whips.

Suggested whips and sauces shown in colour picture No. 25 are cream cheese whipped with a little cream to make it smooth, and garnished with chopped olives, Tartare sauce (Recipe 250) and Tangy sauce (Recipe 338).

338 TANGY SAUCE

1 tablespoon corn oil	*1 level tablespoon brown*
1 clove crushed garlic	*sugar*
2 level teaspoons	*1 4-oz. tin tomato juice*
cornflour	*salt*
1 tablespoon lemon juice	

Mix the corn oil, cornflour and sugar together and cook for 1 minute. Add the tomato juice and cook for a further 2 minutes, stirring all the while. Add the rest of the ingredients, season and serve.

339 BACON ROLLS

These make an excellent hot cocktail savoury. Choose thin streaky bacon, remove the rinds and cut the rashers into halves. Wrap round chicken's livers (frozen or fresh) — these should be well seasoned — round small pieces of kidney, round pieces of pineapple, squares of cheese or liver pâté. Stand cocktail sticks in the rolls and either put under a hot grill or better still cover the dish with foil and cook in a moderately hot oven (400°F. — Gas Mark 5) until the bacon and filling are cooked. Keep hot until ready to serve. For more elaborate savouries try small pieces of scallops, oysters or stuffed prunes. *Illustrated in colour picture No. 24.*

340 MUSHROOMS ON FRIED BREAD

This is one of the easiest and most delicious hot cocktail savouries. Choose small button mushrooms, and if cultivated the skins need not be removed. Just wash them very thoroughly.

Fry small rounds of fried bread and drain well. Cook the mushrooms, having removed the stalks. Put on to the fried bread.

These can be prepared earlier in the day and re-heated gently in the oven when desired.

You can give additional flavour if the fried bread is spread with liver pâté — or the cups of the mushrooms filled with soft scrambled egg. This must be done just before serving.

341 SAVOURY EGGS

½ egg per person	*grated cheese*
seasoning	*fingers of toast*
anchovies or anchovy	
paste	

Hard-boil the eggs. Cut through the middle and put the yolks through a sieve. Stir in plenty of seasoning and grated cheese. Fill the whites with this mixture. Dust liberally with grated cheese and brown under the grill. Put on to fingers of toast which should be spread with pounded anchovies or anchovy paste. Serve very hot.

342   CHEESE AIGRETTES

1 oz. butter	pinch salt and cayenne
⅛ pint water	pepper
2 oz. plain flour	1½ oz. grated cheese —
2 eggs	Cheddar and Parmesan
	mixed

Aigrettes are a type of fritter made with a mixture similar to choux pastry. Bring the butter and water to boiling point. Toss in all the flour at once and beat until smooth. Cool, then add the eggs gradually, beating the mixture very well after each addition. Stir in the cheese and seasoning. Drop small teaspoons of the mixture into a pan of hot deep fat (350°F.) and fry to a golden-brown, taking 7—10 minutes. Drain and serve hot, sprinkled with a little grated cheese.

343   Nutty Cheese Aigrettes

Add ½ oz. salted chopped almonds to the mixture together with the grated cheese.

344 SARDINE WELSH RAREBIT FINGERS

2 oz. butter	4 tablespoons milk
12 oz. grated Cheddar	4 large slices toast
cheese	12 sardines
2 level teaspoons made	parsley to garnish
mustard	
pinch cayenne pepper	
and salt	

Cream the butter, add grated cheese, seasoning and milk and mix to a stiff paste. Spread this mixture thickly over the toast and grill to a golden brown. Lay three sardines on each slice and heat through under the grill. Cut into fingers, garnish and serve hot.

345   CHEESEOLETTES

3 eggs	1 tablespoon grated onion
2 oz. flour (with plain	2 tablespoons chopped
flour use ¼ teaspoon	parsley
baking powder)	seasoning
4 oz. grated cheese	fat, oil or shortening for
	frying

Blend all the ingredients together. Heat fat in pan and drop in spoonfuls of this mixture. Fry until crisp and golden brown. Turn, brown on the other side. Drain well and serve with a dish of sliced tomatoes and another of crisp lettuce. These are a cross between pancakes and omelettes.

346   CHEESE WAFERS

Brush ice cream wafers with melted margarine or butter and finely grated cheese. Sandwich 2 together and brush the top with melted margarine. Put into a very hot oven (475—500°F. — Gas Mark 8—9) for 3—4 minutes. Serve at once.

To make a daintier savoury, cut the ice cream wafer into halves before heating.

Hot or Cold Savouries

347 CHEESE PUFFS

4 oz. finely grated	¼ level teaspoon salt
Cheddar cheese	1 egg
pinch cayenne pepper	fat for frying

Mix the cheese, pepper and salt, and stir in the beaten egg yolk. Fold in the stiffly beaten egg white and shape lightly in the hands into small balls. Fry a few at a time in hot, deep fat (350°F. approx. or until a cube of bread turns brown in 1 minute) to a golden brown, taking 3—4 minutes. Drain, and serve as a savoury snack or on cocktail sticks for a party.

348 FRIED CHEESE TRIANGLES

Dip portions of Swiss Petit Gruyère cheese into either a thin batter or beaten egg and fine crumbs. Put into the frying basket and brown in hot deep fat for about 1 minute only. Remove at once and serve.

Variations:

Split the triangles of cheese across the centre and sand-wich the two halves together with a thin slice of cooked ham. Coat again and fry.
Sandwich the triangles of cheese between 2 equal sized pieces of thin bread. Soak in a little beaten egg and fry in shallow fat, turning after browning on the under side.
Cover each triangle of cheese with very thin pastry and bake for approximately 15 minutes in a hot oven (450°F.— Gas Mark 7).

349 SAVOURY FLAPJACKS

6 oz. plain flour	1 egg
2 rounded tablespoons	milk
fine semolina	1 oz. grated cheese
2 rounded teaspoons	2 oz. cooked ham
baking powder	1 oz. fat
shake of pepper	(approximately)
¼ teaspoon salt	

Sieve dry ingredients. Add unbeaten egg and mix well, adding milk to make a thick batter. Stir in grated cheese and chopped ham, mixing well. Beat before using. Melt a very small knob of fat in a thick frying pan, griddle or hot plate, and make smoking hot. Drop on tablespoons of batter from the tip of spoon, making as many circles as the pan will take. Cook over moderate heat until bubbles form and burst, by which time the underside of flapjacks will be golden brown. Flip each flapjack over and cook the other side. As made, slip the flapjacks into a clean teacloth, until all the mixture has been used up. Serve freshly baked. Serve with Onion and Tomato sauce (Recipe 350).

350 Onion and Tomato Sauce

1 or 2 small onions	4 good sized tomatoes
seasoning	

Skin tomatoes and chop finely or rub through a sieve. Season and mix with thinly sliced raw onion. Both to-matoes and onions can be cooked if preferred.

Ideas for Cocktail Parties

351 ## COCKTAIL MEDLEY

Put three or more small tit-bits on to cocktail sticks and put the points into oranges or grapefruit.

Use some of the following: squares of liver sausage, cocktail onions, slices of gherkin, prawns or shrimps, diced cheese, tiny pieces of mustard pickle, salami, diced ham, smoked salmon.

352 ## LOBSTER PYRAMIDS

small rounds of toast
  or biscuits
to about 24 biscuits use
  4 oz. flaked lobster

1 tablespoon mayonnaise
  (Recipe 186)
sieved white of 1 hard-
  boiled egg

gherkins or stuffed olives   seasoning

Mince or flake the lobster very finely, mixing with the mayonnaise and egg white. Season well, then form into little pyramids on the small rounds of toast or biscuits and decorate with a ring of gherkins or olives.

353 ## PRINCESS MUSHROOMS

Choose 12 tiny mushrooms, fry until just tender, drain and cool; cream 2 oz. butter, add sieved hard-boiled egg and 1 oz. grated Parmesan cheese. Put mushrooms on cheese biscuits or fried bread and pipe cheese spread round.

354 ## POPPY SEED FLAKES

6 oz. flour (with plain
  flour use 1¼ level
  teaspoons baking
  powder)
2 oz. fine semolina
¼ level teaspoon salt
good shake cayenne
  pepper

¼ level teaspoon celery
  salt
4 oz. butter or margarine
1 beaten egg to bind
a little milk for brushing
1 level tablespoon poppy
  seeds

Sift dry ingredients into a bowl. Rub in fat till mixture resembles fine breadcrumbs, then mix to a stiff paste with the beaten egg. Turn out on to a lightly floured board, knead quickly, shape into a ball and leave, covered, in a cool place for at least 30 minutes. Roll pastry out into a fairly thin oblong, brush lower half with milk then sprinkle with poppy seeds. Fold top half of pastry over, press lightly with a rolling pin then re-roll till poppy seed 'sandwich' is again fairly thin. Stamp into rounds with a 1½-inch biscuit cutter, transfer to greased baking trays and bake at 400°F. — Gas Mark 5 for 12—15 minutes or till crisp and golden in colour. Cool on a wire tray. Serve with Egg and Anchovy Spread (Recipe 355) and black and green olives.

355 ## EGG AND ANCHOVY SPREAD

2 hard-boiled eggs,
  chopped
1 oz. softened butter
1 tablespoon thick cream

1 teaspoon anchovy
  essence
  (or more or less
  according to taste)
seasoning to taste

Beat eggs to a paste with the butter and cream, then add the anchovy essence and seasoning to taste.

356   PINEAPPLE PARTY

Snacks to serve with drinks

Dunks of blue cheese, black grapes, diced pineapple, gherkins and shrimps are skewered on to one pineapple; the other has been scooped and holds a delicious dip of whipped cream and mayonnaise seasoned with mustard and chives The tiny pastry boats hold finely flaked tuna fish moistened with salad dressing and topped with sliced olives. The cooked and well drained prunes are stuffed with cottage cheese and toasted almonds.

357   STUFFED CELERY

1 head celery or 2 small heads	*little mayonnaise (Recipe 186)*
4 — 6 oz. cream cheese or 6 oz. grated cheese*	*cayenne or paprika pepper*

* Try Danish blue cheese for a change

Mix the cream cheese with the mayonnaise and either pipe or spread this in the centre of each celery stick. Cut into short pieces — about 1—2 inches, and dust tops with cayenne or paprika pepper.

358   BERMUDAS

Stir 1 good tablespoon of chopped canned pimentos into 2 tablespoons condensed oxtail soup, adding 1 tablespoon pickle and a few drops of Tabasco sauce. Spread on buttered fingers of crisp toast or on biscuits and sprinkle first with desiccated coconut and then with a little paprika.

359   TIGERS' EYES

Prepare mixture as for Bermudas and spread over small circles of buttered pastry or crisp biscuits. Top with a slice of cooked egg then with a slice of stuffed olive.

360   CHICKEN CROÛTES

4 oz. finely chopped or minced chicken or ham	*2 tablespoons thick mayonnaise (Recipe 186)*
12 rounds fried bread or crisp biscuits	*butter*
12 stuffed olives	*2 tomatoes*
	seasoning

Mix the chicken with the mayonnaise. Cut the tomatoes into 12 very thin slices. Butter the biscuits or drain the fried bread well. Top with sliced tomatoes and the chicken mixture. Press a stuffed olive on top of this.

Cheese Pastry Savouries

361 QUICK-TO-MAKE CHEESE STRAWS

white bread (several
   days old)
melted butter

finely grated cheese
   (Cheddar and
   Parmesan)
cayenne pepper

Slice the bread about ¼ inch thick and cut straws from the slices making them 3 inches long and about ¼ inch wide. Make rings of bread if liked, to form holders for the straws after they are cooked. The rings are cut from the sliced bread using a cutter of 1½-inch diameter removing the centre with one of 1-inch in diameter. Other fancy shapes may be cut from the sliced bread using small pastry cutters.

Dip the bread shapes in melted butter then toss in finely grated Cheddar cheese to which a little grated Parmesan may be added for additional flavour. Coat thoroughly with cheese.

Place on a baking sheet and put into a moderately hot oven (400°F. — Gas Mark 5) to crisp and brown. They will take about 10 minutes. Serve hot or cold — they are particularly good hot.

362 CHEESE RUSKS, STRAWS AND CROÛTONS

½-inch thick slices of day-
   old white or brown
   bread

melted butter
grated Cheddar cheese

Remove the crust and cut the bread into 'animal' shapes for the rusks; into 3-inch lengths for the straws; or ½-inch dice for the croûtons. Dip the bread shapes in melted butter, then toss in grated Cheddar cheese to coat thoroughly. Place on a baking sheet and put in a moderately hot oven (400°F. — Gas Mark 5) to crisp and brown (about 15—20 minutes). The rusks will appeal to children and may be served on a variety of occasions. The straws are useful as a cocktail or party snack and the croûtons are delicious with many soups.

363 CHEESE PASTRY

2 oz. plain flour
1¼ oz. margarine or butter
1¼ oz. finely grated cheese

seasoning
egg yolk or milk to mix

Rub the margarine or butter into the flour, then add the cheese and plenty of seasoning. Make to a firm dough with egg yolk or milk. Use this pastry for tiny biscuits which you can top with ham, smoked salmon, etc., for boat shapes (you can buy these shaped tins in cocktail size) or for cheese straws.

Always bake the cheese pastry in a really hot oven (450°F. — Gas Mark 7) and cool for a few minutes on baking trays as it is very brittle.

364 SAVOURY BOATS (1)

Cheese pastry (Recipe 363)

Line tiny boat shapes with the cheese pastry bake, cool and fill with the following:
(a) Piped cream cheese topped with small pieces of pineapple
(b) Shrimps in thick sauce or dressing — garnished with capers
(c) Home made or bought pâté — topped with celery curls* (See Recipes 148, 149 for pâté)
(d) Scrambled egg and finely chopped mushrooms

* To make celery curl cut into very thin strips, soak in cold water for several hours

365 RICH CHEESE PASTRY

4 oz. plain flour	*2 oz. grated cheese*
2¼ oz. butter	*1 egg yolk*
salt and cayenne pepper	*little dry mustard*

Sieve the flour and seasoning together, rub in the butter, add the cheese and bind with the egg yolk. If necessary add a very little water as well. Roll out firmly and use for savoury flan or tartlet cases or to make economical cheese biscuits or straws. If baking by itself, use a hot oven for this pastry (450°F. — Gas Mark 7). Handle carefully when hot since it is very light. New Zealand Cheddar cheese is excellent in this recipe as it grates so well.

366 SAVOURY BOATS (2)

Make cheese pastry (Recipe 365). Roll out, fill and bake tiny boat shapes with the pastry. Pipe with ham butter (Recipe 367) and decorate with strips of tomato or red pepper; coat with aspic jelly.

367 HAM BUTTER (2)

2 oz. lean ham or bacon	*2 oz. butter or margarine*

Chop, mince and sieve the ham. Work in butter and mix to a smooth paste.

368 HAM SAVOURIES

Cut out rounds of cheese pastry (Recipe 365). Bake as directed until crisp or golden brown. Lay on rounds of ham or cooked bacon, pipe with sieved cream cheese and decorate with tomato coated with aspic.

369 HAM BUTTERFLIES

Cut cheese pastry (Recipe 365) into tiny rounds and cut half of the rounds to make wings. Pipe with ham butter (Recipe 367). Decorate wings of pastry with red pepper and coat with aspic jelly.

370 RADISH CROWNS

Cut out rounds of cheese pastry (Recipe 365). Bake as directed. Pipe with ham butter (Recipe 367) decorate with slices of radish and coat with aspic jelly.

371 BACON BOUCHÉES AND FINGERS

Fill cooked bouchées (tiny Vol-au-vent cases) of cheese pastry (Recipe 365) or puff pastry (Recipe 483) with chopped lean bacon mixed with aspic. Pipe with sieved cream cheese, decorate with fancy shapes, cut out of cucumber skin, and coat with aspic jelly.

Little Bacon Savouries

372 KEBABS

Arrange on cocktail sticks cooked bacon rolls or cubes of ham, pineapple chunks, cubes of cheese, slices of cooked sausage, gherkins and button onions. Serve cold, or brush with melted butter and grill gently for 4—5 minutes.

373 BACON TITBITS

Remove rind from streaky rashers, cut each rasher in half, and spread with mustard or chutney. Roll a piece of bacon round any of the following: a cube of cheese or pineapple; a cocktail sausage or a prawn; sweet gherkins or stuffed olives; a piece of banana or a date. Place on a cocktail stick, grill or bake until the bacon is cooked. Serve hot or cold.

374 HAM BITES

Spread thin slices of ham or lean bacon with cream cheese or peanut butter, seasoned with grated onion or horse-radish sauce. Roll up tightly, leave in the refrigerator or a cold place for several hours. Cut into bite-sized pieces.

25   NEW POTATOES FOR A COCKTAIL PARTY
(Recipe 337)

Savouries, Canapés and Sandwiches for every occasion

As well as cocktail savouries sandwiches are ideal party food. Tiny unusually shaped sandwiches will be very popular and these should, like all sandwiches, be kept covered with foil or damp cloths until the last minute, so that the bread does not dry. Try open sandwiches for a change — they look gay and attractive and can either be small enough for a cocktail party or large and sufficiently substantial for a main meal.

Sandwiches and Cheese Savouries

375 SWISS CHEESE FANS

In the colour picture opposite you can see how effective Swiss Petit Gruyère cheeses look as open sandwiches. Either use whole or split through the centre for a thinner sandwich. Put the cheese on thin triangles of bread and butter or savoury mixture.

1. Spread bread with butter mixed with anchovy essence
   Top the cheese with anchovy fillets
2. Spread the bread with butter flavoured with garlic salt or crushed garlic
   Top the cheese with black olives
3. Spread the bread with mayonnaise
   Top the cheese with gherkin 'fans'
4. Spread the bread with peanut butter
   Top the cheese with sliced salami
5. Spread the bread with horseradish cream
   Top the cheese with shrimps or prawns
6. Spread the bread with ham paste or chutney
   Top the cheese with crisp bacon rolls

376 CANAPÉS

These are tiny pieces of toast, small biscuits, bread and butter cut into small shapes, or fried bread.

In colour picture No. 1. you see (starting from the top of the picture):

Small round biscuits (or rounds of fried bread), topped with butter, sliced hard-boiled egg, anchovy fillets and sliced stuffed olives

Heart-shaped pieces of fried bread topped with salami and sliced stuffed olives

Diced Camembert cheese, topped with diced Cheddar cheese and olives

Baby sausage rolls

Slices of salami rolled round gherkins

More sausage rolls

Heart-shaped pieces of fried bread topped with same shaped pieces of cheese, cucumber rings and radish rings

Rounds of fried bread or buttered biscuits, topped with a little mayonnaise and prawns

Assorted shaped pieces of toast or fried bread topped with cream cheese, olives and walnuts

Assorted shaped pieces of brown bread and butter or fried bread topped with smoked salmon

377 LAYER SANDWICHES

In the colour picture opposite, layer sandwiches are made by putting several slices of bread and butter and two fillings together. Here are a few suggestions:

Mash two portions of Swiss Gruyère cheese with a little butter, 1 teaspoon French mustard and 2 chopped anchovies. Spread on alternate slices of white and brown (or black rye) bread.

Mix Swiss Gruyère cheese with chopped mint, chives and butter. Spread between brown and white bread.

Spread Swiss Gruyère cheese on buttered white bread, sprinkle with caraway seeds, spread with mayonnaise and thinly sliced tomato. Cover with buttered brown bread.

378 HOLLOW SANDWICHES

Take the tops off rolls, pull out the crumb, and rub this until very fine. Mix with flaked tuna or other fish and diced Swiss Petit Gruyère cheese. Use either oil from the tuna or mayonnaise to bind, and mix in chopped watercress or parsley.

379   CHEESE TWISTS

cheese pastry   *vegetable extract*
(Recipes 363 or 365)

Knead the pastry scraps lightly and re-roll to a thin oblong strip. Cut across in half, spread one half with vegetable extract and place on the plain half. Roll lightly together; cut into ¼-inch strips. Twist the strips and bake in a moderate oven (400°F. — Gas Mark 5) for approximately 10 minutes.

380   CHEESE BUTTERFLIES

cheese pastry   *a little seasoned whipped*
(Recipes 363 or 365)   *cream and finely chopped*
vegetable extract   *celery*

Roll out cheese pastry about ¼-inch thick, prick and cut out an equal number of 1½-inch and 1-inch rounds. Brush the 1-inch rounds with beaten egg and cut in half for the 'wings'. Bake in a moderately hot oven (400°F. — Gas Mark 5) for 10—15 minutes. Cool. Put some celery cream on the pastry rounds, fix 'wings' and garnish.

381   CHEESE BROCHETTES

6 medium-thick slices   *fat for frying*
of bread   *1 lb. cooked spinach*
1 lb. Cheddar cheese   *½ pint cheese sauce*
¼ pint milk   *(Recipe 243)*
2 oz. seasoned flour

Egg dip

2 egg yolks   *pinch cayenne pepper*
¼ teaspoon salt   *1 tablespoon water*

For each brochette take six 1-inch squares of bread and five 1-inch squares of Cheddar cheese, approximately ¼ inch thick, and spear alternately on to a small skewer so that they just touch. Soak the brochettes in milk, roll in seasoned flour and then in the egg dip. Fry in deep fat at 350°F., i.e. when a cube of bread turns golden brown in 1 minute, to a golden brown. Drain and serve hot on a bed of spinach with cheese sauce.

382   ASPIC FINGERS

3 slices bread   *smoked salmon*
¼ pint aspic jelly   *sardines*
anchovies   *hard-boiled egg*
tiny pieces of salami or   *tomato*
liver sausage

Lightly toast the bread, then brush one side with half set aspic jelly. Arrange the fingers of food — cutting the egg into thin slices, also slicing tomato. Make as definite a pattern as possible. Spread the rest of the half-set jelly over the top, spreading it evenly with a warm palette knife. Cut into fingers with a very sharp knife when the jelly has become *quite* firm.

383   GOLDEN PUFF STICKS

4 oz. plain flour   *4 oz. cottage cheese*
¼ teaspoon salt   *1 egg yolk*
4 oz butter or luxury   *1 tablespoon milk*
margarine   *2 oz. finely chopped*
     walnuts

Sift flour and salt and cut in the butter or margarine with a knife until it is well blended. Stir in cottage cheese. Wrap in waxed paper and chill well. Turn on to a lightly floured board and roll to about ¼-inch thickness. Brush with the egg yolk beaten with milk and sprinkle with chopped walnuts. Cut into strips about 5 inches by ½ inch and place on greased baking sheet. Bake near top of very hot oven (450—475°F. — Gas Mark 8) for about 7 minutes or until golden and puffed. Remove from tray carefully and at once. Serve with party drinks.

384 CRISP SAVOURY SQUARES

12 oz. short crust pastry
(Recipe 485)
6 oz. boiled bacon or ham
2 tablespoons shredded
pineapple

1 or 2 hard-boiled eggs
1 level tablespoon mild
mustard
1 egg or milk for glazing

Chop ham and mix with pineapple, eggs, and mustard. Roll the pastry to a thin sheet and cut into about 40 2-inch squares. Put a good teaspoon filling on half the squares and moisten edges. Cover with remaining squares. Seal edges and place on baking sheets. Brush with beaten egg or milk and decorate tops with stars cut from the pastry trimmings. Bake near top of hot oven (425—450°F. — Gas Mark 6—7) for 15 minutes or until golden brown. Re-heat just before serving.

385 ECONOMICAL CHEESE BISCUITS

3¼ oz. whipped-up
cooking fat
3 tablespoons cold water
3 oz. finely grated cheese
egg and milk to glaze

8 oz. flour
1 level teaspoon
salt
1 level teaspoon
mustard
pinch of pepper

} *sieved together*

Place the whipped-up cooking fat, water and 2 rounded tablespoons of the sieved flour and seasonings and the cheese in a basin. Whisk together with a fork, about half a minute, until well mixed. Add the remaining flour, and stirring, form into a firm dough. Roll out, fairly thinly, on a lightly-floured board. Prick all over with a fork. Cut into plain and fluted biscuits using 2-inch cutters. Glaze with beaten egg and milk. Bake near the top of a moderately hot oven (400°F. — Gas Mark 5) for 10—15 minutes.

Decorations

2—3 tomatoes sliced
2—3 hard-boiled eggs
sliced
4 oz. cream cheese

2 oz. ham sliced
stuffed olives
gherkins
parsley

Spread all biscuits with margarine or butter and finish as follows:

1. Decorate with sliced tomato, and top with a piped star of creamed cheese.
2. Decorate with sliced hard-boiled egg and top with stuffed olives, cut in halves.
3. Top with rounds of ham, cut to same size as biscuits, and decorate with a piece of gherkin.
4. Cream Butterflies: place a teaspoon of cream cheese in centre of half the biscuits. Cut remaining biscuits in two and place the halves at an angle, sticking into centre of cream cheese. Decorate with parsley.

386   SAUSAGE ROLLS

8 oz. sausage meat   egg and milk to glaze

Pastry

3¼ oz. whipped up   8 oz. flour   sieved
    cooking fat*   ¼ level   together
3 tablespoons cold water   teaspoon salt

* For specially rich pastry use 4 oz. whipped up cooking fat and only 2 tablespoons water

Place the whipped up cooking fat in one piece, water and 2 rounded tablespoons of the sieved flour and salt into a basin. Whisk together with a fork for about half a minute until well mixed and fluffy. Add remaining flour, and stirring, form into a firm dough. Very lightly knead with the fingertips on a lightly-floured board, moulding to a smooth ball. A little kneading does *not* harm the dough.

Roll out the dough, on a lightly-floured board, into an oblong 12 inches × 6 inches. Trim edges. Divide into two 3-inch wide strips. Roll three-quarters of the sausage meat into two 12-inch sausages. Damp edges of pastry strips. Place the sausages in the centre of each strip; fold over and press the long edges together. Flake edges and mark tops diagonally with a knife at ¼-inch intervals. Cut each diagonally into six sausage rolls. Repeat with the pastry trimmings and remaining sausage meat. Place well apart on baking tray. Brush with beaten egg and milk. Bake near the top of a moderately hot oven (400°F. — Gas Mark 5) for 20—25 minutes.

387   TWOS AND FOURS

Use a hot knife to cut slices from a large block of Cheddar cheese. Trim slices to approximate size and shape of a playing card. Prepare thinly sliced bread to match cheese slices. Butter bread and spread some with yeast extract and rest with tomato ketchup. Using miniature playing card cutters, remove pieces from cheese slices to represent the 2 and 4 of each suit. Lay cheese slices on prepared 'black' and 'red' bases.

388   CHEESE FLAN
Cheese Pastry

pinch salt and cayenne   4 oz. grated Cheddar
    pepper   cheese
4 oz. butter   approx. 2 tablespoons cold
8 oz. plain flour   water to bind

Filling

4 oz. cut-up bacon   3 eggs
    lightly fried   pinch cayenne pepper and
6 oz. thinly sliced   salt
    Cheddar cheese   ¼ pint single cream or
2 raw tomatoes to   milk and cream
    garnish

Make pastry, roll out ¼ inch thick and line a heart-shaped sandwich tin, about 8 inches long and 1 inch deep. Bake 'blind' for 20 minutes in a moderately hot oven (400°F. — Gas Mark 5). Remove from tin when cool. Arrange fried bacon in pastry case and cover with sliced cheese. Beat eggs and seasonings, stir in cream and pour over bacon and cheese. Bake in a moderately hot oven (400°F. — Gas Mark 5) for 15 minutes, then reduce heat slightly for a further 15 minutes until golden brown. Decorate with tiny hearts cut out in tomato, and serve hot or cold.

389   COTTAGE CHEESE AND OLIVE BALL

1 lb. cottage cheese   1 tablespoon chives or
12 stuffed olives (or   parsley
    stoned green or black   1 oz. walnuts
    olives)   1 oz. fresh butter or 1 or
4 oz. blue cheese (or   2 tablespoons whipped
    less)   cream

Chop chives or parsley and the walnuts. Blend cheese and butter — crumbling blue cheese first. Mix in chopped olives and chives or parsley. Chill slightly for easier shaping. Form round shape or pile in centre of serving dish. Chill thoroughly. Just before serving sprinkle ball with chopped walnuts. Serve on platter with a variety of small savoury biscuits. Sufficient for 6 — 8 servings.

390   STILTON CHEESE AND CELERY FILLING

4 oz. Stilton cheese   1 tablespoon chopped
2 tablespoons cream or   celery
    top of milk   salt to taste

Mash the Stilton cheese with a fork, beat in the cream or milk and add the chopped celery and salt to taste. In the picture small sandwiches are 'threaded' on cocktail sticks and garnished with olives.

391   CELERY CHEESE BOATS

Stuff celery stalks with Stilton filling (Recipe 390). Cut into 1-inch lengths and garnish with toasted almonds.

392   TRUMP CRACKERS

white bread (several days   finely grated Cheddar
  old)   cheese
melted butter   cayenne pepper

Using playing card cutters, cut thinly sliced bread into shapes, dip them in melted butter and toss in finely grated cheese to coat thoroughly. Place on a baking sheet in a hot oven (425°F. — Gas Mark 6) for about 10 minutes, until a rich golden brown. Serve hot or cold.

393 FOUR-SUIT CHEESE SANDWICHES

Basic Cheese Spread

12 oz. grated Cheddar   good pinch cayenne pepper
  cheese   approx. 6 tablespoons
3 oz. butter   milk

Add the grated cheese to the creamed butter, beat in the seasoning and sufficient milk to make a creamy consistency. A variety of different spreads can be made by additional flavourings, and any of the following are suitable:
  chopped chives
  finely chopped ham or walnuts with Worcester sauce
  chopped pickle

To make the sandwiches

From thin slices of white and brown bread cut equal numbers of diamonds, hearts, clubs and spades using playing card cutters. Butter the bread shapes and cover with any of the above suggested cheese spreads. Pile together in fours using a matching white and brown shape alternately.

394   SHOOSKA PIROSHKI

8 oz. puff or flaky pastry (Recipes 483 or 484).

Filling

4 oz. grated Cheddar   pinch of sugar and salt
  cheese   few drops vanilla essence
1 oz. white breadcrumbs   little beaten egg to bind
¼ oz. melted butter   little beaten egg to glaze

Prepare pastry and lay aside in a cool place. To make the filling, mix together cheese, crumbs, butter and flavourings and enough beaten egg to bind. Roll mixture into small balls. Roll out pastry about ¼ inch thick. Using playing card cutters stamp out the different shapes allowing two matching shapes for each piroshki. Dip cutter in flour each time before using it to make a clean cut. Place a cheese ball in the centres of half the pastry shapes and flatten a little. Brush remaining pastry shapes with beaten egg and lay on top of matching bases, egg-side down. Press edges together, brush tops with beaten egg and bake just above centre of a hot oven (450°F. — Gas Mark 7) for 20—25 minutes until well risen and golden brown. Serve hot or cold.

395   20 SANDWICH FILLINGS

With Egg

1. Chopped hard-boiled eggs, mixed with chopped diced crisp bacon and a little salad dressing or mayonnaise (Recipe 186)
2. Chopped hard-boiled eggs, mixed with sweet chutney, and chopped watercress
3. Scrambled eggs, mixed with chopped chives and a little sliced tomato
4. Soft-boiled eggs, chopped finely, mixed with butter and seasoning (ideal for keeping moist or for young children)

With Cheese

5. Cream cheese mixed with little well drained and finely chopped pineapple
6. Cream cheese mixed with chopped dates and chopped walnuts, spread on crisp lettuce
7. Slices of Gruyère or Cheddar cheese spread lightly with made mustard and sprigs of watercress
8. Grated cheese mixed with grated raw carrot and moistened with little mayonnaise (Recipe 186)

With Fish

9. Chopped cooked cod's roe mixed with a little mayonnaise (Recipe 186) celery salt and chopped watercress
10. Mashed sardines mixed with finely diced or sliced cucumber and a little lemon juice
11. Mashed tuna fish mixed with chopped skinned tomatoes and chopped watercress, moistened with a little mayonnaise (Recipe 186) and well seasoned

12. Salmon on crisp lettuce, spread lightly with horse-radish cream and sprinkled with grated cheese
13. Lightly cooked kippers, the flesh flaked from the bones, well seasoned with a little lemon juice or vinegar added and mixed with little butter and chopped watercress

With meat

14. Flaked corned beef, mixed with a little made mustard, mayonnaise (Recipe 186), and chopped spring onion
15. Flaked corned beef, mixed with sweet chutney or chopped pickle, and a little grated cheese

16. Finely chopped tongue mixed with a little mayonnaise pinch curry powder and chopped hard-boiled egg
17. Chopped cooked ham or boiled bacon, mixed with skinned chopped tomatoes and shredded lettuce
18. Thin slices of cooked beef spread with horseradish cream and finely chopped beetroot
19. Chopped cooked pork and chopped watercress, bound with soft cream cheese
20. Crisp lettuce covered with thin slices of cooked pork and spread lightly with redcurrant jelly and or chopped stoned prunes.

More Savouries and Sandwiches

396   CHEESE-STUFFED ROLLS

Allow 1½ oz. Cheddar cheese, cut into tiny squares and 1 tablespoon chutney or pickle per large soft roll

Remove a 'cap' from the top of each roll and hollow out the centre (this may be cut up and added to the filling if liked). Butter inside roll. Stuff the rolls and replace the 'cap'. For ease of eating at a picnic, half-cut the stuffed roll before placing on the 'cap'.

397   Devilled Mustard Butter

This is excellent with fish sandwiches, hot or cold. Blend 4 oz. butter or margarine with 1 dessertspoon made mustard, ½ teaspoon curry powder, 1 tablespoon lemon juice and ¼ teaspoon finely grated lemon rind.

398   SUNSHINE CUTLETS

1 oz. butter or margarine	6 hard-boiled eggs
1 oz. flour	salt and pepper
¼ pint milk	1 egg for coating
1 tablespoon made mustard	breadcrumbs for coating
1 tablespoon tomato ketchup	deep fat for frying

Chop the hard-boiled eggs finely. Make a thick white sauce, with butter or margarine, flour and milk. Add the mustard, tomato ketchup, chopped eggs and pepper and salt to taste. Leave the mixture to cool, then form into 6 cutlets. Coat each with beaten egg and breadcrumbs and fry in deep fat till golden. Drain on crumpled kitchen paper or kitchen roll. Serve hot or cold.

399   SWEET CORN AND MUSTARD DIP

Blend 1 dessertspoon made mustard with a few drops of lemon juice and 1 teaspoon tomato purée. Add 1 table-spoon dry white wine and a small can creamed sweet corn, or cooked corn and a little white sauce.
Garnish with shrimps, prawns and small fish croquettes (Recipe 468) on cocktail sticks. Serve also small plain savoury biscuits.

REMEMBER FOR AN EARLY START YOU CAN CUT SANDWICHES THE NIGHT BEFORE. WRAP IN ALUMINIUM FOIL AND STORE IN THE REFRIGERATOR

400   INTERESTING SANDWICH SHAPES

Sandwiches look more interesting if cut into fancy shapes.

For children sandwiches cut into animal shapes (as shown in the picture) will be very appealing. The sandwiches in the second picture are cut into heart shapes, and some of the top layer is removed to show the filling.

Toasted Sandwiches

Toasted sandwiches are a very pleasant way of serving a hot dish with the minimum of trouble. Make the sandwiches in the usual way then toast first on one side then on the other side. The following are just suggestions; any other sandwiches can be toasted.

401   TOASTED BACON SANDWICHES

Since bacon takes longer than the bread to cook, it should be grilled lightly first. Butter one side of the bread if wished — this is not really necessary as the bacon fat keeps it moist. Sandwich the bacon between the bread, and toast on both sides of the sandwich. Bacon and cheese sandwiches are a good mixture. Put the bacon and sliced cheese between the bread and butter. Add chutney if wished. *Illustrated in colour frontispiece.*

402   TWO-DECKER CLUB SANDWICHES

Flake fish from a 7-oz. can of middle-cut tuna or salmon and heat with 2 tablespoons of finely chopped celery or 1 tablespoon capers, and 1 tablespoon salad cream. A little chopped onion and parsley can be added to taste. Lightly toast 9 slices of bread, trim and butter. Place thinly sliced tomato on 3 of the slices, cover with a thin layer of cheese then grill until the cheese begins to melt. Top each with another piece of toast. Spread with tuna mixture and then cover with remaining slices of toast, buttered side down. Cut the sandwiches across diagonally and spike each with an olive on a cocktail stick. Serve at once with a salad garnish.

403   HOT WESTERN SANDWICHES

Beat 2 eggs; stir in flaked fish from a 7-oz. can of tuna in tomato, 1 tablespoon finely chopped onion, 1 tablespoon chopped parsley and 1 tablespoon mild mustard. Fry in spoonfuls on a hot greased pan or griddle, turning to brown. Serve between buttered toast or soft rolls.

404   GRILLED OPEN SANDWICHES WITH MUSHROOM SAUCE

Toast 2 slices of bread or halved Bap rolls. Butter and spread lightly with made mustard. Cover with tuna fillets from a 4½-oz. can, then top with bacon rashers, cut to fit and with rind removed. Heat under griller until the bacon is cooked and beginning to brown. Serve topped with a piping hot sauce of thickened mushroom soup or mushroom sauce (Recipe 254).

405 FRIED CHEESE SANDWICHES

8 large thin slices
  wholemeal bread
8 oz. thinly sliced
  Cheddar cheese

2 oz. butter
2 tomatoes
4 teaspoons chutney

Cover the sliced bread with the thinly sliced cheese, and spread over a little chutney. Put two cheese-covered slices together and press firmly. Cut into neat shapes and fry to a crisp golden brown on both sides in butter. Serve hot, garnished with tomato.

406 DOUBLE DECKER SANDWICH

2 slices of bread —
little made mustard

little tomato chutney
2 cheese slices

Toast bread on both sides. Spread a little mustard on one piece of toast, place slice of cheese on top, and return to grill for a few minutes. Meanwhile spread second piece of toast with tomato chutney, cut second slice of cheese diagonally into four and arrange decoratively on top of chutney. Lay second tier on first, and grill for another minute. Garnish and serve hot (1 serving only).

407   30 DANISH SANDWICHES

Fish

1. Lettuce topped with rollmop or Bismarck herring garnished with red cabbage and rings of onion
2. Lettuce topped with scrambled egg and anchovy fillets, garnished with gherkin
3. Hot fried fillet of plaice topped with thick tartare sauce or mayonnaise (Recipes 250 or 186) garnished with lemon or Russian salad
4. Crisp lettuce — tuna fish topped with mayonnaise and garnished with thin rings of tomato and a gherkin
5. Crisp lettuce topped with lots of fresh or defrosted frozen prawns or shrimps and garnished with thick mayonnaise (Recipe 186) and lettuce leaf; served with a thick wedge of lemon
6. Watercress topped with slices of cod's roe, garnished with sliced onion and gherkin
7. Crisp lettuce covered with slices of smoked eel, garnished with either scrambled egg or a spoonful of well seasoned egg custard.

Meat

8. Thin slices of cooked pork, topped with either apple jelly or thick apple sauce and onion ring
9. Thin slices of roast lamb topped with cucumber or gherkin and redcurrant jelly
10. Crisp lettuce, covered with a thick layer of cooked ham, topped with either fried egg or scrambled egg
11. Crisp lettuce covered with cooked roast beef (or salted beef) garnished with potato salad and beetroot
12. Crisp lettuce, covered with sliced cooked tongue and asparagus tips. Garnish with thick mayonnaise
13. LIGHTLY buttered bread covered with crisp rashers of fried bacon and topped with apple rings and onion rings
14. Crisp watercress covered with slices of cooked veal garnished with potato salad and chopped chives

15. Raw minced steak on bread and butter. Make a hollow in the centre and serve with egg yolk and plenty of seasoning
16. Slices of hot fried liver, rings of onion and a roll of crisp bacon
17. Liver pâté, topped with thinly sliced raw mushroom and gherkin or cucumber
18. Crisp lettuce, topped with a meat ball (or rissole) and cucumber or gherkin
19. Watercress, topped with sliced cooked duck, garnished with red cabbage and apple or orange slices
20. Crisp lettuce, topped with sliced cold chicken, plenty of Russian salad and thick mayonnaise (Recipe 186)

Cheese etc.

21. Crisp lettuce topped with Danish blue cheese, garnished with potato salad and chives, gherkin, or chopped cucumber
22. Watercress and slices of Danish blue cheese topped with crisp celery and tomato slices
23. Slices of cheese, topped with scrambled egg, chopped onion or chives and sliced tomato
24. Slices of cheese covered with sliced hard-boiled egg and garnished with pickled red cabbage or radishes
25. Hard-boiled egg, garnished with thick mayonnaise (Recipe 186) and a roll of smoked salmon or a sardine
26. Sliced hard-boiled egg, covered with a curried potato salad (add a little curry powder to the mayonnaise when making the salad)
27. Fried egg, with fried tomato and onion rings
28. Crisp lettuce, covered with thinly sliced tomatoes and topped with scrambled egg garnished with chives
29. Thinly buttered bread topped with fried mushrooms
30. Scrambled egg topped with flakes of fresh cooked salmon and rings of cucumber

Toasted Sandwiches and Danish Sandwiches

28 **DANISH SANDWICHES**
(Recipe 407)

29 **STUFFED GAMMON STEAK**
(Recipe 458)

30   **MACARONI CHEESE** (Recipe 436)

31   **BACONBURGERS** (Recipe 587)

32 CANTERBURY OPEN SANDWICHES

WATER LILY LAMB SALADS

LAMB AND TOMATO BASKETS

All recipes on facing page

Salads and Quick Savouries

In this section you will find savoury dishes that can be prepared within a very short time. There are also new salad dishes and old favourites.

408 CANTERBURY OPEN SANDWICHES

1 lb. lean cooked New Zealand lamb	4 oz. butter
4—6 rather thick slices wholemeal bread	salt
	pepper
1 teaspoon chopped chives or onion	radishes
	tomatoes
	cucumber
	gherkins
	lettuce

Put the New Zealand lamb through a mincer, using the fine cutter. Cream the butter and chives, mix with the lamb and season well. Spread this mixture on to the slices of bread — which can be cut into rounds as in the coloured picture opposite. Garnish with half slices of cucumber and slices of radish. Top with 'fans' of gherkin and serve with lettuce and tomato.

409 WATER LILY LAMB SALADS

3 or 4 globe artichokes	mayonnaise (Recipe 186)
8 oz. cooked New Zealand lamb	French capers
pepper	lettuce
salt	radishes

Soak the artichokes if possible for about 2 hours before cooking in salted water. Cook in boiling salted water for approximately 25 minutes until sufficiently tender to pull out the leaves easily. Drain artichokes and allow to cool. Trim the bottoms of the stems, so they stand easily, and remove the centre leaves, leaving a row of two leaves round the outside. Remove the hairy 'choke', so that the bottoms only are left. Fill the centre of the artichoke 'baskets' with finely diced lamb moistened with mayonnaise. Garnish with the capers. Serve the leaves that have been pulled from the artichokes as a border round the dish and put the artichokes on a bed of lettuce. Top with rings of radish. *Illustrated in colour picture opposite.*

Serve extra mayonnaise or French dressing (Recipes 186, 190) to accompany the additional artichoke leaves.

410 LAMB AND TOMATO BASKETS

6 large tomatoes	sprigs of mint
1 lb. lean cooked New Zealand lamb	mayonnaise (Recipe 186)
	juice of ½ lemon
1 teaspoon finely chopped mint	cucumber
	salt
4 oz. skinned grapes	pepper
3 tablespoons sweet corn kernels (canned or cooked)	

Cut the tops off the tomatoes, scoop out all the pulp, and drain the hollowed cups. Season well with salt and pepper. Put the lamb through a medium cutter on a mincer, or chop finely, then mix with the sweet corn, mint and de-seeded grapes. Bind with the lemon juice and mayonnaise. Fill the tomatoes with this mixture, and garnish with either sprigs of mint or grapes. Serve with thin slices of cucumber.

411 APPLE WALDORF SALAD MOULDS

1 packet lemon jelly	12 oz. diced unpeeled red apples
¼ pint hot water	
¼ pint cold water or apple juice	¼ cup thinly sliced celery
	¼ cup chopped nuts
2 tablespoons lemon juice	¼ teaspoon salt

Garnish

Apple slices dipped in lemon juice to preserve colour

Dissolve jelly in hot water. Add cold water or apple juice, lemon juice and salt. Chill until slightly thickened. Fold in remaining ingredients. Turn into individual moulds. Chill. Unmould and garnish with slices of eating apple. Serve with cheese or cold ham. *Illustrated in colour picture No. 17.*

412 APPLE AND HAM LUNCHEON SALAD

6—8 eating apples	4 tablespoons light cream or top of milk
juice of 1 lemon	
1 lb. cooked ham	2 oz. crumbled blue cheese
2 oz. green pepper or celery	¼ pint mayonnaise (Recipe 186)

Garnish

apple slices	lettuce
fresh parsley	

Cut balls from peeled apples, using melon-ball cutter or a sharp teaspoon, or cut into neat dice. Soak apple balls in lemon juice to preserve colour. Drain and combine with diced ham and sliced celery or pepper. Blend mayonnaise and cream; add to apple mixture and toss. Sprinkle with blue cheese and garnish salad with parsley and a star of red-skinned apple wedges, dipped in lemon juice to keep colour bright. Serve in lettuce-lined salad bowl. *Illustrated in colour picture No. 18.*

413   CHEESE WINDMILL SALAD

4 cheese slices	parsley or watercress
1 lettuce	cocktail sticks
2 tomatoes or 4 radish roses	salad cream

Slash diagonally towards the centre from the four corners of each cheese slice, leaving about 1 inch uncut in the centre. Gather alternate points together in the centre and secure with a cocktail stick to form a windmill.

Arrange on a bed of salad and garnish attractively. Serve with salad cream.

414   SUMMER SALAD

8 oz. cottage cheese	1 slice pineapple, fresh or tinned
4 gherkins, halved	2 teaspoons grated carrot

Place cottage cheese in a mound on a plate. Top with pineapple and grated carrot and surround with gherkin halves.

415 ROQUEFORT FRENCH DRESSING

Add 1 oz. Roquefort or blue cheese, crumbled into Spicy French Dressing (Recipe 416).

416   SPICY FRENCH DRESSING

1 level tablespoon sugar	½ teaspoon salt
1 level teaspoon dry mustard	12 tablespoons corn oil
¼ teaspoon paprika	4 tablespoons wine vinegar
	1 clove garlic

Combine all ingredients in a screw top jar and shake well until blended. Add 1 clove garlic. Store, covered, in refrigerator. When ready to use, shake and remove garlic. For another French dressing, see Recipe 190.

417   SALAD CREAM

2 oz. butter or 2 tablespoons olive oil or corn oil	2 eggs
1 level tablespoon cornflour	¼ teacup vinegar
½ pint milk	1 teaspoon sugar
	good pinch pepper, salt and dry mustard

Blend cornflour with milk, put into a saucepan with butter or oil and plenty of seasoning and sugar. Bring to the boil and cook until thickened. Let it cool slightly, add beaten eggs and cook WITHOUT BOILING for several minutes. Cool again slightly, then whisk in the vinegar. If wished the cornflour mixture can be transferred to a double saucepan or basin over hot water so the eggs can be cooked with the sauce without fear of curdling. For classic mayonnaise, see Recipes 186—9.

418 PINEAPPLE AND CHEESE SALAD MOULDS

thin slices of gherkin and radish }optional
¼ pint aspic jelly
1 small can crushed pineapple
pinch salt
½ oz. powdered gelatine (level tablespoon)
2 tablespoons cold water
2 tablespoons lemon juice
4 oz. grated Cheddar cheese
¼ pint double cream
lettuce, cucumber and tomatoes
salad cream

If liked decorate top of each mould with thin slices of gherkin and radish set in aspic jelly. Heat pineapple and add salt. Soak gelatine in the cold water, add to hot pineapple mixture and stir until well mixed and dissolved. Cool until mixture begins to thicken then add lemon juice and grated cheese, finally fold in whipped cream and turn into prepared moulds. Leave to set in a cool place. Turn out on to a bed of lettuce and serve with tomato slices, cucumber wedges and salad cream.

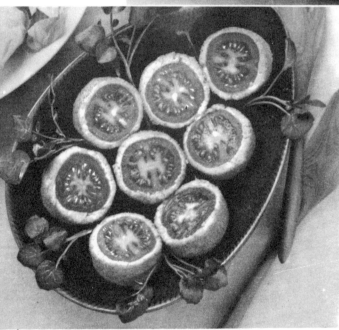

419 TOMATO SURPRISES

6 oz. Cheddar cheese
½ teaspoon Worcestershire sauce
salt and cayenne pepper
3 tablespoons salad cream
4 skinned tomatoes
2 tablespoons breadcrumbs
½ teaspoon grated nutmeg
lettuce
French dressing (Recipe 190)

Mix the grated Cheddar cheese with the Worcestershire sauce, salt, cayenne pepper and salad cream, and divide the mixture into four. Using wet hands coat each tomato completely with one portion, flattening either end. Roll them in crisp breadcrumbs mixed with grated nutmeg. Chill. Cut across in half and serve with lettuce salad.

420 CHEESE AND MACARONI SALAD

8 oz. grated Cheddar cheese
6 oz. cooked macaroni
pinch cayenne pepper and salt
lettuce and radishes to garnish
few chopped spring onions or chives
3 tablespoons French dressing (Recipe 190)

Toss together the cheese, macaroni, seasoning, onions and French dressing. Pile on lettuce and garnish with radish roses or slices.

421 TUNA COLE SLAW SALAD

7-oz. can middle-cut tuna
1¼ cups finely chopped celery
1 tablespoon horseradish sauce
3 tablespoons salad cream or mayonnaise
salt and pepper
1 small savoy cabbage, finely shredded
3 tablespoons grated carrot
2 hard-boiled eggs
2 tomatoes

Mix flaked tuna with the celery, horseradish sauce, salad cream and a sprinkling of pepper and salt. Pile on a bed of finely shredded cabbage mixed with the grated carrot. Garnish with sliced egg and tomato wedges.

To vary this salad add to taste chopped apple, shallot, onion, sweet pepper (capsicum) or capers.

422 CHICKEN COLE SLAW SALAD

As Recipe 421. Use approximately 8 oz. diced cooked chicken instead of the tuna. The horseradish can be omitted and extra mayonnaise used or blend little tomato purée with the mayonnaise.

423 HAM COLE SLAW SALAD

Use approximately 8 oz. cooked diced ham instead of the tuna in Recipe 421. Horseradish is very good with ham or a little made mustard can be stirred into the mayonnaise.

424 BANANA JELLY SALAD

1 packet lemon flavoured jelly*
mayonnaise (Recipe 186) or yoghurt
2 ripe bananas, yellow peel flecked with brown

* Orange can be used instead

Mix jelly according to packet directions. Chill only until slightly thickened. Partly fill 1 pint-sized mould with jelly. Peel bananas, slice and arrange on top of the jelly. Fill mould or individual moulds with remaining jelly. Chill until firm. Unmould. Garnish with additional slices of ripe banana or other fruit, if desired. Serve topped with yoghurt or mayonnaise and garnished with crisp lettuce.

425 HOT POTATO SALAD RING

1¼ lb. potatoes
1 tablespoon finely chopped onion or shallot
2 tablespoons finely chopped celery
2 tablespoons finely chopped parsley or sweet pepper (capsicum)
1 tablespoon made mustard
3 tablespoons salad cream

Filling

1 small can tomatoes
4 hard-boiled eggs
1 tablespoon grated cheese

Cook the potatoes in their skins. Peel and dice while hot. Add the onion, celery, parsley or sweet pepper; blend with the mustard and salad cream. Pile in a ring on a hot dish. Heat the tomatoes from the can and add to this the sliced eggs and turn into the centre of the ring. Top with grated cheese.

To vary this salad fill the potato ring with flaked tuna from a 7 oz. can of tuna in tomato, heated and mixed with 2 slices hard-boiled egg.

426 NORWEGIAN HERRING SALAD

2 salted herrings	2 cups diced cooked
1¼ cups cooked meat	potatoes
1¼ cups diced beetroot	3 raw apples
⅜ cup sour cream	2 tablespoons sweet pickle
2 tablespoons sugar	5 tablespoons vinegar
	pinch pepper

To garnish:

2 hard-boiled eggs	whipped cream or
cooked beetroot	mayonnaise
parsley	(Recipe 186)

Clean the salted herrings and soak overnight. Skin, bone and fillet. If still too salty soak in milk for 2 hours. Wipe dry on cloth. Cut the herrings into ⅓-inch cubes or even smaller, dice the meat about the same size and mix with the herring. Add the diced beetroot and diced potato. In a separate bowl mix the finely chopped apple, sour cream, sugar, vinegar and pickles. Add to herring mixture and season well after tasting. This salad should be served very cold, so either pack tightly into a mould then chill or put on to a flat platter and chill if possible. To garnish arrange sprigs of parsley round the edge of the dish. Chop the yolks and whites of the eggs separately, and grate the beetroot or chop finely. Arrange on top of the salad and serve either with whipped cream or mayonnaise, which can be tinted pale pink with beetroot juice.

427 CHEESE AND BEETROOT SALAD

8 oz. Cheddar cheese	French dressing
8 oz. diced cooked beetroot	(Recipe 190)
1 small onion	2 teaspoons salad oil
1 small green pepper	chicory
	2 skinned tomatoes

Prepare the French dressing and pour over the diced beetroot. Slice the onion and the cored green pepper wafer thin, and cut the skinned tomatoes into neat rings: dress them with salted salad oil. Arrange piles of ½-inch cubes of Cheddar cheese and the dressed beetroot on a flat salad plate, place alternate slices of tomato and onion and the green pepper rings to make an attractive arrangement, and garnish with chicory.

428 LOBSTER BANANA SALAD ROLL

1¼ breakfast cups lobster	¼ teaspoon salt
meat (fresh or canned)	¼ teaspoon ground pepper
1 breakfast cup diced	1 cup sliced ripe bananas
celery or cucumber	(1 — 2 bananas),
3 dessertspoons French	6 — 8 split bread rolls,
dressing (Recipe 190)	plain or toasted
2 dessertspoons salad	salad for garnish
dressing or mayonnaise	2 dessertspoons chopped
(Recipe 417 or 186)	pickle

Combine pieces of lobster meat, celery or cucumber and pickle. Add French dressing, salad dressing or mayonnaise, salt and pepper. Mix lightly. Just before serving, peel and slice bananas. Fold carefully into mixture. Fill bread rolls with salad mixture. Garnish with crisp salad. *Important:* the chopped sweet gherkins and French dressing add considerably to the flavour of the salad, but may be omitted, if desired. To further enhance flavour and colour, finely diced green pepper and chopped pimento may be added to mixture.

429 FRUIT AND CHEESE SALADS

Pears, pineapple, rings of apple, bananas, all blend very well with cheese in salads. Use either cream cheese or diced Cheddar cheese, and toss in French dressing (Recipe 190). Serve the fruit on crisp lettuce and pile the cheese on top. Garnish with dates, walnuts or ginger.

Quick Hot Dishes

430 STUFFED ROLLS

Cut the tops off crusty rolls and remove the centre. Carefully break an egg inside, season, adding a knob of butter or a little grated cheese. Put into a moderately hot oven (400°F. — Gas Mark 5) for about 7 minutes. *OR*: Fill the roll with flaked, cooked, smoked haddock mixed with a creamy sauce. Cover top with grated cheese and heat well.

431 CHEESE STUFFED BAKED POTATOES

4 really large potatoes   *seasoning*
margarine or butter   *grated cheese*

Bake the potatoes in the oven until tender. This depends on how quickly you wish to do them, but the best result is obtained by baking fairly steadily for about 1½ hours in the centre of just a very moderate oven (350°F. — Gas Mark 3). Cut the potatoes on half, scoop out the pulp and put it into a basin. Mash well, add margarine or butter, seasoning and as much grated cheese as you like. Pile back again into the potato cases and return to the oven to brown. If wished a little grated cheese can be sprinkled over the top. *Illustrated in colour picture No. 44.*

432 SURPRISE ROLLS

4 large round rolls   *1 small can evaporated*
1 can tuna fish or salmon   *milk*
1 small can peas or packet   *salt and pepper to taste*
frozen peas   *4 slices cheese*
    tomatoes
    lettuce

Put the evaporated milk, tuna fish, drained peas and seasoning into a pan and heat gently until smooth and creamy. Split the rolls and cover with slice of cheese. Pour over the hot fish mixture, and cover with the top of the rolls. Serve at once with tomatoes and lettuce.

433 CAULIFLOWER CHEESE

1 medium sized   *1 oz. grated Cheddar*
cauliflower   *cheese*
½ pint cheese sauce   *1 tablespoon crisp*
(Recipe 242)★   *breadcrumbs*

★ If desired use half milk and half cauliflower stock to make this

Soak the cauliflower in cold water for about 15 minutes, then break into flowerets. Cook in a little boiling salt water in a covered pan until tender and arrange neatly in buttered scallop shells or a fireproof dish. Make the cheese sauce. Coat the cauliflower with the cheese sauce. Sprinkle with the mixed grated cheese and crisp breadcrumbs, brown under a hot grill or in a fairly hot oven (425°F. — Gas Mark 6). Serve hot.

434 TONGUE AND CHEESE BALLS

1 oz. butter or   *4 oz. chopped tongue*
margarine   *2 — 3 oz. grated cheese*
1 oz. flour   *seasoning*
¼ pint milk   *1 egg*
1 teacup breadcrumbs   *fat for frying*
crisp crumbs for coating
salad

Make a very thick sauce of the butter, flour and milk. Add the crumbs, chopped tongue and cheese. Form into balls, coat with beaten egg and roll in crumbs. Brown in hot fat; if using deep fat they take a very short time, since all the ingredients are cooked. Drain on crumpled tissue paper or kitchen roll. Serve hot or cold with salad.

Variations:

Use chopped ham or chicken or minced cooked meat or flaked fish. This is a very good way of using up pieces of meat or fish left over. If wished the cheese can be omitted or you can use chopped hard-boiled eggs in place of meat.

435   STUFFED CAULIFLOWER

1 medium sized cauliflower	*¼ pint thick tomato sauce*
1 — 2 chopped hard-boiled eggs	*1 tablespoon grated cheese*
1 tablespoon chopped gherkin or cucumber	*few capers*

Cook the cauliflower whole in boiling, salted water, then when soft scoop out centre, mix with all the other ingredients, pile into the centre of the cauliflower, dust with cheese and brown under grill or in the oven.

436   MACARONI CHEESE

3 oz. macaroni	*2 oz. grated cheese*
¼ pint cheese sauce (Recipe No. 242) ★	*1 tablespoon crisp breadcrumbs*
	1 oz. margarine or butter

★ *If you like a more moist Macaroni Cheese, then use ¾ pint cheese sauce to the same quantity of cooked macaroni*

Put the macaroni into about 1½ pints boiling water, to which you have added a level teaspoon salt. Cook steadily until the macaroni is just tender. Do not overcook; elbow length quick cooking macaroni takes only 7 minutes. Drain in a colander, arrange it in a hot dish and pour the cheese sauce over it. Sprinkle cheese and breadcrumbs on top and put the margarine or butter on in several small pieces. Either bake for about 25 minutes near the top of a moderately hot oven (400°F. — Gas Mark 5) until crisp and brown, or put under a hot grill. *Illustrated in colour picture No. 30.*

437   MACARONI AND CHEESE FRITTERS

fritter batter (Recipe 464)	*seasoning*
2 oz. quick cooking macaroni	*fat for frying*
2 oz. grated cheese	

Cook macaroni in boiling salted water for 7 minutes. Meanwhile make fritter batter. Add well drained macaroni, grated cheese and seasoning. Drop spoonfuls into shallow fat, cook steadily until golden brown on under side, turn then cook as under side. Serve with salad or with fried tomatoes and green vegetables.

438   CHEESE POPOVERS

4 oz. flour	*12 tablespoons milk*
¼ teaspoon salt	*2 oz. grated Cheddar cheese*
2 eggs	*pinch cayenne pepper*
	butter

Put a knob of butter in the centre of each little tin of a bun tray and place in a hot oven (450°F. — Gas Mark 7) for about 5 — 7 minutes until the butter is thoroughly hot.

To make the batter sieve the flour and salt into a mixing basin. Beat the eggs well and add the milk to them. Stir the liquid ingredients into the sieved ingredients and beat well until thoroughly blended. Pour a scant tablespoon of the batter into each tin. Put a teaspoon of grated Cheddar cheese in the centre of each and cover with a teaspoon of batter. Bake in a very hot oven (475°F. — Gas Mark 8) for approximately 15 minutes until well risen, crisp and golden brown.

439   GRIDDLECAKES

6 oz. self-raising flour
¼ level teaspoon salt
⅜ pint milk

2 tablespoons melted
butter or luxury
margarine
1 or 2 eggs

Sift flour and salt well. Mix beaten egg and milk and add to the flour mixture, beating until smooth. Add the melted fat. Drop from spoon on to a hot ungreased griddle. Turn only once during baking and before they are dry on top. Serve with cheese.

440   Tuna Griddlecakes

Add to the above recipe flaked tuna from a 7-oz. can of middle-cut tuna. Add a squeeze of lemon juice and, if liked, 1 or 2 tablespoons fine grated cheese and a few drops of Tabasco or Worcestershire sauce.

441   Corn Cakes

Substitute 2 tablespoons drained canned corn kernels for 2 oz. flour. Blend 1 dessertspoon mild mustard with the batter. Serve with fried bacon or tomatoes. Or serve with roast or fried chicken.

442   Apple Griddlecakes

Substitute 2 oz. fine semolina for 2 oz. flour. Sift with 1 level teaspoon cinnamon, 1 tablespoon castor sugar and stir in 1 large apple chopped into small pieces. Serve with pork sausages, or with brown sugar and butter, or with honey.

443   Cottage Cheese Griddlecakes

Add 3 oz. cottage cheese to the batter. Serve with butter or jam, or with bacon or as an accompaniment to a fricassee of lamb, tripe or veal.

More Salads with Cheese and Fruit

444   Cottage Cheese with Orange Salad

Slice orange very finely and arrange around the cheese with unpeeled cucumber slices.

445   Tuna Fish and Cheese Salad

Flake the fish and combine with cottage cheese in equal parts, seasoning with pepper, salt, mustard. Arrange on pineapple slices.

446   Minced Ham and Pineapple Salad

Chop ham and pineapple, mix with cottage cheese and serve on lettuce.

447   Peach Cheese Salad

Halve fruit and pile high with chive-flavoured cottage cheese and serve on lettuce. Garnish with grape or cherry (see picture).

448   Apricot Cheese Salad

Halve apricots, pile high with cottage cheese and chopped peanuts. Top with a slice of ginger. Serve with cress.

449   Banana Split Salad

Split banana lengthwise, spoon cottage cheese liberally in the centre. Add a garnish of sliced strawberry or chopped nuts and watercress.

450   APPLE PINEAPPLE COLE SLAW

1 small head cabbage
* finely shredded*
2 unpared eating apples,
* diced*

9-oz. can pineapple chunks
1 stalk celery sliced
¼ pint mayonnaise
* (Recipe 186)*

Garnish

1 eating apple, cored
* and sliced*

lettuce
lemon juice

Toss all ingredients in mayonnaise. Serve in lettuce-lined bowl; trim with apple wedges dipped in lemon juice to preserve colour. *Illustrated in colour picture opposite.*

33   **GALANTINE OF CHICKEN AND HAM** (Recipe 455)

CHICKEN BROTH (Recipe 66)

FRICASSÉE OF CHICKEN (Recipe 453)

FRIED CHICKEN AND BACON WITH DEVILLED SAUCE (Recipe 454)

34   **APPLE PINEAPPLE COLE SLAW** (Recipe 450)

35   VEAL ESCALOPES WITH TOMATO SAUCE
(Recipe 451)

36   SAUTÉ CHICKEN AND WALNUTS (Recipe 452)

Supper Savouries and One-dish Meals

In this section are more substantial savoury dishes that can be served as a main meal, and dishes that can be cooked in one container, so are ideal when you are short of cooking space.

451 VEAL ESCALOPES WITH TOMATO SAUCE

4 veal escalopes	4 oz. mushrooms
cornflour for coating	1 clove garlic
butter for frying	cooked beans

Sauce

1 level tablespoon cornflour	pepper
¼ pint tomato juice	salt
squeeze lemon juice	pinch sugar

Coat the escalopes with cornflour to which a little salt and pepper has been added. Shape well with a meat bat or palette knife. Brown gently in a little butter in a frying pan, and remove to a hot baking dish. Pound the garlic and cook gently in the butter with the mushrooms. Add to the veal in the dish reserving a few mushrooms for garnish. To make sauce add the cornflour to the butter remaining in the frying pan and cook for 1 minute. Add tomato juice, stir until boiling and cook for 1 minute. Stir in lemon juice, seasoning and sugar to taste. Pour over the veal, cover and bake about 20 minutes in a moderate oven (375°F. — Gas Mark 4). Arrange some green beans in the bottom of a serving dish. Place the escalopes on top and pour the sauce over. *Illustrated in colour picture No. 35.*

452 SAUTÉ CHICKEN WITH WALNUTS

2 tablespoons corn oil	salt and pepper
1 oz. shelled walnuts	4 shallots
1 small chicken —	¼ pint dry white wine
about 2 lb.	cornflour for coating

Lightly fry the walnuts in the corn oil, drain on paper. Joint and skin the chicken and coat well with cornflour to which salt and pepper has been added. Fry chicken pieces in oil with the finely chopped shallots until golden brown. Add white wine and simmer gently for 15—20 minutes or until the chicken is tender. Add the fried nuts a few minutes before the end of the cooking time. Remove the chicken to a serving plate and pour the sauce over, adding a little extra wine if necessary. Serve with green salad. *Illustrated in colour picture No. 36.*

453 FRICASSÉE OF CHICKEN

breast of 1 chicken	seasoning
2 hard-boiled eggs	chopped parsley
1 oz. butter or	little red pepper
margarine	6 slices toast or fried
1 oz. flour	bread
¼ pint milk	creamed potatoes or about
1 or 2 tablespoons	4 oz. cooked rice
cream from top of milk	¼ pint chicken stock

Heat the butter in a large pan, stir in the flour and cook for several minutes. Add the milk and chicken stock, bring to the boil and cook until thickened. Add the seasoning. Cut the breast into fairly thick slices and heat very gently in this sauce. Just before serving add the cream and chopped egg whites. Arrange 4 pieces of toast on a hot dish, put each serving of chicken on a piece of toast, pouring the rest of the sauce round. Garnish with a border of rice or piped potatoes, triangles of fried bread or toast and neat lines of chopped egg yolk, parsley and red pepper. *Illustrated in colour picture No. 33.*

454 FRIED CHICKEN AND BACON WITH DEVILLED SAUCE

cooked drum sticks and	corn on the cob
thighs of chicken	4 tomatoes
8 small rashers of bacon	8 small mushrooms
breadcrumbs — crisp	watercress
crumbs for shallow	fat for frying
frying — soft white	1 egg
crumbs for deep frying	

For the sauce

1 bottle tomato juice	seasoning
¼ pint chicken stock	few drops Worcestershire
1 oz. margarine	sauce
1 oz. flour	little mustard

Dry the legs and thighs well — having made these into 4 joints — by tossing in seasoned flour, then coat with egg and crumbs. If frying in shallow fat use crisp crumbs, and brown in the fat and then put into the oven for about 15 minutes to make sure the chicken is very hot. For deep fat use the soft crumbs and fry steadily to heat through to the middle.

Fry the bacon rashers, halved tomatoes and mushrooms. Arrange with the chicken on a hot dish and garnish with cooked corn on the cob and watercress. Serve with the devilled sauce made by heating the butter or margarine, stirring in the flour. After cooking this roux for a few minutes, add the tomato juice and the chicken stock.

Bring to the boil and cook until thickened, then add lots of seasoning, mustard and Worcestershire sauce. *Illustrated in colour picture No. 33.*

455 GALANTINE OF CHICKEN AND HAM

wings and meat from back
  of 1 boiled chicken
cooked giblets
2 teacups soft
  breadcrumbs
1 chopped onion*
good pinch mixed herbs
1 oz. flour
2 oz. butter or margarine

6 oz. diced cooked ham
¼ pint stock or milk
seasoning
2 or 3 hard-boiled eggs
few crisp breadcrumbs, or
¼ pint aspic jelly and tiny
  pieces of gherkin
tomato to garnish

* and/or 2 oz. mushrooms

Heat butter and fry mushrooms or onion until very soft. Stir in flour and cook gently, then add stock or milk, bring to the boil and cook until very thick. Stir in minced or very finely-chopped chicken meat — you can use all the skin of the chicken if you put it through the mincer. Add minced meat from giblets, crumbs and ham and season well, adding herbs. Press mixture out into oblong shape on a floured board, put shelled, hard-boiled eggs on this, then roll up. Put into well-greased paper, foil or a cloth and steam for about 35—45 minutes. If serving hot remove paper or cloth and coat in crisp crumbs.

If serving cold either coat in crumbs or allow to cool and then coat with half-set aspic jelly and arrange tiny pieces of gherkin and tomato on this to form a delicate pattern. If preferred the mixture can be baked for about ½ hour in a moderate oven in a loaf tin (375°F. or Gas Mark 4). *Illustrated in colour picture No. 33.*

456 VEAL FRICASSÉE

1 lb. veal
salt and pepper
1 oz. butter
1 small can evaporated
  milk
1 small packet frozen peas
small can or 4 oz. button
  mushrooms

1 onion
1 bay leaf, sprig parsley
  and little thyme
1 oz. flour
1 teaspoon lemon juice
1 slice lemon
1 tomato
little extra butter

Wash the veal and cut it into small cubes; put these in a large saucepan, cover with cold water and bring to the boil. Remove the scum. Peel and slice the onion and add it to the meat together with the salt and pepper to taste and the bay leaf, parsley and thyme tied in a small piece of muslin. Cover the pan and simmer gently for 1 hour. Drain meat, reserve stock, discard muslin bag.

Melt the butter in a saucepan, stir in the flour and cook for a few minutes over a low heat. Dilute the milk with enough veal stock to make ½ pint liquid and gradually add this to the fat and flour, stirring all the time. Bring to the boil, reduce the heat and add the lemon juice, meat and peas. Cook for 5 minutes. Meanwhile heat or cook mushrooms in little butter. Turn the veal on to a dish, garnish with lemon slice, mushrooms and tomato.

457 · HAWAIIAN CHICKEN

4 oz. chopped mushrooms
1 small onion chopped
1¼ lb. roasting chicken
  joints
2 oz. butter
1 oz. plain flour

1 small can evaporated
  milk
seasoning
4 oz. boiled Patna rice
1 small can pineapple
8 rashers streaky bacon

Melt butter and lightly fry the mushrooms, onion and chicken. Add the flour and cook for few minutes. Dilute evaporated milk to ¾ pint with cold water and add gradually to chicken. Season and put lid on top and simmer until chicken is tender (30—40 minutes). Cook rice and arrange on serving dish, arrange joints on top, pour sauce over. Meanwhile cut bacon rashers in half, form into bacon rolls and grill. Serve with pineapple chunks.

458 STUFFED GAMMON STEAK WITH
APPLE RINGS

4 eating apples
juice of 1 lemon
2 cups soft breadcrumbs
¼ cup raisins
¼ cup peanuts

2 tablespoons golden syrup
½ teaspoon mustard
2 tablespoons butter or
  margarine
2 slices gammon, ½ inch
  thick
cloves and parsley

Core, but do not peel eating apples. Slice them crosswise into ¼-inch rings and soak in lemon juice to keep colour bright. Combine breadcrumbs, raisins, chopped peanuts, syrup, mustard and butter. Chop 3 apple slices coarsely and add to mixture. Cut the fat around gammon steaks to prevent curling and place 1 slice of gammon in greased shallow baking dish. Spread stuffing liberally over gammon and top with second slice. Stick whole cloves in fat. Bake in centre of a very moderate oven (350°F. — Gas Mark 3) 1 hour, or until done. Baste several times with melted butter or margarine. Serve on a platter garnished with fresh apple rings. *Illustrated in colour picture No. 29.*

459   BEEF SUKIYAKI
(from Japan)

1 tablespoon olive or corn oil	2 tablespoons sugar
8 oz. good quality beef★	½ tablespoon sake or sherry
¼ cup stock	1 onion, sliced
2 — 6 tablespoons Soy sauce★★	1 leek, sliced
4 oz. shredded cabbage	¼ cup spinach
2 — 4 oz. mushrooms	2 eggs
	1 — 2 tablespoons sugar
	seasoning

* *The meat should be cut very thinly, steak or a slice of top side or sirloin — it can be diced if wished*
** *Add gradually as this is quite strong*

Heat the oil in a large frying pan, brown the meat on both sides. Mix the stock, soy sauce, sugar and sherry. Add only half of this to the meat in the pan. Push the meat to one side of the pan then add the sliced onion, leek and cabbage and cook gently for 3 minutes. Add remaining liquid, the very finely shredded mushrooms and spinach. Cook for a further 3 minutes. Beat and season the eggs and heat in a separate large pan, stirring until slightly thickened, but not set. Dip the hot meat and vegetables into this. Serve with cooked rice.

460   GOLDEN CROWN BAKE
Mince

2 oz. cooking fat	2 rounded tablespoons flour
1 medium onion	10 tablespoons stock or water
8 oz. carrots	pepper and salt
1 lb. lean minced beef	

Topping and Garnish

¼ pint milk	pepper and salt
3 level tablespoons fine semolina	1 oz. finely grated Cheddar cheese
1 level teaspoon made mustard	red or green pepper or sliced olives

Peel and chop onion and grate carrots rather coarsely. Melt fat in a pan and fry onion in it till golden. Add carrot and meat and cook until mixture changes colour. Sprinkle in flour and cook mixture slowly 3 minutes, stirring. Add stock or water, cover pan and gently simmer mince for 1 hour, stirring occasionally. Season to taste. About 7 minutes before mince is ready prepare the topping.

Heat milk and sprinkle in semolina. Bring slowly to the boil, stirring, then simmer for 3 minutes. Remove from heat and stir in mustard and other seasonings to taste.

Turn mince into a serving dish and cover with a wide ring of the topping mixture. Sprinkle with grated cheese then brown under a medium grill. Garnish with rings of red or green pepper or sliced olives. Serve piping hot with a crisp salad.

461   RISSOLES

6 — 8 oz. freshly minced meat	good pinch mixed herbs
1 small grated onion	¼ teacup thick brown sauce or egg yolk to bind
¼ teacup breadcrumbs	seasoning

Mix all ingredients together, form into round cakes, flour well and either fry or grill for 15 minutes — quickly at first then lower the heat to make sure they are cooked through to the middle.

462   FAGGOTS

These are made with the same method as Rissoles (Recipe 461) but the heart, liver and kidney of pig are used instead of meat — this should be well minced, preferably twice.

463   KROMESKIES

6 — 8 oz. minced cooked meat	2 oz. margarine or cooking fat
approximately 2 large rashers bacon or 4 small	1 oz. flour
2 oz. mushrooms	¼ pint brown stock
1 small onion	seasoning
	herbs

Divide bacon into 8 pieces about 2½ — 3 inches long; — any tiny pieces of bacon left can be chopped and added to onions and mushrooms. Heat margarine and cook finely chopped onions and mushrooms until tender. Add flour and stir well, then gradually add stock. Bring to the boil and when thick, add meat, herbs and seasoning. Allow to cool and form into 8 finger shapes. Wrap these in the bacon, then coat in thick batter (Recipe 464) and fry until crisp and brown. Drain well. If serving hot, fairly fat bacon is excellent, but for a cold dish choose lean bacon or even slices of cooked ham.

464 BATTER

Mix 2 oz. flour (plain or self-raising) with 1 egg, seasoning and ½ teacup milk.

465 MINCED BEEF ROLL

8 oz. minced raw beef or veal
4 oz. bacon rashers
good pinch powdered mixed herbs
1 egg
4 oz. stale bread (not too crusty)
salt
pepper
(onion can be added if desired)

Break the bread into small pieces, remove rind from bacon. Put bacon and bread through mincer, also the meat if not already minced. Add the herbs, a seasoning of salt and pepper and a well beaten egg. Mix well together and form into a roll shape, wrap in grease proof paper and tie in a cloth. Put into boiling water and boil for 1½ hours. BE SURE THE WATER KEEPS BOILING ALL THE TIME. If during cooking more water is needed to keep roll covered, boiling water must be added. Take out roll and carefully remove cloth. Leave until quite cold then peel off the paper. To serve for special occasions the roll can be brushed over with a little glaze and left to set. Decorate with tiny sprigs of parsley. This beef roll is also delicious hot.

466 MANILA CURRY

4 oz. rice
¾ oz. butter or margarine
1 small onion
1 dessertspoon curry powder
¾ pint water or milk or stock
1 heaped tablespoon semolina
1 pint fresh prawns or shrimps (or use frozen or canned)
2 hard-boiled eggs
1 tablespoon raisins and/or a sliced banana
pepper and salt
lemon and parsley

Cook the rice in fast boiling water until tender, drain and rinse. Meanwhile melt the fat, add the chopped onion and brown lightly. Stir in the curry powder and liquid, heat and sprinkle in the semolina, stirring. Simmer 3 minutes. Add the prawns, sliced eggs, raisins or sliced banana. Season further to taste. Serve piping hot with the rice, garnished with lemon and parsley.

467 FISH CAKES

8 oz. mashed potato
8 oz. cooked fish
salt and pepper
1 egg or ¼ pint thick white sauce
(Recipe 241)

For coating

1 egg
flour
crisp breadcrumbs
fat for frying

Mix the potatoes and cooked flaked fish (cod, hake or other white fish) thoroughly with a fork. Add the beaten egg or sauce, salt and pepper. Form into about 8 flat cakes. Roll these cakes in a little flour, then brush lightly with beaten egg and coat with breadcrumbs. Heat the fat in the frying pan and when a faint haze is seen fry quickly on one side, turn and fry again on the other side. Drain on crumpled tissue paper or kitchen roll for about 2 minutes and serve at once.

468   FISH CROQUETTES

Follow directions for Fish Cakes, but use the white sauce, and 1 teacup breadcrumbs instead of mashed potato.

469   SWISS FISH PIE

6 oz. fine soft
  breadcrumbs
8 small fillets whiting,
  plaice or sole
seasoning

2 — 3 oz. butter
6 portions Swiss Gruyère
  cheese

Butter a dish, and arrange a layer of crumbs. Cut fillets into halves and spread these on the crumbs — using half the amount of fish. Cover with half the diced cheese. Put rest of crumbs over this, the fish, made into neat rolls, cheese, seasoning and plenty of butter.

Cook for approximately 30 minutes in centre of a moderate oven (375°F. — Gas Mark 4). If wished brown under grill before serving. *Illustrated in colour picture No. 37.*

470   CASSEROLE OF SOLE AND ONIONS

4 very large fillets sole
  (plaice could be used)
seasoning
3 oz. butter

4 good-sized potatoes
4 medium sized onions
lemon
parsley to garnish

Cut fillets of sole into fingers about 1 inch by ½ inch. Peel and slice onions and potatoes until wafer thin. Arrange layer of potatoes in a well-buttered casserole, then a layer of onions, then fish. Season each layer well and add plenty of butter. Fill casserole like this, ending with potatoes. Put a tightly fitting lid over top and bake for about 30 minutes in centre of moderate oven (400°F. — Gas Mark 5). Then reduce heat to very moderate (300°F. — Gas Mark 2) for a further 30—40 minutes. Serve garnished with border of parsley.

471   SALMON RING

8 — 12 oz. canned or
  flaked cooked salmon
¼ pint mayonnaise or
  salad cream or white
  sauce (Recipes 186
  or 241)
2 level teaspoons powdered
  gelatine

2 eggs
¼ teacup water
2 tablespoons cream from
  top of milk
1 tablespoon vinegar or
  lemon juice
salt
pepper

Garnish

lettuce
8 oz. potatoes

tomato
cucumber

Beat the egg yolks into the white sauce or mayonnaise. Soften gelatine in the vinegar, add very hot water and stir until dissolved. Add this to the egg mixture. Fold in the fish, cream, then stiffly beaten egg whites, season well. Pour into a ring mould rinsed out in cold water or brushed with a little olive oil. When set turn out on to a bed of lettuce and garnish with tomato and cucumber slices. Fill the centre with a potato and cucumber salad made by mixing 8 oz. diced cooked potatoes with ½ teacup diced cucumber, chopped parsley, 1 or 2 sliced olives and mayonnaise.

Variation

Use this recipe with flaked fish — flavouring it with a little anchovy essence.

472   CHEESE AND TUNA MOULD

2 teacups breadcrumbs
1 teacup grated cheese
1 egg
1 can (medium size)
  tuna fish

1 small onion
1 oz. margarine
seasoning
little chopped parsley
1 teacup milk

Fry the finely chopped onion in the margarine. Flake the fish and mix with all the other ingredients. Put into well greased loaf tin, cover with greased paper, and bake for approximately 1 hour in centre of moderate oven (375°F. — Gas Mark 4). Turn out and serve with baked tomatoes, peas and creamed potatoes.

473   FISH PIES

There are many ways of making fish pies, which can be varied according to the ingredients available.
Method 1. Mix fish (cooked and flaked) with white sauce or cheese sauce, add hard-boiled eggs, and any cooked vegetables and top with creamed potatoes and more grated cheese — OR top with pastry.
Method 2. Mix the flaked fish with a more savoury sauce, mushroom, tomato, curry. Put into the dish and cover with a thick layer of crumbs, knobs of butter or margarine.

In either case put into the oven to brown potato or crumbs or cook pastry.
Suitable sauces will be found under Recipes 242—260.

474 BRAWN

1 sheep's head or pig's head	good bunch mixed herbs
2 carrots	little lemon juice
8 oz. stewing steak, if wished	seasoning
	1 onion

Clean head and put it into the pan, half covering with water and adding all ingredients. Simmer gently for about 1 hour, then add diced stewing steak and continue cooking until all the meat is tender. Remove meat from head, dicing neatly, put into a basin with the steak.

Boil stock down until only about 1½ teacups remain, strain, then clear with egg shells — so tiny pieces of meat etc. adhere to this. Pour over meat and allow to set.

476 CHICKEN AND HAM MOUSSE

1 packet aspic jelly	2 oz. flour
1 oz. powdered gelatine	1 large can evaporated milk
1 firm tomato	
capers	little chicken stock
1 hard-boiled egg	12 oz. minced cooked chicken
2 oz. butter	
4 egg whites	4 oz. minced cooked ham
parsley to garnish	salt, pepper, cochineal

Dissolve aspic jelly in 1 pint of hot water. Dissolve gelatine in 2 tablespoons hot water and add this to the aspic. Set 6 tablespoons of aspic in the bottom of a 7-inch round cake tin. Cut tomatoes into 6 or 7 pieces and slice hard-boiled egg. Dipping pieces of tomato, capers and egg slices in liquid aspic, arrange them in a pretty pattern on top of the set aspic round edge of base. Allow decorations to set firmly. Pour 6 tablespoons of liquid aspic on top of decorations, allow to set.

Melt butter in a saucepan, add flour and cook gently for few minutes. Make milk up to 1 pint with chicken stock and add this liquid gradually to the fat and flour, stirring all the time. Bring to the boil and cook over gentle heat for 3 minutes. Add minced chicken and ham, and cool. Season with salt and pepper then add remainder of liquid aspic and stir well. Whisk egg whites until very stiff and fold them into the chicken mixture. Add a few drops of cochineal to give attractive colour. When mixture is cold but not set, pour into tin and leave to set. Turn out on to a dish to serve, and garnish with sprigs of parsley. 8 servings.

475 HAM MOUSSE

8 oz. cooked and finely chopped ham	¼ gill water
	1 level dessertspoon powdered gelatine
2 eggs	
¼ pint good Béchamel sauce (Recipe 245)	seasoning
	¼ gill cream or evaporated milk
1 tablespoon sherry	

Separate the whites from the yolks of the eggs. Stir the yolks into the hot sauce and cook gently for a few minutes. Add gelatine which should be dissolved in the water. When cool stir in the ham, seasoning, sherry and cream and lastly FOLD in stiffly beaten egg whites. Put into four individual dishes to become firm. Garnish with salad and serve with potato and other salads.

477 GARDEN JELLIED RING

1 envelope (level tablespoon powdered gelatine)	¾ pint water or you can use very clear white stock (made from simmering chicken bones)
1 tablespoon lemon juice	
¼ teacup malt vinegar	seasoning
1 or 2 teaspoons sugar	1 teacup cooked peas
2 tablespoons tomato juice (see Method)	1 teacup shredded cabbage
	1 teacup diced cooked young carrots
2 skinned and sliced tomatoes	about 1 teacup thinly

For the centre

diced cooked ham	mayonnaise (Recipe 186) or diced cheese

Dissolve powdered gelatine in boiling water, then add tomato juice (either use canned or bottled juice or rub 2 or 3 tomatoes through a fine sieve), lemon juice, vinegar, sugar and seasoning. Allow to cool, but not set, then put a little at the bottom of a rinsed mould. Cover with a layer of vegetables, then leave until firm. Continue filling mould like this, and allow to set. If you are in a hurry stir all the vegetables into the cold and slightly thickened jelly, then pour into a mould. Use either a ring mould or plain round mould. When firm turn out, serve on a bed of lettuce. Fill centre with cornets of ham and mayonnaise (Recipe 186).

478   BACON CRUST PIE

1 lb. minced cooked lean bacon   *1 small chopped onion pepper*

small can tomato purée   *¼ cup chopped green pepper*

¼ cup breadcrumbs

Mix these ingredients together, knead well and press into the bottom of a 9-inch pie tin, making a fluted edging all round.

Filling

1 cup cooked rice   *1¼ cups grated Swiss*

1 small can tomato purée   *Gruyère cheese*

Combine rice, tomato purée, part of the cheese, salt and pepper, and spoon into the bacon shell. Cover with grease proof paper. Bake in centre of a moderate oven (375°F. — Gas Mark 4) for 15 minutes. Remove paper, sprinkle remaining cheese over the top and slip under the grill to brown lightly.

479   CREAMED EGG CRUNCH

Pastry Triangles

4 oz. plain flour   *1 level teaspoon dry*

2 oz. fine semolina   *mustard*

¼ level teaspoon salt   *2 oz. cooking fat*

shake of cayenne pepper   *approx. 2 tablespoons*

2 oz. margarine   *cold water to mix*

Sift dry ingredients into a bowl. Rub in fats until mixture resembles fine breadcrumbs. Mix to a stiff paste with the cold water. Turn out on to a lightly floured board and knead quickly till smooth. Roll out into an 8-inch round, keeping it as neat as possible. Pinch up edges between finger and thumb then cut into 8 equal sized triangles. Transfer to lightly greased trays and bake near top of hot oven (425—450°F. — Gas Mark 6—7) for 17 minutes or until crisp and pale gold.

480   Creamed Eggs

4 eggs   *1 oz. plain flour*

1 oz. butter or margarine   *¼ pint milk*

2 oz. mushrooms   *seasoning to taste*

Bring eggs to boil in a pan of water and boil steadily for 10 minutes. Meanwhile make mushroom sauce. Melt fat and gently fry peeled and chopped mushrooms in it for 5 minutes. Stir in flour and cook mixture for 2 minutes. Remove from heat and gradually add milk. Re-heat, stirring, till mixture thickens, then simmer gently for 3 minutes. Shell eggs, cut in halves and put into a small bowl. Cover with mushroom sauce and sprinkle a band of paprika across the top. Stand bowl on a platter and surround with pastry triangles. Serve with crisp leaves of chicory or sticks of celery.

481   CORNISH PASTIES

10 oz. short crust pastry (Recipe 485)   *1 large onion*

6 oz. uncooked rump steak or good quality stewing steak*   *¼ teacup stock or gravy (or water flavoured with little yeast extract)*

2 medium size potatoes or equivalent in small potatoes   *salt and pepper*
     mustard
     egg or milk to glaze

* Canned meat can be used instead in which case shorten cooking time

First make the pastry. Roll this out to about ¼ inch thick, then cut into 4 rounds about the size of a large tea plate. Cut the meat into tiny pieces then dice the potatoes and onion. Mix these together, adding seasoning. Put a good pile in the centre of each round, and moisten with a little of the stock. Brush the edges of the pastry with water, then bring these together in the centre. Press them tightly, so that there is no possibility of their opening during cooking, and stand the pasties on a baking tray. Brush the outside with either a little milk or beaten egg to give a slight glaze. Stand the pasties in the centre of a hot oven (450°F. — Gas Mark 7) and bake for about 25 minutes. Lower the heat to moderate (375—400°F. — Gas Mark 4) for a further 35 minutes to make sure the meat is cooked inside.

482 CHICKEN AMANDINE PATTIES

1 tablespoon oil	5 tablespoons cream
1 small onion — chopped	2 oz. mushrooms
¼ green pepper — shredded	1 oz. blanched toasted and shredded almonds
1 level tablespoon cornflour	squeeze lemon juice seasonings
¼ pint chicken stock	1 egg yolk
1 tablespoon white wine	6 large or 12 small vol-au-vent cases
8 oz. diced cooked chicken	(Recipe 486)

Heat the oil in a saucepan. Sauté the onion, pepper and chopped mushrooms for a few minutes without browning the onion. Add the cornflour and mix well. Cook for a few minutes then remove from the heat and stir in the chicken stock and white wine. Return to the heat and stir till boiling. Add diced chicken, toasted almonds, add lemon juice and seasoning. Mix the egg yolk and cream together and stir into the chicken mixture just before it is required for use. Serve in vol-au-vent cases.

483 PUFF PASTRY

8 oz. plain flour	cold water to mix
7 — 8 oz. fat.*	good pinch salt
	few drops lemon juice

You have a good choice of fats here. Use:
a) Butter — the economical New Zealand butter is excellent *or*
b) Table or luxury margarine *or*
c) ⅔ table margarine and ⅓ modern whipped-up light cooking fat

Sieve flour and salt together. Mix to rolling consistency with cold water and lemon juice. Roll to oblong shape. Make fat into neat block and place in centre of pastry and fold over it first the bottom section of pastry, and then the top section, so that fat is quite covered. Turn the dough at right angles, seal edges and 'rib' carefully (see Recipe 484 for Flaky Pastry) and roll out. Fold dough into envelope, turn it, seal edges, 'rib' and roll again. Repeat 5 times, so making 7 rollings and 7 foldings in all. It will be necessary to put pastry to rest in cold place once or twice between rollings to prevent it becoming sticky and soft. Always put it to rest before rolling it for the last time, and before baking. Bake in very hot oven (to make it rise, and keep in the fat). Bake for the first 10 to 15 minutes at 475 — 500°F. — Gas Mark 8 — 9, then lower to Gas Mark 5 — 6 or turn electric oven right out or re-set to 400°F. to finish cooking at lower temperature. Well made puff pastry should rise to 4 or 5 times its original thickness. When making vol-au-vent cases it may be necessary to remove a little soft dough and return to oven to dry out.

484 FLAKY PASTRY

8 oz. plain flour	pinch salt
5 — 6 oz. fat.*	water to mix

* *Use* a) All butter *or*
b) All table margarine or superfine or luxury margarine *or*
c) ⅔ table margarine and ⅓ modern whipped-up light cooking fat

Sieve flour with salt. Divide fat into 3 portions. Rub 1 portion into flour in usual way and mix to rolling consistency with cold water. Roll out to oblong shape. Now take second portion of fat, divide it into small pieces and lay them on surface of two-thirds of dough. Leave remaining third without fat. Take its 2 corners and fold back over second third so that dough looks like an envelope with its flap open. Fold over top end of pastry, closing the 'envelope'. Turn it at right angles, seal open ends of pastry and 'rib' it. This means depressing it with the rolling-pin at intervals, so giving a corrugated effect and equalising the pressure of air. This ensures that pastry will rise evenly. Repeat process again using remaining fat and turning pastry in same way. Roll out pastry once more but should it begin to feel soft and sticky put it into a cold place for 30 minutes to become firm before rolling out. Fold pastry as before, turn it, seal edges and 'rib' it. Altogether the pastry should have 3 foldings and 3 rollings. It is then ready to stand in a cold place for a little while before baking, since the contrast between the cold and the heat of the oven makes pastry rise better. To bake, use a very hot oven (475°F. — Gas Mark 8) for first 15 minutes, then lower the Gas Mark to 5 or 6, or turn the electric oven off to cook for remaining time at a lower temperature.

485 SHORT CRUST PASTRY

8 oz. flour	cold water to mix — approx. 2 tablespoons
4 oz. fat *	
good pinch salt	

* *There are many fats and combinations of fats that give a first class short crust pastry. Choose between:*

a) Modern whipped-up cooking fat. Use 3½ oz. only as it is very rich
b) Pure cooking fat or lard
c) Margarine — for best results use a table margarine, a superfine or luxury margarine
d) Butter
e) 2 oz. margarine and 2 oz. cooking fat

Sieve flour and salt and rub in fat until mixture looks like fine breadcrumbs. Using first a knife and then the finger-tips to feel pastry, gradually add enough cold water to make dough into a rolling consistency. Lightly flour rolling-pin and pastry board. If a great deal of flour is necessary to roll out pastry you have made it too wet. Roll pastry to required thickness and shape, lifting and turning it to keep it light. Exact cooking times for pastry are given in the recipes but as a general rule it should be cooked in a hot oven (425 — 450°F. — Gas Mark 6 — 7).

Vol-au-vent

486 TO MAKE VOL-AU-VENT CASES

Method 1 Roll out puff pastry until just under ½ inch thick. Cut into rounds. From half the rounds make a circle by cutting out centre. Place circle on top of complete round. Seal edges and put on to *damp* baking trays. Glaze with beaten egg.

Method 2 Roll out pastry until a good ¾—1 inch thick. Cut into rounds or required shape. Put on to damp baking trays. With a smaller cutter press half way through pastry. Glaze with beaten egg.

Bake in very hot oven (475°F. — Gas Mark 8 or 9) until well risen and brown then reduce heat slightly to make sure pastry is cooked.

With Method 2, lift out the centre portion — this is quite easy to do with the point of a sharp knife, and return to oven for a short time to dry out.

487 FILLINGS FOR VOL-AU-VENT CASES

Minced or chopped chicken in creamy white sauce
Cooked mushrooms in a thick sauce
Shell fish in a creamy white sauce, mayonnaise, or mixed with lightly scrambled eggs
Thick cheese sauce
Cream cheese and chopped cucumber
Thick meat or vegetable creamy mixture
Steak and kidney
If serving cold allow pastry to cool before adding filling.
If serving hot put hot filling into hot pastry at the last minute.

488 SALAD PUFFS

3 or 4 thin slices ham, minced
piece of cucumber (diced small, sprinkled with salt, left a while then drained)
vol-au-vent cases

1 good teaspoon mustard (moistened with vinegar or lemon juice)
few radishes
1 or 2 tablespoons mayonnaise (Recipe 186)

Line cases with tiny lettuce leaves. Mix filling ingredients adding, if liked, some grated radishes and a few chopped gherkins. Heap mixture into cases and garnish each with tulip-cut radishes.

489 BACON AND MUSHROOM PUFFS

4 oz. chopped raw mushrooms
few cooked button mushrooms for garnish
1 gill white sauce (Recipe 242)
pinch cayenne
salt to taste
vol-au-vent cases

1 or 2 rashers of bacon, grilled and minced
1 dessertspoon French mustard (or less of dry mustard moistened with vinegar or lemon juice)
1 teaspoon chopped chives or parsley

Mix chopped mushrooms into white sauce when being cooked. Cook for several minutes, then add bacon, mustard and seasoning. When cool, sprinkle in chopped herbs. Use as filling for pastry cases, adding 'cap' of mushroom to each.

490 BEEF AND WALNUT PUFFS

1 teacup minced cooked beef (or corned beef)
2 or 3 pickled walnuts, chopped
vol-au-vent cases

1 gill white sauce (Recipe 242) (well flavoured with mustard and seasoned to taste)
watercress for garnish

Mix filling ingredients and fill pastry cases. Garnish with sprigs of watercress.

491   HOT-WATER CRUST PASTRY or RAISED PASTRY

(for raised pies)

12 oz. plain flour	¼ pint water
3 — 4 oz. fat*	pinch salt

* The modern whipped-up light fat is excellent for this pastry. Clarified dripping or lard or pure cooking fat can also be used

Sieve flour and salt. Melt fat in warm water and add to flour. Mix with knife and knead gently with fingers. Unlike other pastry this should be used when warm. Bake in moderately hot oven (400°F. — Gas Mark 5).

492   VEAL AND HAM PIE

Raised pie pastry

12 oz. raised pastry (Recipe 491)

Filling

1 lb. fillet veal	½ level teaspoon grated
6 oz. ham	lemon rind
1 — 2 hard-boiled eggs	1 level teaspoon gelatine
7 tablespoons, water or	½ level teaspoon meat
bone stock	extract
salt and pepper	beaten egg for glazing

Make pastry and keep warm in basin until ready to use. Remove pastry from basin and with two-thirds of the dough line a 6-inch cake tin or 1-lb. loaf tin. Wash and dry meats removing any skin, and cut into 1-inch cubes. Roll meats together in salt and pepper and lemon rind. Place half the meat in the bottom of the pastry-lined tin, cut eggs into halves, place on top of meat, cover with remaining meat. Pour into the pie 3 tablespoons of water or stock. Turn top edge of pastry lining in over meat, damp it all round, roll out remaining third of pastry to make a lid. Press down well all round edge and cut at ½-inch intervals with a sharp knife to secure. Make a hole in centre and brush over with beaten egg. Place in centre of a moderate oven (375°F. — Gas Mark 4) for 2—2¼ hours. Leave to cool. Melt gelatine in remaining water or stock and stir in meat extract. When pie is cool and

gelatine mixture just setting, pour into pie through the hole in the centre and leave to set before serving. Serve with salad and cold pork sausages. *Illustrated in colour picture No. 20.*

493   SWISS CHEESE ROLL

1 lb. puff or flaky pastry (Recipes 483 and 484)
2 — 3 tablespoons cream to Glaze

Filling

8 oz. Swiss Gruyère	6 tablespoons cream
cheese	salt
2 eggs	red pepper
1 tablespoon butter	

Mix all ingredients for filling together until smooth. Roll out pastry very thinly until about 18 inches × 18 inches, place filling over this — being sparing at the edge — and roll pastry as a Swiss roll. Bake in centre of a moderately hot oven (400°F. — Gas Mark 5) for about 30 minutes. While baking brush roll frequently with cream to give glaze.

494   LIVER SUPPER SNACKS

8 oz. New Zealand	pepper
lamb's liver	salt
2 oz. bacon	large pinch dried sage
2 — 3 small onions	8 oz. short crust pastry
butter	(Recipe 485)

Lightly fry slices of liver and bacon in a little butter. Put through mincer or chop finely. Season to taste and add a sprinkling of sage. Roll out pastry thinly to a long oblong about 6— inches wide. Spread filling mixture along one side of pastry ¾ inch from the edge. Moisten along one side of pastry with water and fold over, making a long sandwich. Press edges firmly together to seal. Mark firmly into portions, arranging them on lightly greased and floured baking sheet. Brush over with a little beaten egg and bake in hot oven (425—450°F. — Gas Mark 6—7) about 20 minutes. Serve hot or cold with a little green salad.

495   LISETTE'S SUPPER PIE

6 oz. short crust pastry   4 oz. bacon
    (Recipe 485)   1 medium onion
¾ – 1 lb. cottage cheese   1 rounded teaspoon made
2 eggs   mustard
1 oz. margarine or butter   seasoning to taste
parsley   1 or 2 tomatoes

Sieve cottage cheese, beat eggs and fry onion in margarine, then fry diced bacon. Roll out pastry and line an
8-inch plain flan ring standing on a greased baking sheet
or sandwich tin. Turn cheese into a bowl and add eggs,
bacon, onion, and made mustard. Season well to taste.
Beat thoroughly to blend all ingredients then turn mixture into pastry flan case. Bake in moderately hot oven
(400°F. – Gas Mark 5) for 10 minutes, then lower heat
to 350°F. – Gas Mark 3 for a further 40 – 50 minutes,
or until filling is firm and top golden brown. Transfer to
serving dish, garnish with fresh tomato wedges and parsley. Serve with a green salad.

497   BEEF AND CHEESE TURNOVERS

12 oz. short crust pastry   ¼ teaspoon dry mustard
    (Recipe 485)   ¼ cup soft bread crumbs
1 lb. minced beef   1 tablespoon
2 onions, chopped finely   Worcestershire sauce
2 tablespoons salad oil   1 tablespoon sour cream
4 oz. Danish blue cheese   ½ teaspoon garlic salt
¼ teaspoon paprika   ¼ teaspoon basil

Melt oil in a pan. Cook onions until light brown. Add
beef, breadcrumbs, seasonings and fry gently until beef
is cooked. Allow to cool. Add cheese and cream. Make
pastry and divide into 8 parts. Roll out each ball of dough
into a circle. Cut slits into one half of the circle. Place
spoonful of mixture on other half, damp edges, turn top
over evenly, pinch edges together, press with fork to seal.
Bake in hot oven (425 – 450°F. – Gas Mark 6 – 7)
and cook for 20 – 25 minutes until crust is golden brown.

496   BAKED APPLE AND CHEESE FLAN

4 oz. cheese pastry:

4 oz. flour   1½ oz. butter
pinch salt, cayenne pepper   2 oz. finely grated
    and baking powder   cheddar cheese
                           cold water to bind

Filling

8 oz. cooking apples   little egg white or
¼ oz. granulated sugar   milk
½ teaspoon nutmeg   ¼ teaspoon finely
2 oz. diced Cheddar   grated Cheddar
    cheese   cheese
                         } to glaze

Sieve flour, salt, cayenne pepper and baking powder. Rub
in butter. Add grated cheese and sufficient cold water to
bind. Leave to stand in a cool place. Peel, core, quarter
and slice apples, and mix with diced cheese, sugar and
nutmeg. Roll out pastry to a square, about 8 by 8 inches.
Cut six ½-inch strips off one side, and keep for latticing:
use rest of pastry as base of flan. Lift on to baking tray.
Spread filling over centre of this strip and fold over
¼ inch of pastry on each side. Place diagonal strips of
pastry ½ inch apart down the length of the flan. Glaze top
of flan with egg white or milk, and sprinkle with very
finely grated cheese. Bake in centre of a moderately hot
oven (400°F. – Gas Mark 5) for 25 – 30 minutes. Serve
hot or cold.
Note. The cheese pastry given in Recipe 365 is a little
too rich for this flan.

498   PASTA PASTRY

8 oz. plain flour   2 oz. butter
pinch of salt   lukewarm water to mix

Rub butter into flour and add water to make a dough that
is soft but not sticky when kneaded. Shape into a ball and
leave standing for an hour.

499   CHEESE CUSHIONS

6 oz. grated cheese   1 egg
2 oz. butter   pepper and salt to taste
a little extra cheese   pasta pastry (Recipe 498)

Make filling by creaming butter, beating in cheese and
then egg and seasoning. Roll out dough *thinly* on a lightly
floured board, and with a serrated cutter make rounds 2½
inches in diameter.
Damp edges, put a good ½ teaspoon of filling in each
round, fold over and press edges together. Fry cushions
in deep fat until nicely browned. Drain and serve hot,
sprinkled with finely grated cheese.

500   CHOUX PASTRY

*3 oz. flour (plain or
  self raising)*
¼ pint water
pinch salt and pepper

1 oz. margarine or butter
*2 whole eggs and yolk
  of 1 egg (or 3 small
  eggs)*

Put the water, margarine and seasoning into a saucepan. Heat gently until margarine has melted. Stir in the flour. Return the pan to a low heat and cook very gently, but thoroughly, stirring all the time, until mixture is dry enough to form a ball, and leave the pan clean. Once again remove from the heat and stir in the well beaten eggs very gradually. Do this slowly to produce a perfectly smooth mixture. Use for small buns or éclairs, which can then be filled with any savoury mixture. Choux pastry for savouries should be kept to very tiny shapes.
Buns — Pipe into tiny rounds on well greased baking tins and bake for approximately 15 minutes in centre of a hot oven (425—450°F. or Gas Mark 6—7).
Éclairs — Pipe or make into tiny finger shapes and bake as above.

501   CHEESE ÉCLAIRS

*4 oz. choux pastry
  (Recipe 500)*
yeast extract

4 oz. cream cheese
little whipped cream
salt and cayenne pepper

Make éclairs in the usual way (Recipe 500) and when baked and cool fill with cream cheese, blended with a little cream and seasoning. Brush the tops of the savoury éclairs with softened yeast extract. If preferred you can fill with cheese cream (Recipe 503) instead.

502   SAVOURY CREAM HORNS

*cheese cream
  (Recipe 503)*

*8 oz. flaky pastry
  (Recipe 484)*

Roll out the flaky pastry on to lightly floured board, and cut into long ½-inch strips. In order not to stretch the pastry, it is better to cut these strips on the cross. Grease metal horn tins and wind the pastry carefully round these, allowing it to overlap slightly, and at no time pulling the pastry out of shape. Put on to baking tin, brush with a little beaten egg or milk to glaze and bake for a good 10 minutes in a hot to very hot oven (450—475°F. — Gas Mark 7—8). Pull out the metal horns very carefully and if necessary put the cases back again for a few minutes in the oven, lowering the heat, to dry out. Fill with cheese cream.

503   CHEESE CREAM

¼ oz. cornflour
¼ pint milk
salt and pepper

3 oz. grated cheese
1 egg
*1 or 2 tablespoons
  whipped cream*

Blend the cornflour with a little cold milk. Bring the rest of the milk to the boil, pour over the cornflour and return to the pan and cook until smooth and thick, stirring well. Continue cooking for 3 minutes, then remove from the heat and allow to cool slightly, add the egg, grated cheese and seasoning. Allow to cool, stirring from time to time to keep mixture smooth, and when cool add the cream and fill the cases. Top with paprika pepper and garnish with chopped parsley.

504   CHEESE AND BACON PIE

*8 oz. short crust pastry
  (Recipe 485)*
6 oz. rashers of bacon

*8 oz. finely sliced
  Cheddar cheese*
pinch of cayenne pepper

Make the short crust pastry, divide into two and roll out each piece to fit a 9-inch plate. Line the plate with one pastry round and prick the bottom. Trim the rashers and cut across once or twice. Lay alternate layers of the thinly sliced cheese and bacon on the pastry-lined plate sprinkling the cheese well with cayenne pepper. Damp the pastry rim and cover with the second piece of pastry. Knock up and decorate the edge, make a hole in the centre, and decorate the pie with pastry leaves. Brush lightly with milk and bake in the middle of a hot oven (425 to 450°F. — Gas Mark 6—7) for 30—40 minutes. Serve hot with tomato sauce or cold with salad. This makes a good packed lunch.

505 PIZZA
(Italian Tomato Pie)

1 lb. flour
¼ oz. yeast
1 lb. or can tomatoes
tin of anchovies
few black olives

1 clove garlic, chopped
4 oz. Parmesan cheese
4 tablespoons olive oil
salt and pepper

Dissolve the yeast in tepid water. Mix the flour with a tablespoon of olive oil, then add the dissolved yeast.

507 TOMATO AND CHEESE PIZZA

Pizza pastry

5 oz. plain flour
pinch salt
1 tablespoon fine semolina
3 oz. butter or margarine

1 egg yolk
1 teaspoon mild mustard
1 tablespoon water

Filling

1 4-oz. can tomatoes
¼ pint milk
1 heaped tablespoon fine
  semolina
2 oz. grated cheese

1 small onion
salt
pepper

To garnish: fried onion rings, anchovies, olives

Sieve flour and salt. Sprinkle in semolina. Rub in fat.

Knead until the dough is smooth. Leave it in a covered bowl for 2 hours. Peel and chop the tomatoes, or drain canned tomatoes, and put them in a pan with the oil and garlic. Add the anchovies and the cheese just before the tomatoes are ready. Season with salt and pepper and simmer gently for 30 minutes. When the dough has risen, roll it until it is very thin and spread it over a large, well oiled baking tin. Cover it with the tomato mixture and bake in the centre of a hot oven (425–450°F. – Gas Mark 6–7). Top with grated Parmesan cheese and black olives.

506 CHEDDAR PIZZA

Use the recipe for Pizza, but omit the Parmesan cheese and black olives (and garlic if wished). Instead put plenty of grated Cheddar cheese over the tomato mixture before being baked.

Garnish with anchovy fillets when ready to serve.

Individual pizza pies look most attractive. Make small rounds of the dough and cover as described in Recipe 505. These will take about 15–20 minutes only to cook instead of the 30–35 minutes required by the larger Pizza.

Beat yolk of egg and mustard with water and stir into flour mixture, adding carefully as required any extra liquid to make a firm light dough. Roll out to a large rectangle, trim and place on oven tray. Roll trimmings and cut a long ½-inch wide strip and place round the edge of rectangle to form raised border. A further rim can be added to give deeper space for filling. Mark with fork to give a fancy edging and prick centre of pastry all over. Glaze border with milk or beaten egg white. Bake in centre of a hot oven (450°F. – Gas Mark 7) until crisp and golden, about 15 minutes.

Drain and rub tomatoes through sieve. Heat milk and slowly shower in semolina. Cook and stir until mixture thickens. Thin down gradually with sieved tomato, still stirring, and cook until blended. Stir in grated cheese and onion, cook for a few minutes and season to taste. Re-heat pastry case, pour in filling and slip into hot oven for a few minutes. Garnish as liked with sauté onion rings and/or sliced olives or anchovy fillets or parsley.

Vegetable Dishes

508 GARDEN HOTPOT

1 can cut celery	*3 oz. grated cheese*
1½ oz. butter or margarine	*1 level teaspoon made mustard*
1½ oz. plain flour	*pepper and salt*
¼ pint milk	*12 oz. cooked potatoes or*
4 oz. boiled bacon	*1 can potatoes*

Remove vegetables from cans and reserve ¼ pint celery liquor. Melt fat in pan and add flour and cook for a minute. Remove from heat and stir in the milk and celery stock; cook, stirring, until sauce thickens. Simmer 2 minutes. Cool slightly and add chopped bacon, 2 oz. cheese, mustard and pepper and salt to taste. Put layers of celery and then sauce and then sliced potatoes in a greased heat-proof dish, finishing with a layer of potatoes. Sprinkle with remaining cheese. Heat for 20 minutes in a moderate oven (375°F. — Gas Mark 4). Serve piping hot with a crisp salad. As an extra try tomato chutney with this dish.
Variation: Instead of bacon add 3 hard-boiled eggs and 3 chopped anchovy fillets or 1 tablespoon capers. Or try the delicate and creamy flavour of 4 oz. cottage cheese, rubbed through a sieve and whipped into the sauce, omitting the grated Cheddar cheese.

509 BRAZILIAN BEANS

3 oz. beans — haricot, butter or black beans	*8 oz. lean pork*
4 oz. corned beef	*4 tablespoons orange juice*
4 oz. pork sausages	*4 tablespoons red wine*
1 rasher bacon	*1 dessertspoon olive oil*
¼ clove garlic	*1 small onion*
4 oz. cooked rice	*pepper and salt*
	1 sliced orange

Soak beans overnight, then cover with fresh water and simmer until almost tender. Cut pork into 1-inch cubes, add to beans and simmer for about 1 hour. Add diced corned beef, bacon and sausages and cook for a further hour. (By this time mixture should be about half covered with liquid — if much more than this remove some of surplus liquid when removing beans. If less, add a little more water or stock.) Remove a cupful of beans and rub through a sieve, return to pork mixture, stir until thickened by bean purée, add orange juice, wine and seasoning to taste. Fry sliced onion and crushed garlic until golden coloured, lift sausages out of meat mixture and slice. Put rice in a deep dish, pour meat mixture on top, garnish with fried onion and garlic, sliced sausages and orange. Serve with Avocado pear salad (Recipe 510).

510 AVOCADO PEAR SALAD

2 Avocado pears	*4 stuffed olives*
2 hard-boiled eggs	*¼ small onion*
4 tomatoes	*1 tablespoon olive oil*
lettuce	*1 dessertspoon vinegar*
1 rasher crisp cooked	*pinch chili powder*

Mix oil, vinegar and chili powder. Dice all ingredients except lettuce and bacon. Arrange lettuce on a dish, pile Avocado pear mixture on top and garnish with the bacon.

511 CREAMED MUSHROOMS

Simmer mushrooms in milk until just tender. Blend a little cornflour or flour with cold milk, add to hot milk and cook until thickened, put in a good knob of butter and a little cream, season well, add a squeeze of lemon. Serve with toast or bread and butter.

512 LENTIL ROAST

4 oz. lentils	*1 or 2 eggs*
1 tomato	*1 oz. fat*
1 onion	*½ oz. oatmeal or breadcrumbs*
¼ teaspoon sage	*¼ apple*

Soak lentils overnight in cold water — this is not essential, but improves them. Cook in water in which they were soaked, adding seasoning, until tender. Beat until smooth. Heat fat in a frying pan, then fry sliced onion, chopped tomato and chopped apple. When soft add this mixture to lentils, together with sage, oatmeal or breadcrumbs, extra seasoning if necessary and egg. Put into greased tin and cover with greased paper. Bake in centre of a moderately hot oven (400°F — Gas Mark 5) for about 45 minutes. Serve with tomato or mushroom sauce (Recipes 254, 256).

513 HARICOT BEAN ROAST or NUT ROAST

Substitute cooked haricot beans for lentils (sieve these when cooked), or use chopped nuts. Illustrated is a Nut Roast using a mixture of nuts. Follow the same recipe as Lentil Roast, using 8 oz. nuts and 4 oz. breadcrumbs.

514   TO MAKE OMELETTES

Allow 1½—2 eggs per person. Beat eggs in a basin — break each separately in a cup before transferring to basin (in case one is bad). Add a good pinch salt and pepper and for each 1½—2 eggs a tablespoon of water. Put knob of butter into omelette pan and when hot pour in eggs — leave for about 1 minute over high heat to allow bottom to set, then loosen egg mixture from sides of pan and cook rapidly, tipping pan from side to side so that the liquid egg flows underneath and cooks quickly. When egg is as set as you like it (tastes vary) slip palette knife under omelette and fold it away from handle of pan. Grasp handle firmly and tip on to a hot plate.

515   LOOKING AFTER YOUR OMELETTE PAN

If possible buy a special pan and keep it just for omelettes or omelettes and pancakes. Don't wash it, but when you have finished using it, clean it with very soft paper (modern soft kitchen rolls are ideal for this) and put it away. Never get the butter too hot so there is any possibility of anything burning in this pan. If you are careful your pan will repay you with years of wear.

516   OMELETTE WITH CORNFLOUR

4 or 5 eggs	1 tablespoon oil
2 level teaspoons	1 level tablespoon butter
cornflour	cooked mushrooms
1 tablespoon water or	tomatoes
milk	green peppers

Mix cornflour and cold liquid in a bowl. Beat eggs into this. Season. Heat oil in omelette pan and pour in eggs and cornflour mixture. After a few seconds of cooking, reduce heat and loosen omelette around edges of pan with a fork or palette knife so that uncooked mixture has a chance to cook. Continue shaking pan occasionally, until surface of omelette is just creamy. When omelette is cooked, dot with butter, fold in three and serve immediately. Garnish with cooked mushrooms, tomatoes and green peppers.

517   GOLDEN CRUST OMELETTE

1 large slice bread	2 oz. butter
1 teaspoon parsley	3 eggs
1 slice ham	

Heat butter in an omelette or frying pan. Cut bread into tiny dice, removing crusts. Fry until crisp and just golden brown. Add beaten eggs, well seasoned and mixed with finely chopped ham. Cook until lightly set, fold, put on a hot dish and sprinkle with chopped parsley. Enough for 2 people.

FILLINGS FOR OMELETTES

518 • Mixed Herb Omelette • Add finely chopped herbs to your beaten eggs.

519 • Cheese Omelette • Grated cheese should be either mixed with the eggs, or better still put over the eggs just before set and folded.

520 • Macaroni Omelette • 2 oz. cooked macaroni mixed with 3 eggs. Just before folding put grated cheese through the middle. *Illustrated in colour picture No. 43.*

521 • Ham Omelette • Either mix finely diced ham with the eggs or put ham in a creamy sauce through the middle.

522 • Chicken Omelette • Either mix finely diced chicken with the eggs, or put chicken in a creamy sauce through the middle as a filling.

523 • Mushroom Omelette • Cook mushrooms and mix with the eggs, or put through the middle in a creamy sauce.

524 • Tomato Omelette • Simmer tomatoes in butter or margarine until tender, season well, and use as a filling.

525   SOUFFLÉ OMELETTES

A soufflé omelette is a very much thicker omelette with a very light, but to some people slightly drier, texture. It is not difficult to make. Simply beat your egg yolks with seasoning, then fold in the stiffly beaten whites. Heat butter in pan in exactly the same way, pour in egg mixture, and cook steadily. Since this is so thick it is difficult to get it cooking quickly enough from the bottom, so it is generally suggested that the soufflé omelette be put either under a moderate grill, or in the oven, when it is reasonably set at the bottom. In this way you cook it quickly without toughening the eggs. Savoury fillings can be used in the same way as for a plain omelette.

526   SCOTCH EGGS

4 eggs	1 egg for coating
2 tablespoons flour	¼ teacup milk for coating
8 — 12 oz. sausage meat	deep fat for frying
breadcrumbs	

Hard-boil the eggs and cool them. Then roll them lightly in flour. Divide the sausage meat into four, fold evenly and smoothly round the lightly floured eggs. Coat these with the beaten egg and milk blended together: roll each firmly in breadcrumbs. Fry steadily in fat and drain.

Remember that the sausage meat has to cook so do not hurry the frying process. Cut each Scotch egg into half with a sharp knife dipped in hot water. Serve hot with tomato sauce (Recipes 256, 257) or cold with salad.

527   PARTY SCOTCH EGGS

Scotch Eggs (Recipe 526)

Filling

2 tablespoons mayonnaise (Recipe 186) or white sauce (Recipe 242)	2 — 3 oz. chopped ham or chopped celery or grated cheese

Drain Scotch eggs on crumpled kitchen paper and leave to cool. Cut the eggs carefully in halves. Scoop out the yolks and pound with mayonnaise (or cream or white sauce) and mustard. Add the ham or celery or cheese and season further to taste. Dust the top with paprika or chopped parsley or garnish with sliced stuffed olives or butterflies of sliced gherkin or radish. Serve on a large flat platter garnished with salad.

528   CHEESE SCOTCH EGGS

6 oz. grated Cheddar cheese	1 beaten egg
1¼ oz. flour	1 — 2 tablespoons milk or cream
pepper and salt	
¼ teaspoon Worcestershire sauce	4 hard-boiled eggs dried breadcrumbs

Mix grated cheese, flour, seasonings, and beat in egg and milk. Using wet hands coat the hard-boiled eggs with cheese mixture and roll in dried breadcrumbs. Fry in hot deep fat to a golden brown (about 2 minutes). Drain, cut in half, and serve hot or cold.

529   SWISS EGGS

4 eggs	2 tablespoons cream or top milk
4 oz. Cheddar cheese	salt and pepper
1 oz. butter	

Grate about 1 oz. cheese and with a very sharp knife cut the remainder into wafer thin slices. Spread the butter all over the bottom of a fireproof dish. Cover with the thin slices of cheese. Break the eggs carefully on to the bed of cheese, being careful not to disturb the yolks. Season with salt and pepper, put a spoonful of the cream on the top of each egg. Sprinkle over the grated cheese. Bake for 15 minutes in a hot oven (450°F. — Gas Mark 6). Glaze under a hot grill.

See also recipes for scrambled eggs (563 — 570).

37   **SWISS FISH PIE (Recipe 469)**

38   **GNOCCHI (Recipe 279)**

39   CHEESE CUSTARD FLAN WITH BACON
(Recipe 531)

40   CHEESE AND BACON FLAN (Recipe 533)

Television Savouries

This section contains savoury dishes that are comfortable to eat while watching television, and yet at the same time are satisfying and nutritious.

530 GRILLED BANANA SPLIT WITH BACON

firm bananas	8 rashers thin streaky
1¼ oz. butter or	bacon
margarine, melted	parsley or watercress
salt	

Peel bananas. Cut lengthwise into halves. Brush completely with butter or margarine and sprinkle lightly with salt. Place halves, cut sides down, on grill rack or into pan containing rack. Grill about 4 inches from heat about 3 minutes. Turn bananas. Arrange bacon strips on rack. Grill bacon and bananas about 4 minutes, or until bacon is done and bananas are browned and tender. For each serving, arrange 2 banana halves on plate. Place bacon strip on each half. Garnish with parsley or watercress.

531 CHEESE CUSTARD FLAN

4 oz. cheese pastry	1¼ gills milk
(Recipes 363 or 365)	1 egg
3 oz. grated cheese	salt and cayenne pepper

Roll out cheese pastry and line a fairly deep 7-inch flan ring. Beat egg, milk, cheese and seasoning well together. Pour carefully into flan case. Bake in centre of a hot oven (450°F. — Gas Mark 7) for 10 minutes, then lower heat to moderately hot (400°F. — Gas Mark 5) until filling is firm and golden on top — this takes a further 15—20 minutes. *Illustrated in colour picture No. 39.*

532 TOMATO AND CHEESE FLAN

4 oz. cheese pastry	small can tomatoes or
(Recipes 363 or 365)	4 fresh tomatoes
1 small onion	2 oz. butter
2 eggs	1¼ gills milk
3 oz. grated cheese	salt and pepper

Line a deep flan ring with pastry. If using canned tomatoes, drain well and put at bottom of pastry case. Fresh tomatoes should be skinned and sliced. Fry onion in butter and then arrange on top of tomatoes. Pour milk over beaten eggs, add 2 oz. of the cheese and seasoning, pour carefully into flan case. Top with rest of cheese. Bake in a moderate oven (375°F. — Gas Mark 4) for about 40 minutes until firm.

533 CHEESE AND BACON FLANS

Follow Recipes 531 or 532, and when cooked *lightly*, put thin rashers of gammon or ham on top of the flan, return to the oven to cook or heat the bacon or ham. *Illustrated in colour picture opposite.*

534 FRIED CHEESE CRUNCHIES

4 oz. grated	pinch cayenne pepper
cheese	1 egg
1 oz. flour	1¼ tablespoons milk
1 level teaspoon salt	4 large slices bread cut
¼ teaspoon	¼ inch thick
Worcestershire sauce	fat for frying

Mix the grated cheese, flour and seasonings. Beat the egg, add the milk and beat into the cheese mixture. Cut the bread into neat shapes and spread with a thick layer of the cheese mixture. Fry in hot deep fat to a rich golden brown, putting the cheese side down first and then turn over. (The total frying time is approximately 1 minute.) Drain and serve at once as a hot cocktail or party snack.

535   CHEESE AND APPLE RINGS

Fry thick rings of apple in bacon fat. When apples are soft add 1 slice of cheese and leave until beginning to melt. Put both apple and cheese slices on to toast.

536   APPLE RINGS AND BACON

Fry rashers of bacon, then lift on to hot dish and fry thinly sliced rings of apples in the bacon fat.
    Serve with fingers of toast or fried bread.

537   T. V. RISOTTO

2 oz. cooked rice	3 eggs
2 oz. butter	seasoning
2 tomatoes	¼ teacup milk
2 kidneys	crisp toast

Heat the butter, fry the sliced kidneys and tomatoes, add the cooked rice and the milk and heat gently. Now add the beaten and well-seasoned eggs and continue heating until lightly set. Serve with crisp toast and/or crisp bacon.

538   KEDGEREE

6 oz. cooked smoked haddock	pinch cayenne pepper and salt
1 hard-boiled egg	chopped parsley
approx. 8 oz. cooked rice	lemon quarters

Flake fish coarsely with a fork. Chop the egg white, sieve the yolk and put on one side for garnishing. Mix the flaked fish, chopped egg white, cooked rice and seasoning in a saucepan over moderate heat until hot, with a fork, adding a little milk if necessary. Pile the mixture into a hot entrée dish, garnish with chopped parsley and sieved egg yolk and serve at once with lemon quarters.

539   Kedgeree With Onions

Make Kedgeree as Recipe 538, pile on hot dish, top with rings of crisp fried onions.

540   Kedgeree With Cheese

Make Kedgeree as Recipe 538, but stir 4—6 oz. grated cheese in mixture just before serving.

541   Salmon Kedgeree

Use flaked cooked or canned salmon in place of haddock.

542   S.O.S. PLATTER

6 oz. spaghetti   ¼ teaspoon
1 pint onion soup*   Worcestershire sauce
seasoning   small quantity diced
12 oz. sausage meat   carrots and peas

* Either Recipe 30 or ready prepared soup

Cook the spaghetti as directed. Drain and return to the pan. Shape the sausage meat into 4 patties, fry or grill them to a good brown on both sides. Heat the soup, add the sauce and seasoning and pour over the spaghetti. Mix thoroughly. Place in hot dish and top with the patties and vegetables.

544   GOLDEN CRUST BANANAS

1¼ teaspoons salt   2 breakfast cups corn
1 egg   flakes
4 bananas, slightly   1¼ oz. butter or
   under-ripe   margarine

Add salt to egg. Crush corn flakes and melt butter. Peel bananas. Cut into halves crosswise. Dip banana halves into egg, then drain 2 or 3 minutes. Roll in crushed corn flakes until well coated. Place crumbed banana halves into greased baking pan. Sprinkle bananas with melted butter or margarine. Bake in a hot oven (450°F. — Gas Mark 7) about 10—12 minutes, until bananas are golden brown and tender — easily pierced with a fork. Serve hot as vegetable or with grilled bacon or sausages and vegetables, or with cold ham.

   To prepare corn flakes for crumbing, fold the corn flakes in waxed paper or in a dish towel and press with a rolling pin, or grind the corn flakes in a mincer to desired size.

545   FONDUE

This famous Swiss delicacy has become very popular. There are quite a number of variations of it, but this is the classic way to make it:

1 lb. Gruyère cheese   ½ pint dry white wine
seasoning   (Graves ideal)
butter

Butter the bottom and sides of an earthenware casserole, or fireproof dish. An unsalted butter is ideal for this. Add the grated Gruyère cheese, or for a milder flavour

543   SAUSAGE SPIRALS

8 oz. flaky pastry   12 oz. (12) skinless
   (Recipe 484)   sausages
1 egg yolk   or sausage meat shaped
1 dessertspoon water   into sausages

Roll out dough into an oblong 12 × 8 inches, approximately ¼ inch thick. Cut into strips, 1 inch wide, 8 inches long. Wrap each strip round a sausage in a spiral, first dampening the strip on the side which goes on the sausage. Overlap the spiral slightly at each twist. Brush the pastry with a glaze made by mixing together the yolk and water. Don't let the glaze dribble on to the cut edges of the pastry, or it will prevent it from rising. Bake in a very hot oven (475°F. — Gas Mark 8) for 10 minutes then reduce to moderately hot (400°F. — Gas Mark 5) for a further 15 minutes. Serve hot or cold, with mustard and steaming hot tomato soup.

use a Dutch Gouda. Add seasoning and the white wine. Keep warm over a gentle heat and stir from time to time. If desired a little brandy or Curaçao can be added. Some people use cornflour, which prevents the possibility of the mixture curdling. To use this, blend 1 good teaspoon cornflour with a little of the wine. Serve the fondue with toasted or untoasted bread. This is cut into squares and using a fork, or the fingers, rolled quickly round in the cheese mixture, to bread the cheese threads, and eaten. Under no circumstances let your cheese mixture boil quickly, or it becomes tough and is spoilt.

546 CROSS-OVER PATTIES

8 oz. short crust pastry (Recipe 485)

Filling

6 oz corned beef or cold cooked lamb, beef or veal
1 large beaten egg
1 level teaspoon made mustard
1½ oz fresh white breadcrumbs

Roll out pastry and cut into nine 3½-inch squares. Mix meat, crumbs and mustard well together then bind with the egg. Divide into nine equal portions and form each into a sausage shape. Put these diagonally across squares of pastry. Moisten opposite corners of each square with water, then fold one over the other, partially enclosing the meat. Brush tops with beaten egg or milk then transfer patties to a greased baking tray. Bake towards the top of a hot oven (425—450°F — Gas Mark 6—7) for 15—20 minutes. Garnish with parsley.

547 LIVER PIELETS

8 oz. New Zealand lamb's liver
2 oz. bacon
2 medium-large onions
1 oz. butter
pepper and salt
1 egg
pinch mixed crushed herbs
flour
¾ large can onion soup or approximately the same amount of meat stock
4 oz. short pastry (Recipe 485)

Cut up liver and bacon into pieces, using kitchen scissors. Fry peeled and chopped onions in butter until well softened and golden, then add liver and bacon pieces and turn altogether in pan for a moment or two. Divide mixture among individual heatproof dishes. Moisten well with onion soup or thicken meat stock with flour, simmering for a few minutes before adding to dishes. Leave to cool while making pastry. Roll out pastry moderately thinly and stamp out small rings, using cutters of two sizes — or if preferred cut circles of paste to cover top of dishes. The small rings should be arranged overlapping round edges of dish, with a ring for the middle. Large circles should be placed on top lightly. Brush over pastry surface with a little beaten egg and bake in hot oven (425—450°F. — Gas Mark 6—7) about 20 minutes, until pastry is golden brown. Serve piping hot.

548 DEVILLED KIDNEYS

6—8 kidneys or ¾—1 lb. kidney
2 skinned tomatoes
1 teaspoon curry powder
1 level tablespoon flour
1 tablespoon chutney
seasoning
squeeze lemon juice
2 oz. dripping
2 sliced onions
½ pint stock
2 hard-boiled eggs
1—1½ lb. creamed potatoes

Heat the dripping then fry the sliced onion and tomatoes until very soft. Stir in the curry powder and flour and cook slightly gradually adding stock. Bring to boil, add the sliced and halved kidneys, chutney etc., and cook until tender. Make a border of mashed potatoes, put the kidney mixture in the centre and garnish with sliced hard-boiled eggs.

If you use a little less stock, this makes an excellent filling for potatoes baked in their jackets. Cook very large potatoes. Cut off tops. Scoop out the potato, mash and season well. Put kidney filling into potato case, spread or pipe potato on top and return to oven to brown.

549 DEVILLED POTATOES

4 large potatoes
4 rashers streaky bacon
1 onion
2 tomatoes
2 oz. margarine
pinch curry powder
little Worcestershire sauce
seasoning

Bake potatoes. Meanwhile chop 2 rashers bacon and make rest into 4 small rolls. Fry chopped onions, tomatoes and bacon in most of the margarine, adding curry powder and Worcestershire sauce. Season well. Grill or fry bacon rolls. Take tops off potatoes, scoop out centre pulp, mash this with little margarine, season well and press or pipe back into potato cases, leaving a good sized space in the middle. Fill this with bacon mixture and top with a bacon roll.

550   KIDNEY RAMEKINS

12 oz. potatoes
  3 large firm tomatoes
  3 New Zealand lamb's
    kidneys
  1 streaky rasher cut into
    three

2 rashers bacon
  little butter
  salt and pepper
  ready-made mustard
  1 tablespoon cream or top
    of milk

Cook potatoes, mash and cream well, adding a nut of butter, 1 tablespoon cream or top of milk, and a shake of pepper. Line ramekins thickly with potato mixture, piping a little through a coarse icing nozzle, to make a ribbon of potato cream round top edges. Cut a slice from each tomato and scoop out seeds. Drain well and dust inside with pepper and salt. Skin and core kidneys. Cut bacon into small pieces (fat bacon is best) and fry until crisp. Divide pieces between the tomato cups. Fry, or grill kidneys — not too well — and spread with a little mustard before putting the halves together and fitting them into the tomato cups. Put a small square of bacon over each and bake in hot oven (425—450°F. — Gas Mark 6—7) until bacon is crisped and contents of dishes piping hot. Remove pieces of bacon before serving.

551   **STUFFED BAKED POTATOES**
To bake potatoes

Scrub large potatoes, wipe them dry and rub with a little melted fat or oil. This makes the skin thin, shiny and delicious to eat. Place on a baking tray or on the oven shelves. Test with a fork to see if they are cooked and then make a small cross on top and holding the potato in both hands, squeeze gently until the cross opens in four points and allows the steam to escape. The cooking time varies from 45 minutes to 1 hour (400°F. — Gas Mark 5).

The stuffings shown in the photograph are strips of anchovy topped with an olive, a frankfurter or chipolata sausage stuck through a hole in the potato made by an apple corer whilst the potato is still raw. Bacon is wrapped around the potato and secured with a cocktail stick; a fried egg garnished with tomato slices and a little chopped chives; chopped fried mushroom garnished with a strip of bacon rolled up and secured with a cocktail stick; a spoonful of peas mixed with the baked potato flesh seasoned and garnished with butter; a grilled kidney garnished with fried onion rings.

To stuff potatoes you can either remove baked potato flesh, season and mix with filling or put filling on top of the hot potato.

Try spoonfuls of hot cooked chopped meat, mixed with potato flesh seasoned and garnished with parsley; cheddar cheese, softened under the grill and garnished with chopped chives and, for a sweet tooth, sultanas and cubes of cheese.

552   POTATO NESTS

Form mashed potatoes into rounds on glass oven-proof plates put in oven to brown and crisp while you prepare the filling. When ready, put filling in centre of potato round.

SAVOURY KIDNEYS — Fry diced bacon, add little butter and cook diced mushrooms and diced lamb's kidneys — this cooks very quickly.

HAM SCRAMBLE — Scramble eggs lightly, adding diced ham and a chopped red or green pepper, if wished.

HERRING ROES — Cook in milk, top with red pepper.

Pancakes

553   TO TOSS A PANCAKE

When the pancake is cooked on the under side it can be tossed. However, remember the really delicate, very thin pancakes are better turned. Hold the pan *loosely* in your hand, keeping your wrist very flexible. Flick sharply upwards. With practice it will twist in the air and come down in the pan with the cooked side uppermost.

554   TO TURN A PANCAKE

When cooked on the underside put a small fish slice or palette knife under the pancake. Get the knife right to centre of pan. Lift carefully and then flick over to turn.

555   YOUR PAN FOR PANCAKES

Look after the pan in which you cook pancakes just as you do your omelette pan. The same pan can be used for both omelettes and pancakes if wished. See Recipe 515 for directions on seasoning and looking after omelette pans.

556   PANCAKE BATTER

4 oz. flour	1 egg
pinch salt	¼ pint milk or milk and water

Sieve flour and salt, add egg and enough milk to give a sticky consistency. Beat well, then gradually add rest of liquid.

557   RICH PANCAKE BATTER

4 oz. flour	2 eggs
pinch salt	just under ¼ pint milk or
1 tablespoon olive oil	milk and water

As above, adding the oil last.

558   BACON PANCAKES

4 oz. flour	pinch salt
1 egg	¼ pint milk and water

For the filling

4—6 oz. streaky bacon	2 oz. mushrooms
2 or 3 large tomatoes	parsley to garnish
little extra fat	Cheese or Tomato sauce
1 small onion	(Recipes 243, 256)

Make the batter by mixing the flour (sieved with the salt) with the egg and enough liquid to make a stiff batter. Beat well until smooth then add the rest of the liquid. Allow to stand. Meanwhile prepare the filling. Remove the bacon rinds and fry these to obtain the fat from them, lift the rinds from the pan, add a little extra fat if necessary and fry the finely chopped onion, then the bacon, chopped mushrooms and tomatoes. Keep this hot and season well. Cook the pancakes. Fill each and roll firmly, or if preferred put 1 pancake on a hot dish, spread with the filling, cover with a pancake and so on, until all are used. Serve with cheese sauce or a tomato sauce and garnish with parsley.

559   TIERED CHEESE PANCAKES

¼ pint rich pancake batter (Recipe 557)	8 oz. grated Cheddar cheese
	1¼ lb. freshly cooked, chopped spinach

Wash and cook the spinach in the usual way. Drain well and chop. Cook thin pancakes, and pile as made on a warm dish putting a layer of spinach and grated cheese between each fresh pancake. Keep the pile hot in a moderate oven, and build up layer by layer until all the batter is used. Top the last pancake with a little grated cheese and serve hot, cutting into wedges as you would a cake.

560 HAM AND POTATO CAKES

1 lb. mashed potatoes *4 slices ham*
4 slices Gruyère cheese *few tomatoes*
seasoning *chopped parsley*
fat

Add seasoning and little chopped parsley to the mashed potatoes — if the mixture is dry then add a little milk and margarine to moisten. Form into 4 large flat cakes, put a little fat on each and brown in a moderately hot oven (400°F. — Gas Mark 5). Top with a slice of ham and cheese and return to the oven until the cheese is beginning to melt. Decorate with parsley and serve with baked tomatoes.

561 AMERICAN SCRAPPLE

1 pint milk or water
3 oz. fine semolina
¼ level teaspoon salt
¼ level teaspoon pepper
butter, margarine or bacon fat for frying
grated onion and chopped parsley

1. Blend ingredients and bring to the boil, stirring. Cook gently for 3 minutes.

2. Turn into a straight-sided loaf tin, rinsed with cold water, and cover. Chill until firm.

3. Turn out and cut in ½-inch slices.

4. Fry gently in butter, margarine or bacon fat until crisp and brown. For a very crisp crust, the scrapple slices can be dipped in semolina before frying.

5. Serve with bacon or sausages.

562 BOSTON BAKED BEANS

1 lb. haricot beans *¼ cup dark molasses*
8 oz. sliced pork *or treacle*
2 teaspoons salt *¼ teaspoon dry mustard*
1 tablespoon brown sugar *½ teaspoon Worcestershire sauce*

Wash and soak beans in cold water overnight. Drain, cover with fresh water and cook slowly until tender. Turn beans into bean pot. Pour boiling water over pork, scrape rind until white, score in ½-inch strips and press into top of beans, leaving only rind exposed. Mix salt, brown sugar, molasses or treacle, mustard and Worcestershire sauce. Add 1 cup boiling water and pour over beans. Add additional water to cover beans, if necessary. Cover and bake in slow oven (250—300°F. — Gas Mark 1—2) for 6—8 hours, adding additional water to keep beans just covered. Uncover during last 30 minutes to brown pork and beans. *Illustrated in colour picture No. 42.*

VARIATIONS ON SCRAMBLED EGGS

564 With chicken Heat any tiny scraps of cooked chicken in the milk and butter, then add the beaten seasoned eggs afterwards and cook as before.

565 With ham As with chicken, but remember ham is slightly salt, and reduce quantity of seasoning.

566 With prawns As chicken, but remember all shell fish is slightly salt and reduce amount of salt with eggs.

567 With tomatoes Allow 1 good sized tomato for each 2 eggs. Skin and slice thinly and heat in the butter. Beat eggs, ADD NO MILK, season and cook as before.

568 With bacon and macaroni or spaghetti Fry the bacon in the pan — until really crisp, add the COOKED and well drained macaroni, heat for a minute, add the eggs and cook as before.

569 With fried bread and onion Chop 1 onion finely and cook in the hot butter until soft, then add a few cubes of bread and brown these. Add the beaten eggs and cook as before.

570 With cheese Add a little grated Cheddar cheese to beaten eggs. Cook particularly slowly to prevent cheese becoming 'stringy'.

563 SCRAMBLED EGGS

Beat eggs, season well, and for softer mixture add 1 tablespoon milk to each 2 eggs. Heat a knob of butter in pan and pour in egg mixture. Cook as SLOWLY as possible, stirring all the time until lightly set. Remove from heat while still a little liquid, since eggs will stiffen slightly in the pan. Put on to buttered toast. Serve at once.

BUFFET SUPPER

(illustrated opposite)

571 TO COOK A GAMMON OR HAM

Always soak in cold water overnight, changing water once or twice if wished. When cooking allow 25 minutes per lb. and 25 minutes over for fairly small pieces. For very large pieces you need allow only 20 minutes per lb. and 20 minutes over. When roasting instead of boiling soak particularly well — or boil for half cooking time and roast the rest of the time. Allow 20—25 minutes per lb. and 25 minutes over. The skin can be removed and the gammon or ham coated with browned breadcrumbs, or covered with a little brown sugar, spice and cloves, and put into a hot oven for approximately 45 minutes until crisp and golden brown.

572 LAMB CUTLETS WITH CUCUMBER

8 or 9 cutlets from best end neck or 6 from loin	¼ pint gravy
	1 egg
1 large cucumber	breadcrumbs
3 oz. butter	salt and pepper

Peel cucumber, remove seeds and cut into dice. Heat butter in saucepan, put in the cucumber, salt and pepper, cover closely and cook gently in butter for nearly 30 minutes or until pieces are tender. Drain well, trim cutlets, dip them in egg, crumb them and fry in hot butter or fat until brown on both sides. Arrange cutlets neatly on dish with cucumber in centre, and pour hot gravy over.

573 LAMB WITH PINEAPPLE EN BROCHETTE

Cut some lean lamb into cubes about 1 inch square and cut some pineapple in the same way. Alternate these squares on skewers, sprinkle with salt and pepper, dip in melted butter, roll in crumbs and grill under a moderate heat, turning the skewers and basting the meat and fruit with butter while they cook. Serve on a bed of rice.

574 STUFFED HAM ROLLS

Fill thin slices of ham with cream cheese, mixed with chopped gherkins, parsley and capers; or fill with vegetables in a thick mayonnaise; or with diced apple and diced celery mixed with mayonnaise.

575 BACON COCKTAIL SAVOURIES

Roll ½ rashers of streaky bacon round tiny pieces of kidney, pieces of pineapple, Frankfurter sausages (stuffed with a finger of cheese), halved bananas etc. Secure with cocktail sticks and either grill in the oven or cook under grill, turning until bacon is crisp and brown.

RISSOTO

576 Fry slices of onion, tomatoes and mushrooms in hot oil or butter and oil, then toss rice in the oil until golden brown. Add stock (allow 1 pint to 3 oz. rice) bring to the boil, put in the rice, diced bacon and seasoning and cook until the rice is tender and has absorbed the stock. Serve with grated cheese.

577 LAMB IN ASPIC

2 pints aspic jelly	3 tablespoons cooked peas
1 lb. cooked lamb	1 tablespoon chopped mint
1 tomato	cucumber

Make up jelly according to instructions on packet and pour enough of it into a 6-inch cake tin to give a thin layer at the bottom. Allow to set then arrange pieces of lamb and tomato in a design on bottom of tin, first dipping each piece into a little jelly. Allow to set. Cover with another thin layer of aspic. Mix remaining meat and aspic together, and add peas and finely chopped mint. When beginning to set, mix well and pour into tin. Turn out when firm and decorate with thin slices of cucumber.

41   BUFFET SUPPER (Recipes on facing page)

42   QUICHE LORRAINE AND BOSTON BAKED
         BEANS (Recipes 282, 562)

43   MACARONI OMELETTE (Recipe 520)

44 CHEESE STUFFED BAKED POTATOES
(Recipe 431)

45   BARBECUE CHEESES (Recipe 581)

46   STUFFED APPLE BASKETS (Recipe 580)

Teen-age Specials

The savouries in the next few pages have been chosen to appeal to teen-agers for they are particularly easy to make and ideal to serve at record parties.

578   HAMBURGERS (1)

1 lb. minced beef
1 good-sized potato
1 large or 2 medium-sized onions
¼ teaspoon mixed herbs

1 heaped teaspoon chopped parsley
1 teaspoon Worcestershire sauce
seasoning

Put meat into a basin, add grated onion, seasoning, herbs, parsley and sauce. Lastly grate in raw peeled potato. Mix thoroughly together. There will be no need to add liquid as the potato binds the mixture together. Form into large flat cakes and either fry steadily in hot fat or bake on a well greased tin for about 25—30 minutes in a moderately hot oven (400°F. — Gas Mark 5). The cakes can be floured or tossed in crisp breadcrumbs before cooking — don't try to turn into a neat rissole shape. Serve hot and, if wished, with a fried egg on top.

579   HAMBURGERS (2)

1½ lb. cooked minced meat
1 minced onion
1 beaten egg
bacon rashers

1 tablespoon flour
1 tablespoon melted butter or bacon fat
1 dessertspoon made mustard

Pound all ingredients together, shape into rolls and skewer pieces of bacon rasher round each roll. Cook in a moderately hot oven for about 15 minutes. Serve hot on triangles of thick, fresh buttered bread or halved rolls. Each burger can be skewered with a pickled onion. Hot or cold pineapple slices, topped with pepper rings, and a green salad go well with these.

580   STUFFED APPLE BASKETS

To each person allow 1 medium sized dessert apple. Cut a good slice off top of each, but leave peel on. Scoop out centre pulp, chop finely. Sprinkle with lemon juice, also sprinkle lemon juice over 'shell' of apple. Mix diced Swiss petit Gruyère cheese, chopped dates, chopped celery, chicory or grapes, seasoning and few chopped nuts with diced apple, blending with mayonnaise (Recipe 186) if wished. Or add chopped ham or boiled bacon. Pile back into cases, replace lids and serve on crisp lettuce. *Illustrated in colour picture opposite.*

581   BARBECUE CHEESES

Cheese is excellent cooked over a barbecue fire, particularly the firm Swiss processed Gruyère cheese. In the picture portions of this cheese are arranged on fine skewers, with thick slices of tomato (or mushroom can be used) in between, and heated on the wire rack until they begin to melt. For a more substantial snack, slit fresh rolls, butter and put a piece of the processed Gruyère cheese in each slit. Heat gently for a short time. *Illustrated in colour picture opposite.*

582   FRANKFURTER DOGS

Grill small chipolata sausages or use Frankfurters and leave to get cold. Use a whole sausage for the body and an angled piece for the head. Anchor with a piece of cocktail stick. Use these sticks cut into short lengths for legs and tail.

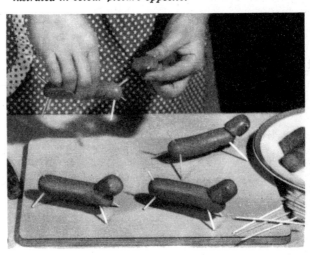

583 BARBECUED ROUND OF BEEF

2 lb. round of beef   4 medium sized carrots
4 medium sized onions   Tangy Barbecue sauce
corn oil   (Recipe 584)

Brush round of beef on both sides with corn oil and
brown over hot coals. Place in sheet of double aluminium
foil, large enough to fold over roast; add quartered onions
and carrots and coat with Tangy Barbecue sauce. Fold
aluminium foil over roast and cook on coals for 45—60
minutes or until meat is tender.

584   Tangy Barbecue Sauce

¼ small onion   2 tablespoons wine vinegar
1 clove garlic   2 tablespoons corn oil
1 sprig parsley   1 teaspoon Worcestershire
¼ pint tomato ketchup   sauce
                      ground pepper to taste

Mince the onion, garlic and parsley and put into a large
screw top jar with all the other ingredients. Cover and
shake vigorously until all ingredients are well blended.
Leave to stand for 24 hours shaking occasionally. Use as
a basting sauce.

585   BARBECUED CHICKEN 'CALIFORNIA'

2 young chickens   juice of 1 lemon
   (2—2¼ lb. each)   pepper
2 tablespoons butter   salt
Tangy Barbecue Sauce
   (Recipe 584)

Prepare birds as usual. Blend lemon juice and butter and
put half of this mixture into each chicken. Truss wings
and legs tightly and place birds on the spit. Baste liberally
with Tangy Barbecue Sauce and cook, basting chickens
from time to time. Serve with additional sauce.

586   HI-HAT BACONBURGERS

8 oz. minced cooked bacon   8 oz. thin streaky rashers
8 oz. sausage meat   1 egg yolk
1 small onion   flour
pinch mixed herbs   2 large tomatoes
clove of garlic   salt
1 oz. butter   pepper
6 button mushrooms

Put minced bacon and sausage meat into a bowl, add
flavourings and moisten with egg yolk. Divide mixture on
a board dredged with seasoned flour, making 6 or 8 portions. Mould into neat rounds and flatten with hands to
the width of a bacon rasher.
Wrap a rasher round each baconburger, securing it with
a cocktail stick. Fry in butter or bacon fat until well
browned on each side. Prepare 6 or 8 slices of onion and
tomato, and heat through in butter, together with the
button mushrooms. To serve, place a slice of tomato and
a slice of onion on each baconburger and top with a button mushroom. Serve piping hot.

587   BACONBURGERS

Recipe as above, but sandwich between fresh rolls and
serve with tomato sauce and mustard. *Illustrated in
colour picture No. 31.*

588 CHEESEBURGER

Hamburger mixture

1¼ oz. breadcrumbs	¼ egg to bind
1 tablespoon minced or grated onion	6 — 8 oz. fairly lean steak, minced
	pinch pepper and salt

Cheese Rarebit mixture

1 oz. butter or margarine	pinch salt and cayenne pepper
1 level teaspoon made mustard	6 oz. grated Cheddar cheese
2 tablespoons milk	
4 hamburger buns or soft rolls	

Make the hamburgers. Mix together all the ingredients, divide into equal portions and shape into round flat cakes slightly larger than the buns. Prepare the Rarebit mixture. Cream the butter or margarine with the seasonings, add grated cheese and milk and mix well. Grill or fry the hamburgers 2 or 3 minutes on each side. Spread a generous helping of the Rarebit mixture over both sides of each split hamburger bun and grill to a golden brown. Put a cooked hamburger on bottom of the grilled bun and close. Serve hot with mustard or ketchup.

589   SANJAOLI BEEFBURGERS

1 lb. minced beef	1 tablespoon thick piquant sauce*
1 oz. dripping or margarine	¼ pint tomato purée
1 small onion chopped	seasoning as required
1 level tablespoon made mustard	4 soft rolls

* Use mushroom or tomato ketchup or chutney if preferred

Fry sliced onion in fat until soft. Remove and keep warm for garnish. Put beef into pan and stir with fork over heat until browned. Add remaining ingredients and simmer over low heat for about 30 minutes. Warm rolls in oven, or toast them under grill, split through centre and place the two halves on warmed plate. Spoon mixture over each of the halved rolls, adding onion rings for garnish. Serve with mustard.

590   MYSTERY SHELLS

2 large baked potatoes	2 oz. grated Cheddar cheese
2 tablespoons crisp chopped bacon	4 eggs

Bake the potatoes in the usual way, and slice in half lengthwise. Scoop out *some* of the cooked centre and use for soup or mashed potatoes. Refill the potato halves with a little fried chopped bacon and grated cheese, and pour one egg carefully into each. Sprinkle over a little more grated cheese and bake in a moderately hot oven (400°F. — Gas Mark 5) until the egg is set. Alternatively, top the half-filled shell with a lightly poached egg and serve at once.

Index

Acknowledgements

Illustrations by courtesy of the following:

Angostura Aromatic Bitters: Black and white photographs accompanying Recipes 37, 204.

The Bacon Information Council Limited: Colour pictures nos. 2, 24, 31, 39, 40, 41, 42. Black and white photographs accompanying Recipes 38, 149, 478, 525, 586.

Batchelors Foods Limited: Black and white photograph accompanying Recipe 115.

Blue Band Luxury Margarine: Black and white photograph accompanying Recipe 552.

Campbell's Soup Company Limited: Black and white photographs accompanying Recipes 167, 321.

The Canned Foods Advisory Bureau: Black and white photograph accompanying Recipe 241.

The Carnation Milk Bureau: Black and white photographs accompanying Recipes 81, 141, 284, 456, 457, 476.

The Cheese Bureau: Black and white photographs accompanying Recipes 16, 20, 26, 31, 45, 110, 156—160, 198, 296, 300, 313, 315, 319, 332, 342, 361, 362, 379—380, 381, 390—1, 396, 405, 418, 419, 420, 427, 438, 496, 499, 504, 506, 528, 529, 534, 559, 570, 588, 590.

Colman's Mustard: Black and white photographs accompanying Recipes 280, 397—9, 490, 527, 546, 578—9, 589.

Colman's Semolina: Colour picture no. 38. Black and white photographs accompanying Recipes 101, 195, 320, 350, 354, 460, 466, 479—80, 507, 561.

Creda Electric Cookers: Colour pictures nos. 1, 5.

Danish Agricultural Producers Information Service: Colour picture no. 28.

Eden Vale Cottage Cheese: Black and white photograph accompanying Recipes 444—449.

Elders and Fyffes: Black and white photographs accompanying Recipes 286, 424, 428, 530, 544.

Express Dairy Products: Black and white photographs accompanying Recipes 231, 316, 384, 389, 414.

The Flour Advisory Bureau Limited: Black and white photographs accompanying Recipes 48, 181, 400, 495, 591.

H. J. Heinz Company Limited, Editorial Service: Colour pictures nos. 12, 13. Black and white photographs accompanying Recipes 18, 91, 124, 125, 168, 201, 227, 288, 359.

Kenwood Manufacturing Company (Woking) Limited: Black and white photograph accompanying Recipe 4.

Ulf Knöppel: Black and white photograph accompanying Recipe 32.

Knorr Swiss Soups: Black and white photograph accompanying Recipe 543.

Kraft Foods Limited: Black and white photographs accompanying Recipes 406, 413, 592.

Mac Fisheries Limited, Food Group Kitchen: Black and white photographs accompanying Recipes 145, 229.

Maggi Soups: Colour picture no. 11.

New Zealand Meat Producers' Board: Colour picture no. 32. Black and white photographs accompanying Recipes 494, 547, 550.

Pepsi-Cola: Black and white photographs accompanying Recipes 426, 459, 509—10.

The Pig Industry Development Authority Home Service: Colour picture no. 20.

The Playing Cards Bureau: Black and white photograph accompanying Recipes 387—8, 392—394.

Paul Popper Limited: Black and white photographs accompanying Recipes 78, 117.

The Potato Desk: Colour pictures nos. 6, 25, 44. Black and white photographs accompanying Recipes 225, 226, 228, 551.

The Prestige Group Limited, Makers of 'Prestige' and 'Sky-line' kitchen equipment: Black and white photographs accompanying Recipes 90, 317.

Public Relations Associates Limited: Colour pictures nos. 3, 4, 5, 7, 9, 10, 17, 18, 19, 21, 22, 29, 34, 35, 36. Black and white photographs accompanying Recipes 42, 122, 274, 482, 516, 583—4, 585.

Quaker Oats Limited: Colour pictures nos. 15, 30, 43.

Radio Times Hulton Picture Library: Black and white photographs of soup garnishes, table setting.

Smedley's Limited: Black and white photograph accompanying Recipe 508.

South African Fruits: Black and white photograph accompanying Recipe 207.

The Spry Cookery Centre: Black and white photographs accompanying Recipe 386.

Swiss Cheeses: Black and white photograph accompanying Recipe 493.

Swiss Processed Gruyère Cheese Bureau: Colour pictures nos. 8, 16, 26, 27, 37, 45, 46.

John West's Middle-cut Brand Tuna: Black and white photographs accompanying Recipes 87, 170, 232, 234, 289, 356, 402, 423, 440.

The White Fish Authority: Colour picture no. 14.

Woman's Day (George Newnes Limited): Colour pictures nos. 23, 33. Black and white photographs accompanying Recipes 184, 185, 233, 237, 400, 434, 471, 477, 512, 513, 536, 541, 542, 558, 560, 580, 582.

1 CANAPÉS (Recipe 376)

2   BACON AND LIVER PATÉ (Recipe 149)

MARGUERITE PATTEN'S

BOOK OF

SAVOURY COOKING

Soups, Hors d'oeuvre, Snacks, Party Savouries

and Supper Dishes for every occasion

PAUL HAMLYN · LONDON

Contents

© Books for Pleasure Ltd. 1961
PAUL HAMLYN • LONDON
SPRING HOUSE • SPRING PLACE • LONDON N.W. 5
Printed in Czechoslovakia
T 743